THE SECRET TO TRUE HAPPINESS

THE SECRET TO TRUE HAPPINESS

Enjoy Today, Embrace Tomorrow

JOYCE MEYER

New York Boston Nashville

FaithWords
Hachette Book Group USA
237 Park Avenue
New York, NY 10017

Visit our Web site at www.faithwords.com.

Printed in the United States of America

First Edition: April 2008

10 9 8 7 6 5 4 3 2 1

Library of Congress Cataloging-in-Publication Data

Meyer, Joyce
The secret to true happiness : enjoy today, embrace tomorrow / Joyce Meyer. — 1st ed.
p. cm.
ISBN-13: 978-0-446-53199-3
ISBN-10: 0-446-53199-5
1. Happiness—Religious aspects—Christianity. I. Title.
BV4647.J68M485 2008
248.4—dc22
2007034401

CONTENTS

INTRODUCTION

I am convinced one of the most important lessons we can ever learn is to choose to be happy every day of our lives as we look forward to the future. One of my greatest desires is to see people thoroughly enjoy the quality of life Jesus died to give us—to actually *be* happy. Not just to read about it or talk about it, but to walk in it and experience true happiness as a daily reality.

Many people, including me, are extremely goal oriented. We are so focused on tomorrow we often fail to appreciate and enjoy today because we are always thinking ahead, looking to the next event, working toward the completion of the next assignment, and seeing what we can check off our to-do lists. Our fast-paced, high-pressure society urges us to accomplish as much as we can as quickly as we can—so we can then accomplish even more. Over the years, I have learned that the intense pursuit of one goal after another can cause us to miss out on some of the happiness life offers us. God does have purposes and plans He wants us to fulfill during the course of our earthly lives, but He also wants us to enjoy and make the most of every day we live.

After years of ministry and interacting with people, I have come to believe that people desperately want to enjoy their lives—to live every day with peace, contentment, and joy, which I like to define as "anything from extreme hilarity to calm delight." In fact, I read recently that some people are so desperate for joy they are joining laughter clubs. In these clubs, people meet together every morning for the sole purpose of finding some way to laugh before they start their day. We may chuckle at the idea of laughter clubs, but their existence clearly reveals a deep hunger for joy in people's hearts.

The Pew Research Center confirmed this when they asked a number of Americans if they were enjoying their lives. What do you think the results were? Only about 34 percent report they are "very happy" in life.[1] This is not hard to believe, because we live in a society that highly values *what people have* over *who they are*. But nothing is worth having if we cannot enjoy it. No amount of money, no measure of fame, no job, no relationship, no talent or skill—nothing does any good at all if we do not enjoy our lives.

What about you? Are you enjoying today as you look toward tomorrow? Are you generally happy, content, and satisfied with who you are and what you do each day? Do you take time to notice and appreciate the everyday experiences that make life rich and rewarding? Or do you race through each day so you can get to the next one? Do you take breaks and find things to laugh about on a regular basis, or do you allow the pressure of your responsibilities to carve a frown on your face as you keep your nose to the grindstone?

Perhaps you desperately want to enjoy everyday life, but fear that actually enjoying something might not be "holy" or pleasing to God. For some reason, many of us have come to believe enjoying our lives is not okay. Often, we are not even aware we think or feel that way, but somehow we have decided we should not enjoy our lives. Instead, we believe we are supposed to be working, accomplishing, following the rules, meeting the deadlines, doing things "right," and keeping people happy at any cost.

I have great news for you: *God wants you to be happy today and every day*. He really does. Jesus' statement about life in John 10:10 is absolutely amazing to me: "The thief comes only in order to steal and kill and destroy. I came that they might have *and* enjoy life, and have it in abundance (to the full, till it overflows)."

What a scripture! Jesus wants us not simply to be alive, but to *enjoy* being alive. You see, Jesus did not come to us so our hearts would beat and our brains would function. He did not come simply to give us physical life, or to give us "just enough to get through" life's challenges and difficulties. You and I were not created to simply exist, pass the time, mope our way through life, dread each new day, or trudge through our jobs with our eyes on the time clock, just waiting to leave work and take our misery home. No, we were made to enjoy every aspect of our lives, every day of our lives. This is what God wants for us and why Jesus came. He came to impart to us true life—the rich, deep, joy-filled, radical life God intended for us, the kind that is "in abundance, to the full, until it overflows."

I'll never forget the woman who thanked me for giving her permission to enjoy life after she heard me teach on this subject. I know she represented countless others who have never felt free to enjoy life, so I want to make clear that we must believe God's will is for us to thoroughly enjoy life. You have permission to enjoy today while you are reaching for and embracing tomorrow—not just my permission, but permission from God Himself.

I challenge you today to go to a new level of enjoyment in your daily life. Determine now that you are going to enjoy where you are today on your way to where you want to be tomorrow. Say it with your mouth; stick it on your bathroom mirror; put it on your screensaver: "I am determined to enjoy today!" And influence everyone around you to do the same.

Whoever you are and whatever your level of happiness, I invite you to step into greater joy. Live with more passion; laugh more; relax more; smile more; do more to make other people happy, and enjoy more. You'll be glad you did, and you will accomplish more because we are the most creative when we are the happiest.

Several years ago, there came a time in our ministry when we changed the name of our television broadcast and our magazine from *Life in the Word* to *Enjoying Everyday Life*. One of the reasons for the change was that I feel so strongly about the importance of enjoying the present as we move toward the future. In John 10:10, Jesus was basically saying: "I came that you might *have life* and that you would enjoy it." Remember, He died so we could experience authentic happiness. Not temporarily, not once in a while, but all the time. He does not want us simply to *have* life; He wants us to *enjoy* and appreciate the gift of life He has given us. That begins by realizing and believing God really does want us to make the most of every day of our lives.

My own journey toward true happiness *every day* has not been easy, and I'll share more about that as we go through this book. Enjoying daily life was something I had to *learn* to do. But now that I know how to do it, I wouldn't want to live any other way. My desire in this book is to share with you some of the truths I've learned about the secret of true happiness. As you read them and apply them to your life, don't be surprised if you find yourself enjoying your life in ways you never dreamed possible. That's my prayer for you today.

—Joyce Meyer

CHAPTER

1

Enjoy Your Everyday Life

"Most folks are about as happy as they make up their minds to be."

—ABRAHAM LINCOLN

The only life you can enjoy is your own. That statement may seem so obvious it's unnecessary, but think about it. One of the primary reasons many people do not enjoy their lives is that they are not happy with the lives they have. When I speak to them about enjoying their lives, the first thought they have is, *I would enjoy my life if I had your life, Joyce!* Instead of embracing the realities of their lives, these people spend their time thinking, *I wish I looked like So-and-So. I wish I had So-and-So's job. I wish I were married. I wish my marriage weren't so difficult. I wish I had children. I wish my children would grow up. I wish I had a new house. I wish I didn't have such a big house to clean. I wish I had a big ministry . . .*

The truth of the matter is, the first step to enjoying our everyday lives is to accept the lives we've been given. We must not allow jealousy or comparison to cause us to be absent from our own lives because we want someone else's life.

The wise king Solomon wrote in Ecclesiastes 5:18, 19:

> "Behold, what I have seen to be good and fitting is for one to eat and drink, and to find enjoyment in all the labor in which

> he labors under the sun all the days which God gives him—for this is his [allotted] part. Also, every man to whom God has given riches and possessions, and the power to enjoy them and to accept his appointed lot and to rejoice in his toil—this is the gift of God [to him]."

I want you to notice the words "allotted part" and "appointed lot" in these verses. What Solomon is basically communicating here is: enjoy your life. Take your "appointed lot" in life and enjoy it. In other words, embrace the life—the personality, the strengths and weaknesses, the family, the resources, the opportunities, the physical qualities, the abilities, the gifts, and the uniqueness—God has given *you*.

Maybe you struggle with things that do not appear to be challenges for other people. For example, you may have a physical handicap or a learning disability. Perhaps you wanted to go to college, but could not. Maybe you do not believe you have as many outstanding qualities or remarkable gifts as someone else. You may wish something were different about your spouse, your children, your job, or your financial situation. Whatever the case, you have to take what you have and decide that you are going to do the best you can with it. After all, your life will not change until you start doing so.

God is asking you to be faithful with your life, not with someone else's. We see in Matthew 25 that the master gave three men talents (a type of money in the New Testament). To one he gave five talents, to another two, and to another he gave one. The Bible states he gave to each one according to his own ability. The master then went on a long journey and later returned for an accounting of what each man did with the talents entrusted to him. The man who received five talents invested his and gained five more. He was able to not only return to the master what was entrusted to him but also give back twice as much as he started with. The same thing happened with the man who was entrusted with two talents. But the man who only had one talent buried it because he was afraid and returned to the master his one original talent. The master was well pleased with the first man and the second man, but he rebuked the third man severely. All the man had to do was embrace his talent, invest it, and be able to give his master back more than he started with, and the master would have said to him, "Well done, good and faithful servant." He did not hear those words, though, because he did nothing with what he had.

> What are you doing with what you have been given?

The fact that the third man did not have as much as the first two men had nothing to do with the reward he would have received had he been faithful with what he had. God only holds us accountable for our gifts, not anybody else's. What are you doing with what you have been given? I believe this is a question we all need to ask ourselves quite frequently.

MAKE THE BEST OF WHAT YOU HAVE

So often, I have heard women say, "I just wish I looked like my friend." I want to respond, "Do you know what? You don't. Take what you do have and make the best of it." I have had firsthand experience with learning to deal with this kind of comparison over the years.

This lesson hit home for me one time in the most ordinary way when Dave and I went on an airplane trip with two of our friends. Now, Dave and I could never be accused of "traveling light." That day, we had nine suitcases. We travel often, and I decided long ago that with our heavy travel schedule, I was going to be comfortable and have everything I could possibly need with me. And I always take too much.

Our friends only had two suitcases—a medium-sized one they rolled and a small one they carried. When I saw them, I thought, *Now wait a minute, Dave and I are two people; our friends are two people. We have nine bags; they have two. Where am I missing it?*

I finally looked at my friend and teasingly said, "Do you know what? Part of the reason I have more luggage than you do is that it just takes me a lot longer than you to look good. I have to have more face paint, more curling irons, more frizzes and sprays and freezes and mousses and everything else."

Some of us simply have to work harder than others to look our best. My friend has nice, thick, naturally curly hair. She hardly has to do anything to make it look good. My hair, on the other hand, has to be washed and spritzed and dried and sprayed and all sorts of things. I need several jars and bottles of hair products to simply do my hair, but my friend has to do little more than wash hers and she's ready to go.

I wish I did not have to spend so much time and energy on my hair. I *really* wish that, but wishing will not change my hair! I have to be happy with what God has given me, and if what He's given me requires more time than what He's given someone else, I have to accept that.

Likewise, you have to be happy with *your* life. God has given you everything He has for a reason—and on purpose. Everything about you is by His design. I am not encouraging you to settle for situations that need to be improved, but I am urging you to accept the way God made you and the life He has given you. Don't complain; don't compare; don't covet someone else's life, and don't spend your valuable time wishing things were different. Realize that every life includes good and bad, happy and sad, easy and difficult, strength and weakness. Your life is really no different than anyone else's when you look at it from a broad perspective. There may be certain specific differences, but *nobody has the perfect life.* Determine today to take the first step toward learning to enjoy your everyday life by making the most of *your* life. Embrace *your* life because God is never going to give you someone else's!

Determine today to take the first step toward learning to enjoy your everyday life by making the most of *your* life.

EMBRACE THE ORDINARY

Another key to true happiness lies in understanding that most of life is "everyday." Most of our lives consist of a routine—an unremarkable series of events that take place day after day, year after year. So if we are really going to enjoy every day, we must learn to embrace the ordinary—to delight in little things, to appreciate small blessings, and to find pleasure in the circumstances and situations other people might overlook.

Another key to true happiness lies in understanding that most of life is "everyday."

Sometimes people think enjoying life means celebrating special occasions, observing important milestones, getting raises and promotions, going on a vacation, buying something new, winning a big game, or closing a significant business deal. The truth is: life is not one big party; we should not expect to giggle our way through every day; and we cannot sit around waiting for the next exciting event. Thankfully, those noteworthy things do happen, but they are few and far between. They certainly do not occur every day, or even once a week or once a month. We need to celebrate life's exciting occasions and its big events, but in between them, we must be able to find joy in fighting traffic, going to work, cleaning house, raising children, taking out the trash, paying the bills, and dealing with grouchy neighbors. We all have responsibilities and things we must do, so when I speak of enjoying each day, I am not talking about entertaining ourselves from daylight until dark or about getting "our way" all the time. I am talking about the "everyday" situations I have mentioned in this chapter and the whole host of others I have not listed, the situations in which we really learn to enjoy everyday life. Enjoying life begins with making a decision to do so, because the truth is, no matter what kind of lives we have, we will not enjoy them unless we decide to do so.

Most of life involves getting up in the morning, going to bed at night, and doing what we need to do in the meantime. This reminds me of Mark 4:26, 27, where Jesus said: "The kingdom of God is like a man who scatters seed upon the ground, and then continues sleeping and rising night and day while the seed sprouts and grows *and* increases—he knows not how." This scripture teaches us that something happens to a seed—a process of growth and nourishment—that no one can see. Much development takes place in the seed while it is underground.

The same principle applies to our lives. Much of life takes place when no one is looking; and God works in our lives during the ordinary times. When nothing remarkable seems to be taking place and everything is "business as usual," that's where we develop character and the ability to enjoy everyday life. And as we enjoy life moment by moment, day by day, week after week, and year after year, we find all of life has become rich, deep, and satisfying. True life is really not found in arriving at a destination; it is found in the journey.

When nothing remarkable seems to be taking place and everything is "business as usual," that's where we develop character and the ability to enjoy everyday life.

THE FREEDOM TO BE HAPPY

Not long ago, I ran across a story about a woman who learned to enjoy everyday life after many years of trying. As we close this chapter, I'd like to share it with you.

> I've never been an athlete. I've never been much interested in sports, ever since I stopped playing touch football with the boys when I hit puberty. I've tried tennis. I hit the ball too high, too long, and way over into left field. I've tried softball. Thank goodness that ball is "soft" and big, because it felt just awful when it hit me in the eye. I tried running, but I couldn't get anyone to chase me.

Finally, I settled on walking, and for a number of years, I walked three to five miles a day. I realize that there is an Olympic sport referred to as "walking," but when I tried that, all I succeeded in doing was throwing my hip out.

I'm definitely not an athlete, but I make do, especially in my mid-life years. Which brings a question to my mind. When did I hit mid-life? I remember when I hit thirty. I had to visit a grief counselor, because I knew my life was over. I remember forty. I had to see a grief counselor the day after my first child graduated from high school and moved out of the house, because I knew my life was over.

Then I hit fifty, and I was all excited, because I was able to join an organization called AARP. My husband was especially excited because he is younger than I, and he got to join too!

Fifty became the magic age. I knew that as long as I was in good health, in this day and age, I probably had a good fifty years ahead of me. Then came the asthma. OK, I had that much earlier, but it only became life-threatening after fifty. Then came the fibromyalgia. OK, I had that earlier, but it's not life-threatening. Then came the arthritis, and more recently at fifty-five, the diabetes. Somewhere in there, I became very interested in pharmaceuticals. But finally one day I became free.

I began by noticing the sunsets, and now I had the time to stop and really wonder at the beauty and the magnitude of it all. Then I moved onto the sunrises, and I quickly found out that if I wasted the early morning, I missed the loveliest part of the day. Then I began to notice how grateful I was to be able to witness the changing of the seasons. The first whisper of spring, the rustling of the leaves beneath my feet in the fall.

When illness would hit me, I found that I actually enjoyed the solitude—a time to reflect, gather my thoughts, and pray, at leisure. I found that I was experiencing this mid-life season, and I was no longer missing every moment, shackled to the chains of worry and what might be. I found that worrying about tomorrow only served to make me overlook the blessings of today.

> It's not always easy. A few loads of laundry and a pile of dishes can take an entire day. But then, I don't push myself a lot. So I forget to make the bed as I watch the rosy glow of dawn meet the rising sun. I have time to walk our wooded acre with my little dachshund straining at the leash.
>
> I get to meet the day every day. I get to say good-night to the sunsets. I've studied a lot of sunsets in the last five years, and I've never seen two that were alike. I get to know my Creator as I never have before, and I've gotten to make my mind up about the mysteries of life. I've grown certain that all this was no accident.
>
> I feed the birds and I take great delight in their multicolored hues, especially in the spring. I drag a chair to stand on so that I can fill the feeders to the brim. I say a little prayer as I wobble, a little cockeyed, on the chair, and I laugh at myself and all the pretensions of my younger life. I take great delight in my life. I thank God for all the precious little things of every day. Friends. Family. Neighbors. And health—a health of the soul. For I have come to understand what real health is, and when you have real health, then you truly have everything.[1]

The author of this story did not truly enjoy life until she experienced illness. Many times, people rush through their days without stopping to delight in the everyday, and then, when they face a crisis, they finally slow down enough to enjoy life, family, friends, work, and simply being alive.

I don't want a crisis or an illness to have to be the catalyst that causes you to enjoy each day of your life. I want you to choose happiness right now—because it *is* a choice. Your life is God's gift to you, even in its common, run-of-the-mill, mundane ordinariness. Decide today you are going to stop waiting for the big breaks and the exciting events before you're happy. In fact, do something today that will raise your joy level in the midst of your everyday life.

CHAPTER

2

Start with God

"We ought to see the face of God every morning before we see the face of man."

—D. L. MOODY

There once was a lady who had to travel extensively for her business, and most of her travel involved flying. But flying made her very nervous, so she always took her Bible to read on long flights because it helped her relax.

On one trip, she was sitting next to a man. When he saw her pull out her Bible, he gave a little chuckle and a smirk, and went back to what he was doing.

After a while, he turned to her and asked, "You don't really believe all that stuff in that book, do you?"

The lady replied, "Of course I do. It's in the Bible."

He said, "Well, what about that guy who was swallowed by the whale?"

She replied, "Oh, Jonah. Yes, I believe that story. It is in the Bible."

He asked, "Well, how do you suppose he survived all that time inside a whale?"

The lady said, "Well, I don't really know. I guess I will ask him when I get to heaven."

"What if he isn't in heaven?" the man asked sarcastically.

"Then you can ask him!" replied the lady.[1]

* * *

This humorous story reminds us we all need a personal relationship with God through Jesus Christ. This relationship is necessary for us to go to heaven when we die and to spend eternity with Him, but it is also essential if we want to enjoy our lives today. The Bible teaches us that in God "we live and move and have our being" (Acts 17:28). That tells me in order to have *real* life, we need to be "in God," vitally connected to Him in an intimate, heart-to-heart communion.

I believe we need to begin each day of our lives talking to God, listening to Him, and spending time in His Word. I encourage you to start every day with God. Before your feet even hit the floor in the mornings, make a habit of meditating on a Bible verse, reminding yourself of a biblical principle, or simply saying, "Good morning, Lord. I love You." Spend meaningful time in God's presence before you go about the other activities of your day.

One of my favorite scriptures to pray first thing in the morning is Psalm 25:1: "Unto You, O Lord, do I bring my life." We need to submit everything about our lives to Him—our work, our relationships, our time, our energy, the decisions we need to make. Whether or not we use the exact words, we can apply the principle of Psalm 25:1, bringing every aspect of our daily lives to Him. This will make an enormous difference in your ability to enjoy our lives today and embrace every day that lies ahead.

LIVE BY THE WORD

The best advice I could ever give you is to live your life according to the truth of God's Word. I believe we should honor God's Word in our lives, and give it a place of priority every day by reading and studying it and doing it to

The best advice I could ever give you is to live your life according to the truth of God's Word.

the best of our ability. From a personal perspective, I can honestly say I love God's Word. Nothing on earth has changed my life—and changed me—the way God's Word has. As a minister, I can say I have seen countless people experience radical transformation and positive, lasting change as they have applied biblical truths and principles to their lives.

The Bible contains answers to every question you could ever have and every situation you will ever face. True, it will not tell you specifically where to go on vacation next year or what color to paint your house, but it will impart to you principles of right living, right thinking, wisdom, and faith. It will instruct you through stories of men and women who lived long ago, but faced many of the same human challenges and relational struggles you and I face today. It will encourage you to persevere, inspire you to overcome, help you make good decisions, and teach you to hear and obey God's voice.

I am always saddened when I encounter people who view the Bible as an outdated, irrelevant religious book. Yes, its words are centuries old, but instead of being old-fashioned or obsolete, they are ancient truths that have stood the test of time and been proven over and over and over again. The words of Scripture are alive; they are saturated with the power of God. They are as real and applicable today as they have ever been—and in our world today, we desperately need to be grounded in this kind of godly truth. The Bible is not only meant for preachers and "church people"; it is a book for everyone in every walk of life. It is spiritual, but it is also extremely practical.

God has given us His Word as a source of strength, wisdom, and guidance in our everyday lives. Just take a look at some of the topics it addresses. Some of these, if not all of them, are sure to be aspects of your daily life:

God has given us His Word as a source of strength, wisdom, and guidance in our everyday lives.

Managing finances: "The rich rule over the poor, and the borrower is servant to the lender" (Proverbs 22:7).

"For which of you, wishing to build a farm building, does not first sit down and calculate the cost [to see] whether he has sufficient means to finish it?" (Luke 14:28).

Choosing friends: "Make no friendships with a man given to anger, and with a wrathful man do not associate" (Proverbs 22:24).

"Go from the presence of a foolish *and* self-confident man, for you will not find knowledge on his lips" (Proverbs 14:7).

Overcoming the temptation to gossip: "He who guards his mouth and his tongue keeps himself from troubles" (Proverbs 21:23).

"Argue your cause with your neighbor himself; discover not *and* disclose not another's secret" (Proverbs 25:9).

Developing a work ethic: "He who cultivates his land will have plenty of bread, but he who follows worthless people *and* pursuits will have poverty enough" (Proverbs 28:19).

"If anyone will not work, neither let him eat" (2 Thessalonians 3:10).

Watching your mouth: "He who guards his mouth and his tongue keeps himself from troubles" (Proverbs 21:23).

"Do you see a man who is hasty in his words? There is more hope for a [self-confident] fool than for him?" (Proverbs 29:20).

Overseeing your household: "Through skillful *and* godly Wisdom is a house (a life, a home, a family) built, and by understanding it is established [on a sound and good foundation]" (Proverbs 24:3).

"Be diligent to know the state of your flocks, and look well to your herds" (Proverbs 27:23).

Raising children: "Train up a child in the way he should go [and in keeping with his individual gift or bent], and when he is old he will not depart from it" (Proverbs 22:6).

"Fathers, do not irritate *and* provoke your children to anger [do not exasperate them to resentment], but rear them [tenderly] in the training *and* discipline and the counsel *and* admonition of the Lord" (Ephesians 6:4).

Disciplining children: "Discipline your son while there is hope, but do not [indulge your angry resentments by undue chastisements and] set yourself to his ruin" (Proverbs 19:18).

"Correct your son and he will give you rest; yes, he will give delight to your heart" (Proverbs 29:17).

Responding to offense or injustice: "Say not, I will do to him as he has done to me; I will pay the man back for his deed" (Proverbs 24:29).

"You have heard that it was said, You shall love your neighbor and hate your enemy; but I tell you, Love your enemies and pray for those who persecute you" (Matthew 5:43, 44).

Dealing with anger: "When angry, do not sin; do not ever let your wrath (your exasperation, your fury or indignation) last until the sun goes down. Leave no [such] room *or* foothold for the devil [give no opportunity to him]" (Ephesians 4:26, 27).

"Understand [this], my beloved brethren. Let every man be quick to hear [a ready listener], slow to speak, slow to take offense *and* to get angry" (James 1:19).

SPEAK THE WORD

For many years, my mouth got me in trouble. Sometimes, I was undisciplined in my speech and made comments I should not have made to other people; sometimes, I said things I later wished I had not said; and a lot of the time, I was grumbling, complaining, and speaking negatively. This made me—and everyone around me—miserable!

As I grew in my personal relationship with God, I came to realize words have power and my negative words were not helping me enjoy my life. Over time, I was able to stop speaking negatively, and I saw some improvement, but not as much as I wanted. Then one day, as I was praying, I sensed God speaking to my heart, *Joyce, you have stopped saying* negative *things, but you have not started saying* positive *things.*

I knew God's Word is full of positive, life-giving, life-changing truth, so I began to make a list of scriptures that reflected the positive changes I longed to see in my life. I then started speaking those words aloud, sometimes several times per day, and the results were amazing.

> Let me encourage you to speak God's Word aloud.

Let me encourage you to speak God's Word aloud too. Go through the Bible and identify scriptures that represent God's truth and perspective on the situations important in your life. Whether you need physical healing, hope for your future, comfort concerning your children, wisdom in relationships, or help getting your fear or anger under control, you can find a scripture on the subject. There are many books that make this easy for you by listing topics such as these (and many others) and then listing corresponding scriptures. One such resource is my book *The Secret Power of Speaking God's Word.*

SAY AND DO

In addition to speaking God's Word aloud, we must also obey it. James 1:22 says, "But be doers of the word [obey the message], and not merely listeners to it." One of the primary ways we position ourselves for God's blessings is by obeying His Word. In fact, this very point is the message of much of the Bible, especially the Old Testament: "If you obey God, you'll be blessed. If you don't, you won't."

God's Word is truth, and we know from John 8:32 that the truth sets us free. But God's truth can only be effective for us if we receive it in our hearts and apply it to our everyday circumstances through obedience. Stop right now and ask yourself if you are applying God's principles to your own situations or if you have fallen into the trap of merely reading it out of duty. If we want the Word to work in our lives, we need to do more than read it, study it, know it, and confess it; we have to do as it says. I understand this is not always easy—especially when we would rather stay angry at someone and we see that the Word says we must forgive; or when we would rather spend a day being lazy and we know the Word teaches us to be diligent—but obedience is necessary if we want to enjoy God's blessings. In John 13:17, Jesus said, "If you know these things, blessed *and* happy *and* to be envied are you if you practice them [if you act accordingly and really do them]."

KEEP COMMUNICATION OPEN

Talking with God about everything gives us a sense of belonging, of being cared for by Someone on our side Who is powerful. One of the phrases I like to use when teaching on prayer is: "Pray your way through the day." This is certainly good advice to follow if we want to enjoy our lives each day. We need to remember we can pray anytime, anywhere. Ephesians 6:18 instructs us to "pray at all times (on every occasion, in every season) in the Spirit, with all [manner of] prayer," and 1 Thessalonians 5:17 tells us to be "unceasing in prayer." In other words, we need to keep the lines of communication open with God. We need to stay in constant fellowship with Him through prayer, all day, every day.

Talking with God about everything gives us a sense of belonging, of being cared for by Someone on our side Who is powerful.

While there are times when we need to be very diligent, focused, and set apart as we pray, we do not have to wait until we are in church or some other designated place, or until we have a specific amount of time, before we pray. The best way I know to be "unceasing in prayer" is to live as though God is constantly paying attention to us, because He is. For example, we can pray quick, simple, effective prayers aloud or silently. We can say silently while sitting in a business meeting: *Oh God, help me make a good decision here. Give me Your wisdom to speak wisely and be a blessing to my company.* We can whisper a prayer as we drop off our children at school: "God, protect them today. Help them learn everything they need to know. Give them favor with their teachers and their friends."

We can also pray prayers of praise and thanksgiving as we go about our daily lives, saying things like: "Thank You, Lord, for helping me through this day," or "I worship You, God, for Your goodness this afternoon." These types of prayers take only a few seconds, but they keep us focused on God, aware of His presence, and in continual communication with Him. They keep us connected to a power source beyond our understanding. Living in the presence of God releases joy in our lives and gives us the ability to enjoy everything we do.

Let me urge you to live your life the way I have described in this chapter. Start every day with God. Read His Word; speak it aloud; and obey it. Determine to live your life and approach the situations you face daily according to His truth. In addition, pray your way through every day. Always remember you do not need to impress God with eloquent prayers; instead, keep them simple and sincere. Make your relationship with God top priority, and refuse to let the pressures of daily living distract you from Him. He is always *with* you and He is always *for* you, so begin your day with Him, walk with Him through all the ordinary things you have to do, and enjoy His presence every day.

Make your relationship with God top priority, and refuse to let the pressures of daily living distract you from Him.

CHAPTER 3

Make the Choice

"All I can say about life is...
enjoy it!"
—BOB NEWHART

I don't have to tell you life is not perfect. That is not breaking news to you, is it? Truly, no one's life is everything he or she wants it to be. We all have challenges and struggles, sometimes even heartbreaks and tragedies. I have never met one person who could honestly say, "Every day of my life is every bit as wonderful as I always dreamed it would be."

What may be news to some people is that God's desire *is not only* to make us happy or to give us the lives we've always hoped for. Often, we so desperately want unsaved people to become Christians we tell them their lives will be better if they will just receive Jesus. In many ways, this is true, but sometimes we paint such a rosy picture we lead people to believe they will never have another problem again for the rest of their lives and everything will be wonderful and sublime if they will simply ask Jesus to be their Lord and Savior. This is not true. Jesus did not come to give anyone a life of leisure; Jesus came to give us *abundant* life, but not a trouble-free life. Part of the abundance He offers those who belong to Him is the power of His Spirit to overcome what others cannot. You see, the good news is that, as a Christian, even if you have a problem you have the Problem Solver living in you, ready to help at any time.

As believers, we have the power of the Holy Spirit to help us deal with circumstances differently than nonbelievers do. When we are in Christ, we are supernaturally anointed to live our natural, ordinary lives in supernatural ways. God's anointing is the presence and power of the Holy Spirit always available to us. We can rejoice in situations in which those who do not have access to God's power could not be happy at all. We can be at peace in the midst of a crisis, and we can be positive when everything around is gloomy and depressing. Why? Because we believe all things eventually work out for good and we do not allow our circumstances or our feelings to determine our decisions. We know we have choices to make—and we can choose joy, peace, positive attitudes, and stability. We can enjoy every day of our lives, but that will not happen by accident; we must choose to do so.

When we are in Christ, we are supernaturally anointed to live our natural, ordinary lives in supernatural ways.

YOU ONLY LIVE ONCE

I have learned some important lessons about choosing to enjoy life through the way I raised my children. I loved them; I was a responsible parent; and I certainly cannot say I never enjoyed my children, but I look back now and realize I did not enjoy them as fully as I could have and wish I had. The reason I did not enjoy them more often is that I was a workaholic. Professionally, I was so busy working, and at home, I was so busy keeping everything neat and tidy and clean I never felt free to relax and enjoy them. (I didn't realize the mess would still be there the next day and that some quality time with my children was more important!)

I can remember many times when my children wanted me to stop working and said, "Come and play with me, Mommy." My immediate response was, "Oh, I can't do that, I've got work to do."

We will *always* have work to do, which means we will have to choose to take a break and enjoy life sometimes. We need balance when it comes to choosing how we spend our time. There are some situations especially where our children are concerned, we will never have an opportunity to relive. If we do not choose to embrace and enjoy them when we can, we will reach the end of our lives and be filled with regret. The only way we can avoid having regrets tomorrow is to make better choices today.

The only way we can avoid having regrets tomorrow is to make better choices today.

This short article below drives home the importance of making good choices each day and reminds us to focus on what is truly important in life.

> Ready or not, some day it will all come to an end.
>
> There will be no more sunrises, no minutes, hours or days. All the things you collected, whether treasured or forgotten will pass to someone else.
>
> Your wealth, fame and temporal power will shrivel to irrelevance. It will not matter what you owned or what you were owed.
>
> Your grudges, resentments, frustrations and jealousies will finally disappear. So too, your hopes, ambitions, plans and to-do lists will expire.
>
> The wins and losses that once seemed so important will fade away.
>
> It won't matter where you came from or what side of the tracks you lived on at the end.
>
> It won't matter whether you were beautiful or brilliant. Even your gender and skin color will be irrelevant.
>
> So what will matter? How will the value of your days be measured?

What will matter is not what you bought but what you built, not what you got but what you gave.

What will matter is not your success but your significance.

What will matter is not what you learned but what you taught.

What will matter is every act of integrity, compassion, courage, or sacrifice that enriched, empowered or encouraged others to emulate your example.

What will matter is not your competence but your character.

What will matter is not how many people you knew, but how many will feel a lasting loss when you're gone.

What will matter is not your memories but the memories that live in those who loved you.

What will matter is how long you will be remembered, by whom and for what.

Living a life that matters doesn't happen by accident. It's not a matter of circumstance but of choice.

Choose to live a life that matters.[1]

CHOOSE TO ENJOY

I truly enjoy what I do, but it hasn't always been that way. Years ago, I realized that as much as I loved being in the ministry and doing what God called me to do, I really wasn't enjoying it. I know it may seem strange to say, "I loved it, but I didn't enjoy it," so let me explain.

I am a hard worker and a very responsible person. I have a lot to keep up with, many activities to oversee, and a great deal of responsibility in life and in ministry. I was doing a good job handling my responsibilities and fulfilling my obligations, and a certain part of me was very satisfied. But, at the same time, I always found myself thinking, *Boy, I sure will be glad when this conference is over so I can get home and enjoy Sunday.*

Many people think the same way I did. We start so many sentences with "I'll be so glad when [fill in the blank]." This kind of thinking keeps us so focused on where we want to go that we do not enjoy getting there. When I realized I was not enjoying the journey, I simply made a decision to change. I made some adjustments that made my intense travel and ministry schedule easier and more comfortable, but most importantly, I decided that if I were going to spend my time flying on airplanes, staying in hotels, and standing on my feet preaching for hours, I was going to enjoy it.

Soon, I did reach a whole new level of joy because I realized that all it takes to begin enjoying something—anything—is a choice. All it takes is a new mindset, a deliberate decision to enjoy what you are doing. Just as you can decide to be frustrated or unhappy, you can also decide to be happy in any situation.

Just as you can decide to be frustrated or unhappy, you can also decide to be happy in any situation.

All of us are tempted at times to complain and say we are not happy in life. We all have moments and seasons when we do not enjoy our lives. Sometimes, getting past that is simply a matter of telling yourself, "Well, I just need to make a decision. If I have to clean house (or change the oil in the car or do the laundry or cut the grass), I'm going to choose to enjoy life while I do it." We must prepare ourselves mentally for what we need to do.

We need to choose to have positive attitudes, because there is so much to be unhappy, concerned, and even disturbed about when we look at the world. If we are going to enjoy our lives, we will have to do so on purpose. If we don't do it intentionally by making a decision, we are not likely to do it at all. Wherever we are, whatever we are going through, we can say, "This is where I am; this is what's going on in my life; and I choose to make the most of it."

THE SECRET OF CONTENTMENT

I believe you can enjoy almost everything about your life if you will make that decision. Unless you are in the midst of a major crisis, there is probably very little going on in your life you cannot find a way to enjoy. Even in challenging situations or relationships, you can find something positive. If nothing else, you can decide to rejoice in the fact they are developing character in you and helping you grow!

We *can* learn to enjoy life even during difficult times.

We *can* learn to enjoy life even during difficult times. The apostle Paul, a man acquainted both with life's comforts and ease and with difficulty, writes:

> "For I have learned how to be content (satisfied to the point where I am not disturbed or disquieted) in whatever state I am. I know how to be abased *and* live humbly in straitened circumstances, and I know also how to enjoy plenty *and* live in abundance. I have learned in any and all circumstances the secret of facing every situation, whether well-fed or going hungry, having a sufficiency *and* enough to spare or going without *and* being in want. I have strength for all things in Christ Who empowers me [I am ready for anything and equal to anything through Him Who infuses inner strength into me; I am self-sufficient in Christ's sufficiency]" (Philippians 4:11–13).

Paul learned to be the same in every season—to be content, or satisfied, in every situation. He made a choice to make the best of whatever came his way, and we can too. What was Paul's secret to contentment? I think he believed the words he wrote in Romans 8:28: "We are assured *and* know that [God being a partner in their labor] all things work together *and* are [fitting into a plan] for good to *and* for those who love God and are called according to [His] design *and* purpose." I believe Paul had enough experience to realize there was no point in fighting the inevitable. Life is not perfect; we have to deal with it as it is; and we can choose whether to enjoy it or not.

I also think Paul believed he developed godly character during the abasing times in his life and enjoyed the growth he attained in the times of abounding. It is in times of difficulty we press deeper into God and His ways. He knows when we need seasons of abounding, and He is always faithful to provide. God will never allow more trouble to come to us than we can bear, but He always provides the way out (see 1 Corinthians 10:13).

As I think about this principle, I am reminded of my work with a strength coach. When he thinks I am ready to develop more muscle, he gives me more weight to lift. But I have noticed that he is always right beside me and if at any time he sees I am having too much difficulty lifting the weight, he quickly takes it from me so I won't hurt myself. God has used this example in my life to show me how He relates to us. If at any time we truly have more than we can handle, He will intervene and help us.

JENNY'S CHOICE

The world is full of people who make difficult choices to enjoy life in the face of suffering and hardship. One of those people is a young woman named Jenny, whose story I want to share with you as we close this chapter:

"A Different Kind of Athlete"

We found out that Jenny was hearing impaired, when she was four and a half years old. Several surgeries and speech classes later, when she was seven, we found out that Jenny had Juvenile Rheumatoid Arthritis.

She could not put pressure on the heels of her feet, so she walked on tiptoe, and when the pain became unbearable, I carried her. Jenny was fortunate, though, because she did not suffer the deformities, often associated with JRA.

All through grade school, and on into high school, Jenny suffered, yet never complained. She took her medicine, and

I would often wrap her feet in steaming towels, and hold her until the pain eased. But, as soon as she could withstand the pain, Jenny immediately carried on, as though she were pain free.

She wore a smile on her face, a song on her lips, and a love and acceptance of others, that was, simply, amazing. I don't remember her ever voicing self-pity. She ran, when she could run. She played when she could play, and she danced when she could dance. And, when she could do none of these things, she took her medicine, and she waited until she could.

Jenny, a beautiful blonde, with warm brown eyes, was never a cheerleader. She never competed in a sport. She could not even take part in a Gym Class, though she took the same health class four years in a row, just so she could pass with a substitute credit each year. She joined the band. She won a place in the Governor's School for the Arts; yet, no one in the Charleston, South Carolina School System knew what to do with Jenny. The perimeters were, simply, not in place to deal with a student, who was both active and handicapped.

Jenny continued to have one surgery after another on her ears, all through school. Her hearing improved to 60%, and she taught herself to read lips. She carried a pillow to school, all through high school, and once, when she suddenly experienced crippling pain, her friends scooped her up, and carried her from class to class.

She was totally mainstreamed, popular, and funny, attending every football game, cheering the team on, carrying her pillow everywhere she went, so that she could cushion the pain, when she sat down. Then came her senior year. She would be considered for scholarships; however school activities, especially sports, could often mean the difference between receiving an award or losing out.

So Jenny came to a decision; and in her quirky, unorthodox manner, she began to bombard the high school football coach. She begged. She pleaded. She promised. She got her best friend to sign up with her. Finally the coach gave in, with the admonition, "If you miss *one* game, you're out!" So, Jenny became Manager of the Garrett High School Football Team.

She carried big buckets of water to her teammates. She bandaged knees and ankles before every game. She massaged necks and backs. She gave pep talks. She was continually at their beck and call, and it turned out to be one of the best years for the Garrett High School Football Team, in its twenty-five-year history. Often Jenny could be seen carrying a bucket of water in each hand, nearly dragging them, along with her pillow tucked under her arm.

When asked why he thought that the team was winning all their games, even in the face of injury, one linebacker explained, in his soft, Charleston drawl, "Well, when you've been knocked down, and you can't seem to move, you look up and see Jenny Lewis, limping across the field, dragging her buckets and carrying her pillow. It makes anything the rest of us may suffer seem pretty insignificant."

At the Senior Awards ceremony, Jenny received a number of scholarships to College of Charleston. Her favorite scholarship, however, was a small one from the Charleston Women's Club. The President of the Women's Club listed Jenny's accomplishments, starting with her grades, and ending with an excited, ". . . and the first girl to letter in football, in Garrett High School history!!"[2]

CHAPTER 4

Laugh a Lot

"Laughter is an instant vacation!"
—MILTON BERLE

I always appreciate humorous stories, so before I share anything else with you in this chapter, here's a story guaranteed to make you chuckle:

> After being nearly snowbound for two weeks last winter, a Seattle man departed for his vacation in Miami Beach, where he was to meet his wife the next day, at the conclusion of her business trip to Minneapolis. They were looking forward to pleasant weather and a nice time together.
>
> Unfortunately, there was some sort of mixup at the boarding gate, and the man was told he would have to wait for a later flight. He tried to appeal to a supervisor, but was told the airline was not responsible for the problem and it would do no good to complain.
>
> Upon arrival at the hotel the next day, he discovered that Miami Beach was having a heat wave. Miami's weather was almost as uncomfortably hot as Seattle's was cold. The desk clerk gave him a message that his wife would arrive as planned.
>
> He could hardly wait to get to the pool area to cool off and quickly sent his wife an email. However, due to his haste,

he made an error in the email address. His message, therefore, arrived at the home of an elderly preacher's wife, whose even older husband had died only the day before. When the grieving widow opened her email, she took one look at the monitor, let out an anguished scream and fell to the floor dead.

Her family rushed to her room where they saw this message on the screen:

Dearest wife,
Departed yesterday, as you know.
Just now got checked in.
Some confusion at the gate.
Appeal was denied.
Received confirmation of your arrival tomorrow.
Your loving husband.

P.S. Things are not as we thought. You're going to be surprised at how hot it is down here.[1]

LIKE A MEDICINE

You and I need to laugh and be lighthearted. Even the Bible says lightheartedness is good for us, and throughout the Scriptures we are encouraged to "rejoice," to "be joyful," and to "be glad." Many of us know Proverbs 17:22 in the old King James Version, which says, "A merry heart doeth good like a medicine." In the Amplified Bible, this verse says, "A happy heart is good medicine." In both translations, we see that being joyful is of great benefit to us.

Most know laughter can pull us out of the pit of depression or sadness; it can even give us boosts of energy; and it can completely change our attitude or outlook on a situation. I did some research on laughter one time and learned some additional information about it. For instance, when we laugh, it actually releases tension, anxiety,

> Most know laughter can pull us out of the pit of depression or sadness; it can even give us boosts of energy; and it can completely change our attitude or outlook on a situation.

anger, fear, shame, and guilt. Laughter also increases antibodies and is believed to have a protective capacity against viruses, bacteria, and other microorganisms.

Science affirms that laughter truly is like a medicine because it causes the release of body chemicals called endorphins. These substances help relieve pain and create a sense of well-being within us. Studies indicate that endorphins may also reduce stress, enhance circulation, improve the immune system, lower blood pressure, stimulate the nervous system, decrease cholesterol, and strengthen the heart. Like a massage, a good belly laugh can stimulate all of our major organs. Laughter, some say, is equivalent to any other standard aerobic exercise. A good, hearty chuckle really is like internal jogging. It's an internal aerobic exercise; we inhale more oxygen when we laugh; and researches say it can increase the capacity of our lungs.

Some of the findings I have mentioned have certainly proven to be true in my life. As just one example, I remember a night when my family and I were playing a game. I had a really terrible headache, but something funny happened and I started laughing hysterically, having several minutes of side-splitting laughter. When I finally stopped, I noticed that my headache was completely gone.

LIGHTEN UP!

> The average child laughs about 150 times per day. No wonder the Bible says we need to approach Jesus as little children.

Did you know that the average man or woman laughs 4 to 8 times per day, but the average child laughs about 150 times per day? No wonder the Bible says we need to approach Jesus as little children. Children are happy!

We adults, on the other hand, need to lighten up. We would be so much better off if we would stop being so very serious about everything and start enjoying our lives more.

One of the dynamics causing adults much trouble is we take our personal faults and mistakes so seriously. We spend too much time opposing ourselves, being our own worst enemies. We often judge ourselves more strictly than we judge others, and we focus on our faults far too intensely. Of course, there are times when situations are grave and there are circumstances requiring us to be serious. But, so many of the little, everyday things we treat as monumental are really not so terribly important. Someone once said, "Blessed are those who can laugh at themselves, for they shall never cease to be amused." So let me encourage you today: give yourself a break!

God knew every flaw and weakness you would have and every mistake you would make when He called you into relationship with Himself. Nothing about you is a surprise to God. Sometimes people think God extends salvation to us and then sits in heaven, looking down at us, saying, "Oh no. *Now* what am I going to do? I didn't know he was going to do *that*!"

The Bible teaches us God knows everything we will ever do or say. He made us; He made us to be imperfect; He made us to need Him. Through His Word, He is still saying to us today what He told Jeremiah centuries ago: "I *know* you." Specifically, He spoke to Jeremiah, "Before I formed you in the womb I knew *and* approved of you [as My chosen instrument]." (Jeremiah 1:5).

God knows—and has always known—everything about you. He knows what you will think, do, and say every day for the rest of your life on earth. He also knows how He will help you, teach you, correct you, encourage you, and give you grace for all your faults and failures. He is always for you, never against you, no matter what you do. This truth should set you free to lighten up, enjoy being whom God made you to be, and have a laugh at your own expense.

You are who you are. You do what you do, and it's not always

American actress and Academy Award winner Ethel Barrymore once said: "You grow up the day you have the first real laugh at yourself."

perfect. In fact, sometimes you really mess up! That's part of being human. But if you also love God, have a heart to change, and ask Him to help you, then you can relax. God is working on you, changing you every day, helping you grow. American actress and Academy Award winner Ethel Barrymore once said: "You grow up the day you have the first real laugh at yourself." I believe she's right about that. We need to have childlike hearts that laugh easily and smile readily, but we also need to have enough maturity to be lighthearted about ourselves. So accept who you are; laugh at yourself; and enjoy your life today.

YOUR JOY IS YOUR STRENGTH

Choosing to laugh, be joyful, and take a lighthearted approach to many things in life will do more than make you a pleasant person. Nehemiah 8:10 says "the joy of the Lord is your strength." Think about it: How strong or confident do you feel when you are discouraged, depressed, or "down in the dumps"? You don't feel strong at all. But when you allow God to fill you with joy, you feel as though you can do anything.

Many times, when Satan comes against us, he is simply trying to steal our joy. He wants us to fear, despair, or have a negative outlook on life because he knows if he can dampen our joy, he can steal our strength. In order to stay strong, we must also stay joyful.

Mark Twain said, "The human race has one really effective weapon, and that is laughter." As believers, we know God has given us many spiritual weapons, but Twain is right in the fact that *laughter is a weapon.* Laughter in and of itself is not the same as joy, but laughter certainly is an aspect of joy.

Sometimes I am amazed at the lack of joy in people's lives, but I understand it. I was once a person who really struggled to enjoy life.

I was legalistic; I was a workaholic; and I grew up in an environment where being happy was not okay and fun was not something we valued. The same dynamics are true for many people. They simply grew up in an atmosphere of fear, stress, strife and anger, confusion, or other dysfunctions. Perhaps they were criticized for being lighthearted or surrounded by such miserable people they dared not appear to be happy. For them, and for me, the goal of each day was to survive it, not enjoy it.

JOY IN THE MIDST OF TROUBLE

There are also people who seem to think they cannot enjoy their lives if they have any problems. If they have problems, they focus intensely on finding a solution, and they will not relax or enjoy life until the problems are solved. Of course, there are times we need to address urgent matters, and there are times we need to apply spiritual disciplines in our lives, but we do not have to live under constant pressure or rigid demands. We can rejoice in spite of and the midst of our problems! Start by smiling a lot; a smile is a way to prime the pump of joy, an effective weapon against all problems. Most of the time, if we will simply begin to find the joy, we will overcome the obstacles against us and be better able to handle the problems we have.

We can rejoice in spite of and the midst of our problems!

I think this is one reason the apostle Paul said, "Rejoice in the Lord always [delight, gladden yourselves in Him]; again I say, Rejoice!" (Philippians 4:4). Paul knew that joy gives us strength. He faced many hardships and difficulties during his life. He had plenty of reasons to be afraid, discouraged, and depressed. Just read his description of his ministry: "But we commend ourselves in every way as [true] servants of God; through great endurance, in tribulation *and* suffering, in hardships *and* privations, in sore straits *and* calamities, in beatings, imprisonments, riots, labors, sleepless watching, hunger" (2 Corinthians 6:4, 5). Now there is a man who had many reasons not to rejoice! Paul could have decided to live his life in "survival mode," but he *chose* to be joyful. In fact, several verses after the passage above, he writes, "[We are treated] as unknown *and* ignored [by the world], and [yet we are] well-known *and* recognized [by God and His people]; as dying, and yet here we are alive; as chastened by suffering and [yet] not killed; as grieved *and* mourning, *yet [we are] always rejoicing*" (vv. 9, 10, emphasis mine). We need to make the same choice Paul did—to rejoice always, even in difficult situations.

Recently, a woman told me that my teaching had changed her life, so I asked her, "What is the most significant way it has changed you?" She responded, "You have taught me that I don't have to 'white knuckle it' through life until I die and go to heaven, but that I can actually enjoy the journey."

We need to remind ourselves often that Jesus died so we could do much more than simply "make it" through another day. Remember, in John 10:10, He said He came so we could "have and enjoy life." He also said, in John 17:13, "I say these things while I am still in the world, so that My joy may be made full *and* complete *and* perfect in them [that they may experience My delight fulfilled in them, that My enjoyment may be perfected in their own souls, that they may have My gladness within them, filling their hearts]." What a scripture! Jesus wants His joy to be made full in us; He wants us to experience His delight. That's what I'm praying for you—that the joy of the Lord would fill your heart and be your strength. Don't let circumstances or situations steal your joy, but be determined to stay strong by staying joyful. Let Jesus' joy be complete in you, and enjoy your life today. Smile, sing, be positive, be lighthearted, hum a tune—and by all means, laugh.

Let Jesus' joy be complete in you, and enjoy your life today. Smile, sing, be positive, be lighthearted, hum a tune—and by all means, laugh.

CHAPTER 5

Know Who You Are

"Know, first, who you are . . ."
—EPICTETUS

How would you respond if I asked, "Who are you?" Would your first inclination be to list the things you do and the roles you play in life? Would you say, "I am a flight attendant," "I am a brain surgeon," "I am a banker," "I am a minister," "I am a wife and a mother," or "I am a high school student"? Would you tell me where you live, what your hobbies and interests are, or what you want to do in the future? Any of these answers would describe *what you do*, but none of them would tell me *who you are*.

As a believer, one of the most important realities for you to understand is who you are in Christ, your identity in Him. When I first heard the phrase "who you are in Christ," I did not know what it meant. But understanding these powerful words is vitally important. When people receive Jesus Christ by faith as their personal Savior, God sees them as made right with Him and as "in" Jesus. Being in Christ provides you with certain rights and privileges, the rights and privileges that belong to the children of God. Being in Christ is not about what you do, but about who you are. It's not about how you view yourself, but about how God sees you. It's

Being in Christ is not about what you do, but about who you are.

not about your activity; it's about your identity. It's not about your "do"; it's about your "who." It is about what you believe.

If the daughter of the queen of England desired to visit the United States, I doubt anyone would ask for a list of what she could do. She would have immediate access and favor because of who she was. If this dynamic works with a human being, just imagine how much more valuable it is to be a child of God. However, if the queen's daughter did not know who she was, she would not use her identity to her advantage. The same principle applies to those who do not know their identity in Christ. They have many rights and privileges they never access simply because they do not know who they are.

There is a big difference between who we are in Christ and who we are in ourselves. In and of ourselves, we are nothing, we have nothing, and we can do nothing of eternal value. In Christ, though, we can be, do, and have everything God promises us in His Word. We can leave a legacy for the world and we can enjoy our journeys through life. The Bible teaches us all kinds of wonderful truths about who we are in Christ. We must know and believe these truths above everything else—above who we think we are, above what other people say about us, and above what the world tells us we should be. God's Word is truth; what others think and say is merely opinion. We must not allow someone's opinion to determine our value.

FINDING FREEDOM

We must know who we are in Christ if we are going to enjoy today and have hope for tomorrow. When we know who we are in Him, we can honestly evaluate ourselves and not feel ashamed or put down because we do not have everything everybody else has or because we cannot do all the things other people can do. It is very liberating to be able to take a realistic inventory of what we cannot do and not feel belittled by it. I may not be able to do everything someone else can do, but I can probably do something he or she can't do. I think the best way to evaluate ourselves is to know that what we do well is a gift from God and that what we don't do well is not a problem. God gives us each a little part of a greater whole, and we are supposed to work together, doing our parts with diligence and excellence, not wishing we could do what He has assigned someone else. Finding the freedom to be ourselves is a major victory that releases amazing joy. Knowing who we are in Christ gives us the confidence to move past the mistakes of the past and embrace the future with expectancy.

Knowing who we are in Christ gives us the confidence to move past the mistakes of the past and embrace the future with expectancy.

Many years ago, I grew tired of feeling bad about myself all the time, thinking something was missing in me, wondering what was wrong with me, and believing I was not everything I was "supposed" to be. During that season of my life, I tried and tried to "be" more by doing more. I tried especially hard to do and be things I saw in other people. If you have ever attempted to do this, you can guess what happened: I ended up completely frustrated. I continued in this cycle of striving and frustration until I finally found out who I was in Christ.

Discovering my identity in Christ was so liberating to me because, as I said, when we know who we are in Christ, then what we cannot do in our natural selves does not matter much anymore. When we find out who we are in Him, we can be comfortable and secure not being everything our friends think we should be. When we understand our identity in Christ, we become much less interested in what others think and expect of us. When we walk in our identity in Christ, we can evaluate ourselves with brutal honesty and still feel great about who we are. We do not feel put down in the least because of what we cannot do; we are completely set free to be the best we can be and to use the abilities we do have.

In Paul's day, social classes and religious groups were clearly defined. The Jews believed they were better than the Gentiles; those who were free thought they were better than the slaves; and men felt they were better than women. Paul liberated everyone and set the record straight when He wrote, "There is [now no distinction] neither Jew nor Greek, there is neither slave nor free, there is not male and female; for you are all one in Christ Jesus" (Galatians 3:28). These words had to be quite shocking to those who felt they were better than others, but quite liberating to those who had always been made to feel inferior. In essence, Paul was saying that nobody had any value apart from who they were in Christ. We are valuable because God loves us, and what we can or cannot do does not add to or delete from that wonderful truth.

I am grieved when I hear people devalue themselves with comments such as, "I am so stupid," "I hate the way I look," or "I never do anything right." These remarks and others are so sad to me because they represent an unbiblical way people think about themselves—and I came to understand years ago how dangerous that kind of thinking and speaking is. It does not reflect the truth of God's Word or align with the way He thinks about us, and it will keep us trapped in ways of living that are far less enjoyable, less fruitful, and less powerful than He desires for us.

When we know who we are in Christ, our freedom and confidence will soar. Being rooted in our identity in Him will keep us from the fear of failure, from excessively trying to please other people, and from being caught in the cycle of trying to perform so others will accept us. It will also enable us to stay strong and steady when adversity comes. People who do not know who they are in Christ can be devastated by difficulties, failures, making mistakes, or the opinions of other people, but a strong

> Being rooted in our identity in Him will keep us from the fear of failure, from excessively trying to please other people, and from being caught in the cycle of trying to perform so others will accept us.

sense of who we are in Christ sets us free from the effects of these things.

AGREE WITH GOD

We can never rise above the thoughts and beliefs we have toward ourselves, so we must make sure we believe what God says about us. We must stop merely agreeing with other people, our circumstances, our flesh, and the devil; and we must begin to agree with God. He says we find our true worth and value in the fact that He loves us and sent His Son to die for us. We have been purchased for God by the blood of Jesus. When God looks at us, He is not looking to see what we do, where we live, who we know, how we dress, or how many educational degrees we hold. He is looking at our hearts, saying, "That man is worth so much that I sent My Son to die for him"; "That woman is so valuable because she belongs to Me and I love her."

Let me be very personal for a moment. I have come to the point that I really know and believe my value as a person is not in the fact that I lead Joyce Meyer Ministries. It is my calling and my job to lead this ministry and teach God's Word. I do it for God. Yes, it's exciting; and yes, I am blessed in doing it. But if I didn't do it, would I be less valuable or worthless? Certainly not! My worth and value in God's eyes would not change one bit.

The same is true for you. God does not measure your worth by what you do. Now, the enemy will try to make you believe you would be worthless if you were to stop doing the things you do. But that is not true, so do not allow yourself to become entrapped in that lie. The truth is that God loves you; He cares for you; He wanted a relationship with you so much that He sent His Son to suffer and die just so you could draw near to Him. You have incredible worth and value to Him. You have to choose to believe that, because the enemy and the world will work hard to convince you otherwise.

Obviously, God has something for each of us to do and we should be busy doing it and bearing good fruit. But the point I want to make is that what we do should not be compared to what someone else does, nor should we seek or derive our worth and value from what we do. One person may be a great singer while another is a great ditch digger, but both are equally valuable to God.

You may be asking, "If I am so valuable to God, why do I feel so bad about myself?" You see, your worth and identity are established in God's heart and recorded in His Word. Your position of value is "legal," spiritually speaking, because Jesus has given it to you. However, you may not feel it experientially because there is a process involved in understanding and receiving what He has done. When I write about "who you are in Christ," I am referring to a work that God has done in your spirit (the inmost part of your being, the spiritual aspect of who you are). When you received Jesus as your Lord and Savior, He made you righteous in the eyes of God (see 2 Corinthians 5:21). That does not mean you do everything right, but it does mean you can press toward better behavior every day of your life and meanwhile God still sees you as righteousness because of your faith in Him. When you received Jesus as Lord and Savior, you were made a new creature (see 2 Corinthians 5:17). Everything about your old self passed away from God's perspective. Receiving Him made you new, clean, and right with God. You received a new heart, a new future, the fruit of the Holy Spirit; you were filled with new possibilities and much more.

This means you have a legal right to feel good about yourself. It's simply not biblical to walk around feeling rotten about yourself all the time and saying, "Oh, I'm just a wretched person, a miserable sinner." You do sin and make mistakes; you still need mercy every day, but you have a new identity in Jesus Christ. You are a blood-bought child of God with more worth and value than you could ever imagine. God has done an awesome work inside you. Experientially, you are moving toward the manifestation of your "legal" position in Christ every day, and for the rest of your life, the Holy Spirit will be working with you to work out *through* you what He has done *in* you. Your job is to cooperate with Him by yielding to His guidance in your life and by believing what God says about you in His Word.

You are a blood-bought child of God with more worth and value than you could ever imagine.

BECOMING WHAT YOU BELIEVE

When you come to know who you are in Christ by believing what the Bible says about you, then no matter how you feel, and no matter what others say, God's promises concerning you will be released in your life through faith. You may make mistakes, but if you keep believing what God's Word says about you, then you will become who God says you can be; you will do what He says you can do; and you can have what He says you can have. On the other hand, you are not likely to experience the blessings of God's promises if you do not believe them.

Let me ask you a few important questions:

- Are you believing God's Word in every area of your life right now? If not, you can change that by simply making the decision to believe.
- Are you applying the truth of God's Word to every situation in which you find yourself? If not, why not make a change today?
- What do you believe about yourself? Does it agree with God's Word? You can decide to believe everything God says about you and to embrace His plan for you. You don't have to wait for a feeling; you can make a decision.
- What do you believe about your future? Does it reflect the truth of God's Word?

- What do you believe about your past? Does it align with God's truth?
- What do you believe about the situations that seem impossible in your life? Are your beliefs scriptural?

The answers to these questions will determine how you see yourself. To really know who you are and walk in the freedom and power of your identity in Christ, your beliefs must align with the truth of His Word.

There was a time in my life when I was convinced I could never overcome the abuse in my past. As long as I believed that, it was my reality; I could not move beyond the abuse. No matter what God did for me, it would not manifest in my life if I refused to believe it. But once I began to believe, things began to change. It did not happen quickly, but over a period of time I started to realize God could heal every area of my life. It has taken more than thirty years, but I have overcome the consequences of abuse by studying and believing God's Word actively and intentionally—day after day after day after day. It has been a process, but every day has brought gradual change, and over time, it has changed me completely.

You may think thirty years is too long to wait, but I really did not have any other options. No one does. Only God can change a person from the inside out; only He can heal the inner man and remove the wounds and bruises from the past. Perhaps it won't take as long for you as it did for me, but however long it does take, it is worth it! Please remember I was seeing progress all along the way, and you will also.

We must believe what God says and align our thoughts with His thoughts. Agreeing with God by accepting His thoughts and His Word as truth enables us to say, "Well, I made a mistake today, but I have faith" or "I did something I shouldn't have, but I have confidence in God's Word and I know He will forgive me if I repent," or "My circumstances are very difficult right now, but I have faith God will come through for me because His Word says He will. I trust Him." We must believe and keep on believing. This kind of confidence in God's Word enables us to overcome every obstacle in life because no matter how difficult things are, faith opens a door for improvement and change. The simple truth is you cannot be defeated when God is on your side.

TRANSFORMED BY THE RENEWING OF YOUR MIND

Romans 12:2 helps us understand why our beliefs are so important: "Do not be conformed to this world (this age), [fashioned after and adapted to its external, superficial customs], but be transformed (changed) by the [entire] renewal of your mind [by its new ideals and its new attitude], so that you may prove [for yourselves] what is the good and acceptable and perfect will of God, *even* the thing which is good and acceptable and perfect [in His sight for you.]." We learn from this verse we must renew our minds, or develop new thoughts, according to God's truth so we can fulfill His plan for our lives.

God has great plans for every person alive. Our enemy, the devil, knows this and tries to keep us from doing what God wants us to do by causing us to believe lies. He may tell us God doesn't love us enough to use us, that we do not have the talents or skills we need to fulfill God's purposes, or we could never do anything well enough to please God. These are all lies! The reason we must know the truth as God gives it to us in His Word is so we can overcome the power of the enemy's lies and walk in the good plans God has for us. We have to know and believe God's Word so we can agree with God and not with the devil.

The reason we must know the truth as God gives it to us in His Word is so we can overcome the power of the enemy's lies and walk in the good plans God has for us.

When we agree with God by believing His Word, we become confident in who we are in Christ and His love for us. We also position ourselves to reach the full potential He has placed within us and to carry out His plans and purposes for our lives. As we do this, we will find ourselves doing what we were made to do. When we are not able to do the things we were created to do, we become frustrated, restless, and unhappy. But when we can do those things, we are energized, passionate, fulfilled, at peace, and successful. We are able to enjoy both the process and the results of what we do; we can enjoy the present and anticipate the future with confidence.

WHAT GOD SAYS ABOUT YOU

The Bible is full of truth concerning who you are and what God thinks about you. I know people who like to read through the New Testament and highlight verses that include the words "in Christ" or "in Him." This is a good exercise—one worth an investment of your time and energy and one that can transform the way you see yourself. In the Appendix of this book, I have provided an extensive list of these scriptures, in the form of confessions to help you become established in God's truth about who you are. I urge you to read, memorize, pray about, and confess these power-filled words because, if you will believe them and renew your mind according to them, they will change your life.

CHAPTER

6

Move Forward in Faith

"The only limit to our realization of tomorrow will be our doubts of today. Let us move forward with strong and active faith."

—FRANKLIN D. ROOSEVELT

A young woman took her fiancé home to meet her parents. After dinner, her mother asked her father to find out about the young man. The father invited the fiancé to his study for a talk.

"So, what are your plans?" the father asked the young man.

"I am a biblical scholar," he replied.

"A biblical scholar. Hmmmm," the father said. "Admirable, but what will you do to provide a nice house for my daughter to live in?"

"I will study," the young man replied, "and God will provide for us."

"And how will you buy her a beautiful engagement ring, such as she deserves?" asked the father.

"I will concentrate on my studies," the young man replied. "God will provide for us."

"And children?" asked the father. "How will you support children?"

"Don't worry, sir. God will provide," replied the fiancé.

The conversation proceeded like this, and each time the father questioned, the young idealist insisted that God would provide. Later, the mother asked, "How did it go, honey?" The father answered, "He has no job and no plans, and he thinks I'm God."[1]

One thing is true about the young man in this story: he certainly had faith! We all need to do our best, work hard, and live wisely, but we must also have faith in God, trusting Him to see us through difficulties, show us how to live, provide for us, and guide us in the affairs of our daily lives. We must mix faith with everything we do because we cannot please God without it (see Hebrews 11:6).

To enjoy today and embrace tomorrow, we must approach life with faith. To embrace tomorrow means to look forward to it with expectancy. Don't dread the unknown or things impending you might not be looking forward to. Dread is a relative of fear, and it is opposed to faith. The Bible says we are supposed to *live* by faith, to approach everything in faith (see Habakkuk 2:4). Faith is not simply a dynamic necessary for us to receive salvation; it is a way of life. We need faith to manage our finances, raise our children, and build successful homes and marriages. We also need faith concerning our jobs—faith to work hard and operate with integrity and faith to look at God as our source of provision rather than at a company or an organization. We need faith to cover the mistakes of our pasts and to boldly face tomorrow. Someday, we will reach the end of our earthly lives and we will even need to die by faith, believing God is waiting to receive us into His eternal presence in heaven.

> Everything else may fail us, but God is our Rock, our Refuge, our Hiding Place, our High Tower, our Stronghold in times of trouble, our Secret Place.

Yes, we need faith for today and faith for tomorrow. Without this confidence in God, we may be doubtful and hesitant about the present and fearful of the future. God alone gives us strength to face each day, so we need to turn to Him and place our faith in Him alone. Everything else—people, material possessions, education, relationships, corporations, paychecks—may fail us, but God is our Rock, our Refuge, our Hiding Place, our High Tower, our Stronghold in times of trouble, our Secret Place. He is our hope, our peace, our joy, our strength, and the source of everything we need. He is the only One who never fails and the only One worth putting our faith in.

ABSOLUTE TRUST

I love the Amplified Bible's definition of faith in Colossians 1:4: "For we have heard of your faith in Christ Jesus *[the leaning of your entire human personality on Him in absolute trust and confidence in His power, wisdom, and goodness]* and of the love which [have and show] for all the saints (God's consecrated ones)" (emphasis mine). It teaches us that faith in God is "the leaning of your entire human personality on Him in *absolute* trust and confidence in His power, wisdom, and goodness." (emphasis mine). When you and I exercise our faith, we lean everything about ourselves on Him and we place our trust and confidence in three specific attributes of His character: His power, His wisdom, and His goodness.

God's Power

When we approach God in faith, we must first realize He has the power, the supernatural ability, to meet our needs and solve our problems. He is able to orchestrate circumstances and events, arrange relationships, open doors of opportunity, rescue us from trouble, send financial or material provision, and work any kind of miracle we need. Jesus Himself said, "*All things* are possible with God" (Matthew 19:26, emphasis mine). You and I are limited in our human strength, but God can do anything. Believing this is essential to having faith.

God's Wisdom

Faith also involves placing absolute trust and confidence in God's wisdom. When we do not know what to do or how to do it, God does. He is powerful enough to do anything! But in His wisdom, He may choose not to do everything He is able to do. He knows what is best for us; and He always works in our lives with our best interests in mind. He knows exactly what to do for us and how to help us. When He answers our prayers in ways we do not understand, we need to lean on the fact He is a wise God who sees the big picture of our lives and works all things together for our good (see Romans 8:28). God is always able to deliver us from difficulty, but He may choose not to do so for our own good. Sometimes we need the experience of going through something, rather than being delivered from it. In Isaiah 41 the people are told to fear not because God is hardening them to difficulties (see v. 10). I think that is an interesting statement and one we should understand. By being exposed to challenges, we learn to overcome them rather than be defeated by them. There are some things in my life God chose not to deliver me from that initially upset me but do not bother me at all now. Why? Because through my experience I discovered I was stronger in God than I thought I was.

God's Goodness

God is a good God, and we need to have faith in His goodness. The Bible is full of scriptures telling us how good He is and how much He loves us. He also has good plans for our lives. In Jeremiah 29:11, God promises, "For I know the thoughts and plans that I have for you, . . . thoughts *and* plans for welfare *and* peace and not for evil, to give you hope in your final outcome." Along the same lines, Ephesians 2:10 says God has planned good works for us "that we should walk in them [living the good life which He prearranged and made ready for us to live]."

When you put your faith in God, you are trusting completely in His power, His wisdom, and His goodness. You are not begging for favors from a heavenly judge who wants to punish you; you are not trying to connect with a distant deity watching the universe from afar. When you have faith, you have complete confidence in the ever-present God Who has the power to accomplish anything on your behalf, the wisdom to know exactly what you need, and the goodness to work in your life in ways that bring the greatest possible blessing.

When you put your faith in God, you are trusting completely in His power, His wisdom, and His goodness.

I like to say it this way: "God is powerful enough to do what needs to be done in my life; He knows how to do it, and He wants to do it because He is good!"

FROM FAITH TO FAITH

Romans 1:17 tells us, "For in the Gospel a righteousness which God ascribes is revealed, both springing from faith and leading to faith [disclosed through the way of faith that arouses to more faith]. As it is written, The man who through faith is just *and* upright shall live *and* shall live by faith." This verse reminds us that we need to learn how to live from faith to faith. It means we approach everything we face, every challenge we meet, every decision we make, and everything we do with faith. Faith should be the posture of our hearts and the attitude of our minds toward every situation.

I certainly need faith in my everyday life and in my ministry. When I travel to conferences, I go in faith that I will arrive safely at my destination. When I begin teaching, I do so in faith that God has given me the right message for the audience. I have faith that I am anointed to teach God's Word, to help people, and to speak the right words. When I walk off of the platform, I have faith that God has used my ministry to change lives. When I leave to go home, I have faith that I will arrive safely. After many years of being doubtful and fearful, I have definitely decided faith is much better. Faith enables us to enjoy our lives and to do amazing things. Living by faith is not a *feeling* we have; it is a conscious decision we must make.

Just imagine what I would be like as a minister if I did not have faith concerning my messages. I would not be very effective if I started teaching, believing it was God's word for a group of people, and then lost my confidence midway through the sermon because someone yawned, grunted, left the room, or looked at me the wrong way. The devil would know I lost my confidence, and that would open the door for him to ruin the entire meeting. The audience would also realize I was not confident about what I was saying and they could not receive help from the message. Doing things in fear not only torments us but also wastes our time. No good can come of it because God does not work through fear; He works through our faith.

Doing things in fear not only torments us but also wastes our time.

Can you apply the principles of my story to your life? Do you ever feel you are doing the right thing and take a step of faith? Then, if you do not see the response you deem appropriate, do you fall into doubt and unbelief and spend the next several days thinking, *Oh, I did the wrong thing. I shouldn't have done that. I shouldn't have said that*? God does not want us to live with this kind of confusion in our lives, never knowing what to do and never being confident about our words and actions. He wants us to live by faith and to do everything we do with confidence in Him.

Even if you come to a place where you know you made a wrong decision about something, you can still have faith that God will work it out for good. Faith really is amazing. It opens the door for God to get involved in everything we do; and with Him on our team, we cannot lose.

We cannot truly live by faith if we waver from faith to fear to doubt to unbelief and then back to faith and again to fear and to more doubt and unbelief and finally back to faith. We need to get rid of the mixture! This unstable way of living causes tremendous torment in people's lives, so we need to come to a point where we make up our minds, once and for all, about what we believe and in whom we believe. We have to decide who can solve our problems and who cannot. Once we have firmly made up our minds, we have to stand firm and hold our convictions tightly. This is what the Bible refers to as "fighting the good fight of faith." Sure, it is challenging to continue having faith when nothing you see, feel, or think supports it. But this is when we need to look deeper to see what is in our hearts. When we do, we will find that God is always there encouraging us to keep on believing.

SIMPLE FAITH

I like to define faith in a very basic, easy-to-understand way: living with a positive attitude. Living by faith is looking at everything in a positive way, not trusting in the power of positive thinking, but trusting in the power of God, who loves us and wants the best for us. When we have faith, we can say with confidence in our hearts:

Living by faith is looking at everything in a positive way, not trusting in the power of positive thinking, but trusting in the power of God, who loves us and wants the best for us.

- "I don't know what to do, but God does."
- "I don't understand what's going on in my life, but God will make a way for me."
- "I don't know how I can pay my bills this month, but God will provide."
- "This trial I have doesn't feel good; I don't like it; but I believe

God works all things out for good to those who love Him and are called according to His purpose" (see Romans 8:28).

- "I don't like the situation I'm going through, but what Satan means for my harm, God intends for my good" (see Genesis 50:20).

These statements and the attitudes they represent demonstrate faith. Faith always trusts in God's love and looks beyond where it is to the end result. Faith is always hopeful and refuses to accept defeat. People who live by faith can enjoy every day of their lives and enthusiastically embrace tomorrow.

FAITH FOR EVERY DAY

Ephesians 2:8, 9 says, "For it is by free grace (God's unmerited favor) that you are saved (delivered from judgment *and* made partakers of Christ's salvation) through [your] faith. And this [salvation] is not of yourselves [of your own doing, it came not through your own striving], but it is the gift of God; Not because of works [not the fulfillment of the Law's demands], lest any man should boast." No one alive today saw Jesus die on the cross, but because we have faith, we sincerely believe that event happened. As Christians, we have deliberately decided to believe in the power of an event we did not witness or even hear about firsthand. When we read the crucifixion stories in the Bible or hear people talk about how Jesus has changed their lives, we can choose to believe them or not; the decision is entirely up to us. I believe faith comes when we hear the gospel, but we still need to make a decision. When we choose to believe Jesus died for us and rose from the dead, that is the beginning of what can be a life of faith. Our initial faith will lead to more faith as we study God's Word and learn how to walk with Him. Each time we see how faith works in our lives, it increases our faith to trust God in other situations.

As I mentioned earlier, God does not want us to limit faith to our salvation experience. Colossians 2:6 says, "As you have therefore received Christ, [even] Jesus the Lord, [so] walk (regulate your lives and conduct yourselves) in union with *and* conformity to Him." So if we receive Christ by faith, we are supposed to live our entire lives by faith. We should not decide to believe God for certain projects or situations and try to handle everything else by ourselves. But sometimes we approach our lives that way, thinking, *Oh, God, I've got a big problem today. I mean, this is major. God, I really need help with this one.*

God wants to help us with the things that seem "big" to us and with the things that seem less significant. He wants to help us when we feel desperate and when we don't. I figured out years ago that everything in life is over my head; it's all too much for me to handle alone. I used to run to God only when I thought I was desperate, but then one day I finally realized I was desperate all the time; I just didn't know it.

God wants to help us with the things that seem "big" to us and with the things that seem less significant.

The same is true for you. You are desperate for God all the time, whether you realize it or not. Jesus says in John 15:5, "I am the Vine; you are the branches. Whoever lives in Me and I in him bears much (abundant) fruit. However, *apart from Me [cut off from vital union with Me] you can do nothing*" (emphasis mine). To abide in Him, we must have faith. We cannot see Him with our physical eyes or reach out and touch Him with our hands, but we can relate to Him in powerful, personal ways when we have faith. As we abide in Him through faith, we can do everything, but apart from Him, we can do nothing that will have any real lasting value.

Our desperate need for God and His desire for us to abide in Him does not mean we have to sit around being "super spiritual" all the time. We do not need to feel obligated to read our Bibles or confine ourselves to a prayer closet for hours each day, but when we really love God and He is first in our lives, everything we do becomes spiritual in a way because we are doing it with Him, in Him, through Him, by Him, for Him, to His glory.

We should study our Bibles and pray because we want to and feel that doing so is an awesome privilege. We should not read and study only out of a sense of duty or because we think we score points with God. It should be part of our lives, but we don't need to feel as if we are being "spiritual" when we do it and "unspiritual" when we do ordinary things. It was very liberating for me to finally realize everything takes on a spiritual nature if we do it through, by, for, and with Jesus. Even picking out the clothes I am going to wear each day becomes more meaningful if I keep in mind I want to dress for His glory.

Let me encourage you to let God into every area of your life through faith. Jesus died so we could enjoy our lives—everything about them. As we grow in faith, we will increase in our abilities to relax and enjoy every aspect of today and look forward to tomorrow.

CHAPTER 7

Trust through the Trials

"Character cannot be developed in ease and quiet. Only through experience of trial and suffering can the soul be strengthened, ambition inspired, and success achieved."

—HELEN KELLER

Wishing to encourage her young son's progress on the piano, a mother took the small boy to a Paderewski concert. After they were seated, the mother spotted a friend in the audience and walked down the aisle to greet her.

Seizing the opportunity to explore the wonders of the concert hall, the little boy rose and eventually explored his way through a door marked, "NO ADMITTANCE."

When the house lights dimmed and the concert was about to begin, the mother returned to her seat and discovered that her son was missing. Suddenly, the curtains parted and spotlights focused on the impressive Steinway on stage.

In horror, the mother saw her little boy sitting at the keyboard, innocently picking out "Twinkle, Twinkle Little Star."

At that moment, the great piano master made his entrance, quickly moved to the piano, and whispered in the boy's ear, "Don't quit. Keep playing."

Then leaning over, Paderewski reached down with his left hand and began filling in the bass part. Soon his right arm reached around to the other side of the child and he added a running obbligato.

Together, the old master and the young novice transformed a frightening situation into a wonderfully creative experience. The audience was mesmerized.[1]

That's the way it is with God. What we can accomplish on our own is hardly noteworthy. We try our best, but the results aren't exactly graceful, flowing music. But with the hand of the Master, our life's work truly can be beautiful.

Next time you set out to accomplish great feats, listen carefully. You can hear the voice of the Master, whispering in your ear, "Don't quit. Keep playing." Feel His loving arms around you. Know that His strong hands are playing the concerto of your life.

The young boy in this story learned a valuable lesson about trust. He was headed for great embarrassment—and probably punishment from his mother—before the masterful pianist came to his rescue. At some point in our lives, all of us find ourselves in some type of trouble. It may or may not be a situation we have brought upon ourselves; it may be much more serious than the little boy's adventure at the concert, but we realize we need the Master's help.

> We can make unwise or unhealthy choices when faced with difficulty; we can try to take matters into our own hands; or we can trust God.

Everyone faces tests and trials over the course of a lifetime, and we can choose how we want to deal with them. We can make unwise or unhealthy choices when faced with difficulty; we can try to take matters into our own hands; or we can trust God. I highly recommend trusting Him. He is the only One Who can truly help us, save us, guide us, give us what we need, and encourage us with His presence when we walk through adversity.

My great hope for you is that you will enjoy every day of your life, but the fact is, you will have challenges and trials. You may have some dark or difficult days over the course of your life; these are simply opportunities to trust God. I have seen God do absolutely amazing things in people's lives over the years, and I have experienced His miracle-working power in my own life, in my family, and in my ministry. I have learned that the best way to position ourselves for a miracle is to trust God through the troubles and trials we encounter in our lives. He is a faithful God; and He will always come through for us when we trust Him.

TRUSTING GOD *IN* AND *THROUGH*

Often when we think of trusting God, we think of trusting Him for things we need or want—financial provision, physical healing, the restoration of a relationship, a promotion at work, a place to live, an opportunity we want, or a big win in some kind of competition. A true relationship of trust in God extends beyond trusting Him *for* something and includes trusting Him *in* certain circumstances or *through* a situation. We need to learn to not simply look to Him for the results we desire; we need to learn to trust Him through the process of attaining them.

There was a time in my life when I focused intensely on trusting God for things, saying, "I want this, God," "I want that, God," and "I need such-and-such, God." In the midst of my requests, He began to show me that getting all those things was not the most important issue in my life at that time. Those things would come later, but right then, He needed to teach me how to trust Him while I was going through situations, how to trust Him enough to walk through situations with stability and with a good attitude on a consistent basis. He wanted me to learn that He may not always rescue us when we want out of circumstances, but He is always with us as we walk through them.

God does not always deliver us *from* everything when we think He should. Throughout His Word, we read about people who had to go

God does not always deliver us *from* everything when we think He should. Throughout His Word, we read about people who had to go *through* things.

through things. One familiar passage to many people is Psalm 23:4: "Yes, though I walk *through* the [deep, sunless] valley of the shadow of death, I will fear or dread no evil, for You are with me." (emphasis mine). Psalm 66:12 says, "You caused men to ride over our heads [when we were prostrate]; we went *through* fire and *through* water, but You brought us out into a broad, moist place [to abundance and refreshment and the open air]" (emphasis mine). The prophet Isaiah, speaking for God, says, "When you pass *through* the waters, I will be with you, and *through* the rivers, they will not overwhelm you. When you walk *through* the fire, you will not be burned or scorched, nor will the flame kindle upon you" (Isaiah 43:2, emphasis mine).

One of the most amazing stories of trusting God through trouble is the account of three courageous young men named Shadrach, Meshach, and Abednego. The Old Testament king Nebuchadnezzar threatened to throw them into a blazing furnace where they were sure to be burned alive if they did not worship his idols. They responded to him: "If our God Whom we serve is able to deliver us from the burning fiery furnace, He will deliver us out of your hand, O king. But if not, let it be known to you, O king, that we will not serve your gods or worship the golden image which you have set up!" (Daniel 3:17, 18). Let me make clear that the phrase "If our God Whom we serve is able to deliver us" does not mean God might not have the power to deliver them; He certainly has the power. In this context, the words mean "if it is in His plan, if it is best for all concerned."

Angry Nebuchadnezzar did throw the three men into the fiery furnace—after ordering the furnace turned up to seven times its usual heat. The flames from the furnace were so hot, they incinerated the men who bound the young men and threw them into it.

When Nebuchadnezzar looked into the furnace, expecting the three men to be incinerated, he said in astonishment, "Behold, I see four men loose, walking in the midst of the fire, and they are not hurt!" (v. 25 [many people believe the fourth man was the pre-incarnate Jesus]). The king called Shadrach, Meshach, and Abednego out of the furnace, and when they emerged, not one hair on their heads had been singed, their clothes were not scorched, and they didn't even smell of smoke.

This testimony of going through difficulty with absolute trust in God has inspired people for generations. Today, we can draw much encouragement from the fact that Shadrach, Meshach, and Abednego went into a terrifying situation, one we can assume they wanted to be delivered from, and Jesus was in the fiery furnace with them. As we follow their example, we can go through trials in our lives with stable, positive attitudes, trusting God completely, even against seemingly impossible odds. Then, other people can gain strength and encouragement from our lives, just as we do from the story of Shadrach, Meshach, and Abednego.

Remember, your attitude in every situation is yours to command. No one can force you to have a bad attitude or a good one; it is entirely up to you. Maintain an attitude of faith, praise, thanksgiving, and positive expectation, and you will definitely come out of your situation victoriously at just the right time.

> Remember, your attitude in every situation is yours to command.

TRUSTING WHEN WE DON'T UNDERSTAND

One of the great mysteries and facts about our walk with God is that we rarely understand everything He is doing in our lives. If we always understood, we would have no need to trust Him. As believers we often find ourselves in places of not knowing, and we catch ourselves questioning God: "What does my future hold?" "Will I ever get married?" "What will my children be when they grow up?" "Will I have the provision I need in my old age?"

We have to learn to trust God when we do not understand what is happening in our lives, and we need to become comfortable with unanswered questions. You and I may never have every answer we want when we want it, so we need to relax and get comfortable knowing and trusting God, the One Who does know. Without trust, it is impossible to enjoy today and be ready to face tomorrow with expectancy.

Job, who had many reasons to question God as he faced a staggering series of crises and losses, said, "Though He slay me, yet will I wait for and trust Him" (Job 13:15). Job did not understand what was going on in his life, but he made the decision to trust God anyway. I believe that was the only way he could find peace in the midst of his terrible circumstances. Similarly, you and I will never have peace in our lives until we learn how to stop trying to figure everything out and how to start trusting God more.

Proverbs 3:5, 6 says, "Lean on, trust in, *and* be confident in the Lord with all your heart *and* mind and do not rely on your own insight *or* understanding. In all your ways know, recognize, *and* acknowledge Him, and He will direct *and* make straight *and* plain your paths." Notice we are to trust in the Lord with *all* our hearts and minds. We cannot say with our mouths, "I trust God," and then allow our emotions to be upset and our thoughts to run wild. We have to be diligent to maintain a steady, unwavering posture of faith and trust toward God in our hearts and minds.

We cannot say with our mouths, "I trust God," and then allow our emotions to be upset and our thoughts to run wild.

In my life, it helped me to finally get really honest with myself about whether or not I was *truly* trusting God. I had to face the truth that if I was worried, I was not really trusting God. Being honest about my level of faith actually helped me grow in faith and get where I needed to be.

If you are the kind of person who has to have everything figured out in order to settle down, let me encourage you today to accept the fact that you are not likely to receive all the answers you want in this lifetime. Choose to stop demanding explanations and to begin practicing trust. Instead of asking God why, tell Him you trust Him. This is part of how you can trust God in a practical way when you do not understand what is happening. There have been many times in my life when I wanted with all my heart to know why something was or was not happening, but I knew God wanted my trust, not my questions.

When you can only see one step ahead of you, but you would prefer to see the entire journey, take that one step and trust God to show you the next one. When you know God could supply a need for you without much effort at all, but His response is delayed, trust Him to answer you in His perfect timing. In Isaiah 55:8, God says, "For My thoughts are not your thoughts, neither are your ways My ways." His thoughts and ways are higher, better, and wiser than ours. He can see the end from the beginning, and He knows answers we cannot yet comprehend. We need to trust Him when we do not understand.

TRUSTING IN THE TESTS

God wants to do good for us. He wants to bless us, but He also wants to be sure we are mature enough for the blessings He wants to pour out. Sometimes, in order to show us what is in our hearts—and what we can or cannot handle, He tests us. That's exactly what He did with the Israelites in the wilderness before they entered the Promised Land, as we read in Deuteronomy 8.

God wants to do good for us. He wants to bless us, but He also wants to be sure we are mature enough for the blessings He wants to pour out.

"And you shall [earnestly] remember all the way which the Lord your God led you these forty years in the wilderness, to humble you and to prove you, to know what was in your [mind and] heart, whether you would keep His commandments or not" (v. 2). Notice first that *God* led the Israelites through the wilderness. They did not get lost and end up in the wilderness. Rather, He led them through the wilderness for the purpose of testing them to see if they would keep His commandments and worship Him in the midst of the difficulties of the wilderness. Likewise, God will lead you through some tests and through some experiences that will try your faith. During these times, He will be watching to see what is in your heart.

Verses 3, 4 describe the Israelites' time of testing in greater detail: "And He humbled you and allowed you to hunger and fed you with manna, which you did not know nor did your fathers know, that He might make you recognize *and* personally know that man does not live by bread only, but man lives by every word that proceeds out of the mouth of the Lord. Your clothing did not become old upon you nor did your feet swell these forty years." As God tested His people, He humbled them, and He caused them to trust Him for their daily provision. They never knew from one day to the next whether manna would fall from heaven the next morning, but God required them to gather only as much manna as they could eat each day. They had no choice but to trust Him for their next meal. He disciplined them in this way, and in other ways, as we read in verses 5, 6: "Know also in your [minds and] hearts that, as a man disciplines *and* instructs His son, so the Lord your God disciplines *and* instructs you. So you shall keep the commandments of the Lord your God, to walk in His ways and [reverently] fear Him."

When God tests us, He does so because He wants to bless us. In the Israelites' case, He tested them and disciplined them for the purpose of taking them into the abundance and blessing of the Promised Land. Verses 7–9 show us His heart for them: "For the Lord your God is bringing you into a good land, a land

When God tests us, He does so because He wants to bless us.

of brooks of water, of fountains and springs, flowing forth in valleys and hills; a land of wheat and barley and vines and fig trees and pomegranates, a land of olive trees and honey; *a land in which you shall eat food without shortage and lack nothing in it;* a land whose stones are iron and out of whose hills you can dig copper" (emphasis mine).

The passage goes on in its description of the good land into which God was leading His people. We need to remember He first led them on a long, hard journey; He tested them and disciplined them in the wilderness before they entered the land He promised. He was testing them centuries ago, and He still tests those He loves today. When you encounter tests and difficulties, remember that blessings are ahead, and move forward with absolute confidence and trust in God. Concentrate more on passing your tests than on how difficult they are. You are capable of much more than you might think, and God will always deliver you at the right time.

TRUSTING WHEN WE CANNOT SEE

Earlier in this chapter, I wrote about Shadrach, Meshach, and Abednego. Those three young men had no idea what would happen to them when they were thrown into the fiery furnace, but they were willing to put their lives on the line instead of disobeying God. We need people today who will take a stand for righteousness, for what is right according to God's Word. If this does not happen, our world will be in serious trouble. But many times, people fail to stand up for righteousness because they are afraid of what will happen when they do. Will they lose their jobs? Will they lose their friends? Will they be ridiculed in the media? In situations such as these, when we do not know what the outcome or result of a situation will be, we need to trust God and press forward to do what we believe is right. Even if

We need people today who will take a stand for righteousness, for what is right according to God's Word.

we are persecuted for the sake of righteousness, God's Word says we are blessed (see Matthew 5:10).

The world desperately needs men and women who will lose jobs rather than compromise their integrity to keep them. We need politicians who will lose votes if necessary rather than sacrifice their integrity. God can put us in better places than people could ever put us if we put our trust in Him and if we are people of integrity and excellence. We need people who will put everything on the line and say, "Even if I lose what I want, I will not compromise and do what I know in my heart is wrong." Sometimes we do not even give God opportunities to work in our lives because we are too busy trying to take care of ourselves. We think, *Well, I better do this because I don't want to lose my job. Well, I better do this because I don't want to lose my friends.* We cannot allow the fear of man to be greater than the fear of God in our lives.

We need to fear the Lord above all else, and to trust Him at all times, in every situation, every day of our lives. Whether you are going through something, walking through a situation you do not understand, being tested, or wondering what will happen if you refuse to compromise, put your trust in God. And don't forget that trust allows you to enter God's rest; only in that place can you truly enjoy your life.

CHAPTER 8

Get Some Rest

"Everything has its wonders, even darkness and silence, and I learn whatever state I am in, therein to be content."
—HELEN KELLER

Most of us understand the value of physical rest and relaxation. We know we need to get enough sleep, take breaks throughout the day, and allow ourselves time to be refreshed and renewed if we want to be healthy and enjoy our everyday lives. We also need rest for our souls; our "insides" need rest as much as our external bodies do.

PEACE AND REST

Several years ago, I heard an old friend was very ill. Though I had not had many opportunities to speak with her for about ten years, I called her to let her know I was praying for her. She was fighting a fierce battle against cancer, but she found time on the phone to be lighthearted and even joke a little bit. She also spoke of her complete trust in God, and I could tell she was truly resting in faith. Toward the end of the conversation, she said, "You know something, Joyce? You sound really peaceful." That observation really blessed me because this woman knew me ten years earlier, and she noticed how much God had changed me.

Back then, I fought worry and anxiety constantly, and I was often frustrated because I really was not trusting God to solve my problems. "I" was working on my problems and not resting in the Lord. I said I trusted God, and then I worried all the time. But when my friend said, "You sound really peaceful," I knew the reason was, for the most part, I have learned to enter the rest of God. That does not mean I never slip out of His rest, but when I do, I am so miserable I will do anything to regain my peace. Once we understand what peace is like, we can hardly bear to be without it. When we've lived with strife, turmoil, and anxiety and then finally found peace and rest in God, we will be diligent to stay in that place.

God's peace and rest are available to every believer. We do not have to live every day stressed out, upset, worried, or exhausted. Hebrews 4:1 tells us, "The promise of entering His rest still holds *and* is offered [today]," and we can enjoy His rest every day of our lives.

REST TAKES WORK

We read in Hebrews 4:10, 11: "For he who has once entered [God's] rest also has ceased from [the weariness and pain] of human labors, just as God rested from those labors peculiarly His own. Let us therefore be zealous *and* exert ourselves *and* strive diligently to enter the rest [of God, to know and experience it for ourselves], that no one may fall *or* perish by the same kind of unbelief *and* disobedience [into which those in the wilderness fell]." These verses call us to work with the Holy Spirit and make an effort to learn how to live in rest. Be radical about rest! Refuse to live your life worried, upset, frustrated, aggravated, and joyless. Decide right now to learn to dwell in peace and enjoy your life.

> Be radical about rest! Refuse to live your life worried, upset, frustrated, aggravated, and joyless.

One way we learn to be at rest internally is by identifying the things that upset us. The enemy loves to lure us out of the rest of God, but he does not use the same tactics on every person. I like to say, "The devil sets us up to get us upset." He often knows what our weak points are and "pushes our buttons" over and over until we want to explode. I encourage you to find out what your "buttons" are; figure out what upsets you and causes you to lose your peace so you can learn to deal with those things and enter into God's rest.

I'm sure you can think of something that really upsets you or causes you to lose your patience. It could be computer problems, co-workers who talk too much, making a trip to the grocery store only to discover they do not have what you need, or a teenage son who responds to every comment by rolling his eyes back in his head, as if he were about to pass out. Personally, I do not do well if I have to hurry, especially if I have to hurry for a long time. I can handle a little bit of a rush, but if I have a day when I constantly have to hurry-hurry-hurry-hurry, I start getting more and more emotionally upset and soon want to throw up my hands and say, "Stop! I am not going to live like this!"

Another example that comes to mind is the way Dave responds to traffic. Now traffic does not bother me much, but Dave can get really upset when people are not driving correctly. If he waits and waits for a specific parking place, and just about the time the car in it moves out of the way, another car zips in and takes it, that really bothers Dave. For some reason, it does not upset me as much, but, as I mentioned, other things do set me off. So we need to know ourselves. We need to know what causes us to lose our peace, and we need to be diligent to learn how to overcome these situations so we can stay at rest in God.

RESTING IN FAITH

Living by faith helps us rest in the Lord because when we have faith, we believe God will somehow work for good whatever is going on

> Living by faith helps us rest in the Lord because when we have faith, we believe God will somehow work for good whatever is going on in our lives.

in our lives. When we live by faith, we trust Him completely and assume He is always working to benefit and bless us. Maybe being stuck in a traffic jam spares us from being killed in an accident. Maybe not getting the parking place we wanted kept somebody from pulling in next to us and denting our car. There are all sorts of reasons things happen as they do, and when we are trusting God with our lives, we choose to believe He is always watching over us and working for our good.

Taking this thought one step further, we need to realize we cannot enter God's rest if we are not living in faith. Hebrews 4:3 says, "For we who have believed (adhered to and trusted in and relied on God) do enter that rest, in accordance with His declaration that those [who did not believe] should not enter when He said, As I swore in My wrath, They shall not enter My rest; and this He said although [His] works had been completed *and* prepared [and waiting for all who would believe] from the foundation of the world." Note that this verse says "we who have believed do enter" God's rest. Faith is the doorway through which we enter the rest of God. When we want to know whether or not we really have faith in a situation, we simply need to do an internal check and see if we are at peace. We cannot enter God's rest if we do not have confidence and trust in God, so when we are resting in Him, chances are we are also living in faith.

WAIT A MINUTE

Psalm 62 teaches us about resting in God by learning to wait on Him:

> "For God alone my soul waits in silence; from Him comes my salvation. He only is my Rock and my Salvation, my Defense

> *and* my Fortress, I shall not be greatly moved. . . . My soul, wait only upon God *and* silently submit to Him; for my hope *and* expectation are from Him. He only is my Rock and my Salvation; He is my Defense *and* my Fortress, I shall not be moved. With God rests my salvation and my glory; He is my Rock of unyielding strength *and* impenetrable hardness, and my refuge is in God! Trust in, lean on, rely on, *and* have confidence in Him at all times, you people; pour out your hearts before Him. God is a refuge for us (a fortress and a high tower). Selah [pause, and calmly think of that]!" (vv. 1, 2, 5–8)

What does the opening statement of this passage mean: "For God alone my soul waits"? The soul is comprised of the mind, the will, and the emotions. When we are trusting God and resting in Him, we do not try to figure out what is going on or speculate about how God might respond to us, but our minds are still, our wills want what God wants for us, and our emotions are calm as we wait confidently for God's answer. We do not try to make anything happen in our own strength; we wait for God to move on our behalf.

As we wait on God, we learn to develop the attitude Jesus demonstrated in the Garden of Gethsemane: "Father, if You are willing, remove this cup from me; yet not My will, but [always] Yours be done" (Luke 22:42). That's the place we need to come to in our spiritual lives. We need to get to the point where we can say, "God, I don't like this; this hurts; this is not what I had planned; this is not what I wanted; and God, I'd like You to take this away, *but* if that's not Your plan, then give me the grace to endure it." We find great peace and enter into supernatural rest when we are able to surrender. I finally had to admit that God is simply smarter than I am. If you have not come to that place in your life yet, this would be a good time! Life becomes much

> Life becomes much easier when we sincerely believe God is in control and really does know what He is doing.

easier when we sincerely believe God is in control and really does know what He is doing.

We get into trouble when our souls decide to stop waiting on God. When our wills don't want to wait anymore and our minds are tired of being still, our emotions find ways to express themselves. When God asks us to be still and wait, but we insist upon trying to make something happen, striving and frustration are the results. On the other hand, when we discipline our minds, wills, and emotions to rest in God, He takes care of everything according to His good plans and in His timing. If you need to, speak aloud to yourself and say, "Stop worrying and trust God!"

GIVE YOUR BRAIN A BREAK

On a practical level, how do we learn to rest in God? I can tell you to wait on the Lord and rest in Him all day long, but that does no good if you do not know *how* to enter His rest. I believe the simplest, easiest way to trust Him is to get your mind off of your problems. You may think you could never do that, but you can. You do it by choosing to think about something else. Sometimes, one of the best things you can do when you have a problem and seem to be unable to get something off your mind is to simply go do something. Call a friend; go to the grocery store; take a walk; change the oil in your car; watch a good, clean, funny movie; read a book; or bake something. Just get busy! Invest your mental energy in something other than your problem. You will find it difficult to trust if you talk about your problems, because the more you talk about them, the more upset you will be. Turn your thoughts elsewhere; give your brain a break; and you'll find yourself better able to rest in God.

> Growing in the ability to trust God and to walk in faith is a lifetime journey.

Growing in the ability to trust God and to walk in faith is a lifetime journey; it does not happen quickly. As we grow spiritually, we have to remind ourselves over and over again: cast your care on God; be anxious for nothing; trust Him in every situation. As we are diligent to do these things, we find ourselves resting in the Lord more and more, and that is where we find peace, clarity, wisdom, and the strength to face each day.

LEAVE THEM ALONE

Before we close this chapter, I want to call your attention to an issue that causes many people to lose their peace and be unable to rest in God, and that is our desire to help, fix, rescue, or change other people. One thing we cannot do with our faith is control someone else's right to free choice. As the old saying goes, "You can lead a horse to the water, but you can't make him drink." We simply cannot make people love God, live right, or do what we think they should do. Sometimes I wish I could just unzip people and stuff them full of God's Word so they would stop making unwise choices and ruining their lives. Most of us want to help people when we see them hurting themselves, but we must remember that one of God's great gifts to humanity is the gift of free will. Every person alive is free to make his or her own choices.

When you are believing God for something in another person's life, your will is not the only will involved. That person's will also affects the outcome—even more than yours does. When you pray for people, you open the door for God to work in their lives, but they still have to choose to cooperate with Him. Refuse to lose your joy over somebody else's bad choice. You have a life to live; and I encourage you to live it by learning to trust, wait on God, and rest in Him. And remember, you cannot help someone who does not want to be helped or who does not believe they have a problem.

When you pray for people, you open the door for God to work in their lives, but they still have to choose to cooperate with Him.

CHAPTER

9

Choose Well

"What we call the secret of happiness is no more a secret than our willingness to choose life."

—LEO BUSCAGLIA

You and I have the God-given privilege of making choices every day. Over the course of time, the choices we make determine the quality, direction, and results of our lives. If we want to enjoy life today and embrace everything the future holds for us, we must learn to make right choices. I recently ran across the story of an elderly woman who understood the power of choice. Its title is "Positive Attitude," but to me it illustrates not only the benefits of a positive approach to every situation, but also the importance of making good decisions.

> She is 92 years old, petite, well poised, and proud. She is fully dressed each morning by eight o'clock, with her hair fashionably coifed, and her makeup perfectly applied, in spite of the fact she is legally blind. Today she has moved to a nursing home. Her husband of 70 years recently passed away, making this move necessary.
>
> After many hours of waiting patiently in the lobby of the nursing home, where I am employed, she smiled sweetly when told her room was ready. As she maneuvered her walker to the elevator, I provided a visual description of her tiny

> room, including the eyelet curtains that had been hung on her window. "I love it," she stated with the enthusiasm of an eight-year-old having just been presented with a new puppy. "Mrs. Jones, you haven't seen the room . . . just wait," I said. Then she spoke these words that I will never forget: "That does not have anything to do with it," she gently replied. "Happiness is something you decide on ahead of time. Whether I like the room or not, does not depend on how the furniture is arranged. It is how I arrange my mind. I have already decided to love it. It is a decision I make every morning when I wake up. I have a choice. I can spend the day in bed recounting the difficulty I have with the parts of my body that no longer work, or I can get out of bed and be thankful for the ones that do work. Each day is a gift, and as long as my eyes open, I will focus on the new day and all of the happy memories I have stored away . . . just for this time in my life."[1]

I strongly suspect the woman in this story spent a long time making good choices in her life. Why? Because in the midst of a difficult situation, the training was there to choose well. When faced with the enormous change that accompanies moving into a nursing home after losing her husband of seventy years, she had the ability to choose to be positive and upbeat instead of negative and depressed. She understood that her ability to enjoy her life in the nursing home depended on *making the choice* to be happy there. The freedom of choice with which God has endowed us is truly one of the greatest gifts of all. It assures us we can enjoy our lives if we really want to.

All of us have to make choices on a regular basis. They may be significant choices, such as what career to pursue or whom to marry, or they may be seemingly minor decisions such as what to wear to work and what to eat for lunch. Any time we have a choice, we have to make a decision. I realize that sounds simple, but my point is that when we have a choice to make, we can only commit to one of two options, or maybe one of several. Sometimes we can choose between good and bad; other times we have to choose between a good option and a better option. Whatever the case, we need the skills to make good choices because our choices chart the courses of our lives.

One of the most powerful scriptures in the Word of God is Deuteronomy 30:19: "I call heaven and earth to witness this day against you that I have set before you life and death, the blessings and the curses; therefore *choose life*, that you and your descendants may live" (emphasis mine).

I like this verse because in it God tells us what our options are and then He tells us which to choose. He says, basically, "These are your choices: life and blessings or death and curses," and then He clearly instructs us to choose life. This is like taking a test in school and having the teacher write the answers on the blackboard! God wants to make it easy for us to experience the life and blessings He wants to give us, but we must choose these things over things that bring death and destruction.

God wants to make it easy for us to experience the life and blessings He wants to give us, but we must choose these things over things that bring death and destruction.

THE AGONY OF REGRET

Some people decide not to choose life. They make decisions that lead to strife instead of peace, to bondage instead of freedom, or to misery instead of joy. I believe the primary result of wrong choices is regret, which means: to feel sorry, disappointed, or distressed about something; to feel sorrow or grief over.

The world is full of people who live with regret. Most of the time, you can identify these people because they seem to have a sense of heaviness, sadness, or grief about them for no apparent reason and for a long period of time. These are people who are sorry about everything. They are sorry about their lives, sorry about what they have done and what they haven't done, sorry they didn't finish their education, sorry they are in debt, sorry they ate so much dinner, sorry they didn't save more money, sorry they messed up their marriage or did not spend more time with their children. Living in an attitude of sorrow and regret simply robs these people of the joy they could experience every day and of hope for a better tomorrow. Wrong choices cause regret, and when we experience regret, we need to deal with it and let it teach us how to make better choices in the future.

Wrong choices cause regret, and when we experience regret, we need to deal with it and let it teach us how to make better choices in the future.

I understand firsthand that wrong choices lead to regret. I looked at myself a while back and regretted never having been serious about exercise in my life. I saw a marked difference between Dave and me because he has exercised all his life and is healthy, strong, and in good physical shape. When Dave and I return home from overseas travel, I struggle with jet lag for several days, but he can take *one nap* and be fine! That used to upset me, but I now realize he recovers more quickly than I do because he's stronger than I am.

Initially, I merely regretted that I wasn't as strong as Dave, but then I realized I could do something about it. It is never too late to make good choices and start reaping good results. I now exercise regularly and have been amazed by how quickly my body has responded by losing fat, building muscle, and producing more energy. So, if you find yourself regretting some of the unwise choices you have made in life, don't be deceived into thinking it is too late to do anything about it. You can get out of debt, make relationships better, increase your energy, or do anything else you want to do. All you need to do is begin and stick with it!

ONE CHOICE AT A TIME

Are you enjoying the life and blessings of God in your everyday life? Or have you made a series of choices resulting in disappointment, pain, or feeling that everything you do requires great effort and produces little reward? If so, there is hope for you! Don't spend your time and energy mourning all the bad decisions you have made; just start making good ones.

Don't spend your time and energy mourning all the bad decisions you have made; just start making good ones.

The way to overcome the results of a series of bad choices is through a series of right choices. The only way to walk out of trouble is to do the opposite of whatever you did to get into trouble—one choice at a time. Maybe the circumstances of your life right now are the direct result of a series of bad choices you have made. You may be in debt because of a series of bad choices with money. You may be lonely because of a series of bad choices in relationships or in the way you treat people. You may be sick because of a series of unhealthy choices: eating junk food, not getting enough rest, or abusing your body through working too much and not having enough balance in your life.

You cannot make a series of bad choices that result in significant problems and then make one good choice and expect all the results of all those bad choices to go away. You did not get into deep trouble through one bad choice; you got into trouble through a *series* of bad choices. If you really want your life to change for the better, you will need to make one good choice after another, over a period of time, just as consistently as you made the negative choices that produced negative results.

No matter what kind of trouble or difficulty you find yourself in, you can still have a blessed life. You may have suffered some losses, perhaps some things you will never get back. You cannot do anything about what is behind you, but you can do a great deal about what lies ahead of you. I believe if you are really faithful to God, He will even give you better things than you would have had previously. You are never hopeless with God! With God, "plan B" can be even better than "plan A" would have been. God is a redeemer; He causes bad things to work for your good; and He will always give you another chance. If you have a situation that is too big for you to solve, then you are material for a miracle. Invite God to get involved, follow His directions, and you will see amazing results.

DON'T PLAY THE BLAME GAME

Many times when we suffer the consequences of bad choices, we want to blame them on someone else. Instead of taking personal responsibility for our decisions and their results, we say, "The devil made me do it," "I am in this condition because of the way my parents raised me," or "If my boss would pay me more, I wouldn't be in debt." Sometimes people do have reasons for making bad choices, but those reasons should never become excuses. We need to use the recognition of those reasons to help us understand how we need to change and make good choices, not to justify continued bad choices. I had a lot of personality quirks because my father abused me sexually, and God had to remind me that even though the abuse was the reason I was the way I was, I could not let it be an excuse for never changing. The Holy Spirit has the job of transforming each of us into the image of Jesus Christ, but we have to stop blaming, stop making excuses, and start making right choices.

Bad choices rarely affect only one person. If you make negative or harmful choices in your life, they will inevitably affect someone else—your spouse, your children, your friends, your parents, and perhaps your co-workers, fellow students, or neighbors.

Bad choices rarely affect only one person. If you make negative or harmful choices in your life, they will inevitably affect someone else.

Sometimes, the impact of others' choices is tragic or devastating. In my case, someone's decision to abuse me sexually affected my life in radical ways. As a result, I made bad choices too—not the same bad choices, but other choices detrimental to me and to my relationships. Over time, my bad choices began to affect my children. But now, thank God, I have learned to make good, wise choices. For years, Dave and I have watched how making right choices has had positive effects on our children. The same can be true for you. No matter how many bad choices you have made in the past, if you will start making good choices *and keep at it,* you will begin to see positive results in your life and the lives of the people around you.

God gives us the ability to make our own choices. No matter what Jesus has done for us, and no matter what the Holy Spirit is trying to do for us now in our everyday lives, we still have the awesome privilege and responsibility of free choice, and we need to exercise it in ways that lead to life and blessing. We must choose to agree with God; we must choose to cooperate with His plan. We have to stop blaming circumstances and people for the problems in our lives and start taking responsibility for our choices.

> If you have a bad attitude, take responsibility for it in your own heart and before God.

If you have a bad attitude, take responsibility for it in your own heart and before God. Say, "This attitude is wrong. It's nobody's fault but mine, God, and I want to change!" If you are in trouble financially, then take responsibility for it! Say, "Well, God, there must be something wrong. I'm either spending too much money, handling my money wrong, or spending my money on things I should not spend it on. I've gone into debt and have not been willing to pay the price necessary to get out of debt. Maybe I have the wrong job and you're telling me to step out and do something else and I'm not doing it. I don't know—I don't know what's wrong, God, but something's wrong and

I'm not just going to blame the devil or inflation or high prices. I will take some responsibility, and I need you to show me what I need to do to get out of this mess." God will come through for you.

WE REAP WHAT WE SOW

My primary goal in this chapter is to help you see where bad choices have led to regret or trouble in your life and to encourage you to start making good choices so you can live a life in which you enjoy God's blessings every day.

Galatians 6:7, 8 teaches us a principle we need to understand: "*For whatever a man sows, that and that only is what he will reap.* For he who sows to his own flesh (lower nature, sensuality) will from the flesh reap decay and ruin and destruction, but he who sows to the Spirit will from the Spirit reap eternal life" (emphasis mine).

This principle of sowing and reaping is foundational to our lives. We all understand that it is true in the natural world. If a farmer plants corn, he will not reap potatoes at harvest time. If he plants soybeans, he will not reap cotton. The farmer will have in full, mature form whatever he planted in seed form. The same is true for your thoughts, words, actions, and choices. If you think about situations that make you angry, you will express anger in your life. If you think and speak positive, faith-filled words, you will have positive results. If you act kindly and generously toward someone, he or she will probably be kind and generous toward you. If you make choices that align with God's Word, you will reap the benefits He promises you. Be careful what you sow as you make choices every day, because whatever you sow, you also will reap. You may not reap immediately, but someday you will have a harvest.

Be careful what you sow as you make choices every day, because whatever you sow, you also will reap.

Romans 8:5, 6 affirms this truth, presenting it in a slightly different way:

> "For those who are according to the flesh *and* are controlled by its unholy desires set their minds on *and* pursue those things which gratify the flesh, but those who are according to the Spirit *and* are controlled by the desires of the Spirit set their minds on *and* seek those things which gratify the [Holy] Spirit. Now the mind of the flesh [which is sense and reason without the Holy Spirit] is death [death that comprises all the miseries arising from sin, both here and hereafter]. But the mind of the [Holy] Spirit is life and [soul] peace [both now and forever]."

In these verses, Paul is writing about the power of choice and reaping what we sow. If we choose to focus our thoughts and actions on the flesh (our worldly feelings and desires), we will be miserable. But if we focus on the Spirit of God and follow Him, we will experience peace and joy.

Unless your life is extremely unusual, peace and joy may seem very hard to find at times. Daily existence is full of challenges, problems, and opportunities to overcome obstacles. Flat tires, dirty diapers, bills, a broken windshield, and other such things will always be part of life, so you might as well accept the fact that problems will never go away completely. But in the midst of big challenges and not-so-big ones, you have the ability and power, through the Holy Spirit, to choose to respond well. People who live happy, enjoyable lives are not without struggles; they simply make good choices.

I encourage you to do the same. Choose life today!

CHAPTER

10

Grieve Your Losses

"Grief is itself a medicine."
—WILLIAM COWPER

In 2005, there were approximately 2.4 million deaths in the United States. That means at least that many suffered the loss of someone they loved. In addition, countless others experienced various forms of significant loss. For instance, a husband leaves his wife of thirty years. A hurricane or natural disaster strikes and wipes out an entire community. Someone's house burns down. A person goes to the doctor feeling fine, but discovers after having tests that he or she has stage-four cancer. A disgruntled employee spreads terrible lies about a former boss and ruins his reputation. These circumstances happen every day, and people have to confront them. No amount of faith can ever prevent us from feeling the pain of loss, but it can help us recover and go on with our lives.

Perhaps something devastating has happened to you—maybe recently, maybe many years ago. In the face of your losses, I want to offer hope to you today. Whatever your situation, God wants to heal you, strengthen you, and lead you to a place where you can enjoy life again. You certainly need to grieve, but you can do so in healthy, appropriate ways that will keep you from getting stuck in your sadness or pain, and enable you to heal and move forward in God's plans and purposes for your life.

GO AHEAD AND CRY

When you have had a loss in your life, you need to go through the grieving process. In fact, the only way to cope with loss in a healthy way is to grieve appropriately. Grief is defined as deep, mental anguish over a loss, or as deep sorrow. It means to be sorrowful, to mourn, or to be distressed. The grieving process is necessary when loss occurs; it is healthy mentally, spiritually, and even physically.

> The only way to cope with loss in a healthy way is to grieve appropriately.

Grieving is necessary and healthy because you must deal with your problems and pain or they will deal with you. Sooner or later, they will catch up with you if you do not confront them honestly and work through them, so determine today that you will grieve the losses in your life. Going through the grieving process is difficult and painful at times, but God will give you the ability to do it and He will be with you through it. Denial is not the answer to difficulty.

Remember, God gave you tear ducts for a reason. He knows you sometimes simply need to cry. Weeping is not a sign of weakness; it's part of the process of healing from painful events and situations. Let me repeat: the grieving process is important, and it is normal. If you are a Christian who has suffered a loss and are having a hard time, if you have some days when you cry easily or for periods of time each day, do not think you are weak or that you don't have any faith. Such expressions of emotion simply mean you are in a stage of grief in which you need to cry, and that is okay. God treasures our tears and keeps them in a bottle; and when you need to cry, He wants you to do so.

THE GRIEVING PROCESS

Grief, like many other things in life, is a process; it has a beginning and an end. Sometimes people do not want to go all the way through this process because they feel guilty about moving beyond the intense pain of their loss. People who have lost a loved one may feel guilty when they even think about not being constantly sad over the person's death anymore. Some have told me they feel guilty when they feel happy. That is merely Satan's way of keeping them trapped in a past they cannot do anything about. When you are grieving, you will have a period of great sadness and a time when you need to cry, but you cannot let yourself stay in that place. You need to go all the way through the grieving process because if you allow prolonged or excessive grief to take over your life, it will become destructive. So, as soon as possible after loss takes place, I encourage you to make a decision and tell yourself, *I'm not going to let this defeat me or overwhelm me. I am going to press on, even if everything's been destroyed. Even if I have to start all over, with God all things are possible.* You have God's permission to enjoy your life again!

When you are grieving, you will have a period of great sadness and a time when you need to cry, but you cannot let yourself stay in that place.

God is a healer of hearts; He wants our hearts to be healed, restored, and strengthened after we have endured the pain of loss. In this section, I want to help you understand the grieving process so you will know what to expect and what is healthy and normal as you mourn the losses you have encountered, or will encounter, and begin to work your way through them. You see, we all experience losses of some kind at times, and in order to enjoy life and not fear tomorrow we must know we can recover from them.

Shock

When you experience a great loss in your life, your first response is likely to be shock. Even if you have been expecting the loss, you will probably still be shocked when it actually happens. Shock is good and healthy because it functions in your life as shock absorbers do on your car. When you hit a pothole while driving, shock absorbers keep you from being jolted or thrown against the ceiling of the car upon impact; they cushion the blow. A period of shock after significant loss will do the same for your emotions.

Expect a period of numbness when you are grieving. Do not feel guilty about not feeling more, but realize that time of shock and numbness is helpful because if you could feel everything all at once, it would be overwhelming; your emotions couldn't handle it. Little by little, God will release those feelings and help you begin to work through them. The shock is temporary. It's like an anesthetic. It will not last forever, but it is part of the process of healing.

Sometimes when you are shocked and numb after a trauma or a loss, you will hurt too much to even pray. You may not be able to do anything more than look out the window and say, "Oh, God, oh, God, oh . . ." That's understandable and perfectly acceptable. It's part of being in shock, which is an important phase of the grieving process.

Feeling

As time passes, the shock will begin to wear off and you will begin to feel the pain of your loss. A friend who lost his son told me the hardest time for him was after the funeral service because that was when people stopped calling, stopped sending flowers, stopped dropping by to visit. He and his wife were simply left with their pain.

Being "left with your pain" is part of the grieving process. It is difficult but necessary. When you reach the point of feeling the pain, you are moving forward in the grieving process. Feeling the pain is vital to mourning a loss. Trying not to feel the pain is not normal; it's unhealthy. In fact, I believe facing and feeling the pain that accompanies loss

Feeling the pain is vital to mourning a loss. Trying not to feel the pain is not normal; it's unhealthy.

is *necessary* to move beyond the loss into the next season God has for you.

Anger

Anger is another aspect of the grieving process, and it often comes after the shock has subsided and while you are feeling the pain of your loss. If you have lost someone you love, you may be angry at that person for abandoning you; you may be angry at yourself for things you did or did not say or do; or you may be angry at friends or family members for various reasons.

Sometimes people are angry with themselves or blame themselves for a loss. They say, "Well, I wish I had . . . Why didn't I . . . ? I could have . . . I should have . . . I shouldn't have . . ." Comments such as these do not help. All of us who have ever experienced loss can look back and wish we had done or said things differently. Under these circumstances, we must believe we did the very best we could in the situation, and we must give ourselves the grace to accept that.

You may also be angry with God, and this is fairly common in the wake of a devastating loss. Anger with God is the primary response the enemy wants to see from you when tragedy comes your way. He wants you to be furious with God, to believe God doesn't love you anymore, and to stop praying and talking to God. He also wants you to get into a place where you cannot receive the comfort of the Holy Spirit, because if that happens, he knows you will never complete the grieving process and move beyond your sadness.

Often, a person who is grieving and angry with God will say something like, "Well, I don't understand. If God is loving, how could He let this happen?" The first thing an angry person wants to do is place blame. That is normal; it's natural. But sooner or later you have to come

> You may not understand some of the things that happen in your life, but that does not make God unloving.

to the point where you say, "You know what? If I'm mad at God, I hurt nobody but myself because He's the only One who can help me." You may not understand some of the things that happen in your life, but that does not make God unloving. If you are angry with God, I urge you to find peace with Him and stop trying to figure Him out. If we ever understood Him completely, He could no longer be our God. God knows things we do not know. His wisdom is infinite, beyond anything we could imagine.

I cannot explain why things happen as they do. I simply know we must trust God in the face of unanswered questions. We live in a world under the influence of sin, and bad things do happen to good people. God never guarantees us trouble-free lives, but He does promise to strengthen us. He enables us to move on with life and enjoy what remains of it rather than wasting it living in a past we cannot change. The fact is, we simply do not have the answers to many things, and when we reach the point where we can accept that, we can stop being angry and start really living again rather than merely existing from day to day.

KEEP MOVING

I want to emphasize again that the grieving process is healthy, but I also want to be clear that it must come to an end. Problems arise when it does not reach a conclusion. There is a time for grieving, mourning, sadness, and weeping. When you have sustained a great loss in your life, you have to do your hurting. If you do not give yourself time to be healed, you will suffer more than necessary. So go ahead and go through the process, but remember there will come a time when God will say, "Now it's time to move on."

Deuteronomy 34:8 teaches us a valuable lesson about grieving losses: "And the Israelites wept for Moses in the plains of Moab thirty days; then the days of weeping and mourning for Moses were ended." As we read this verse, we must remember that Moses was an extremely important person in the lives of the Israelites. When he died, they mourned deeply and cried over the loss of this significant leader. Notice they wept for him "in the plains of Moab thirty days; then the days of weeping and mourning for Moses were ended."

By calling your attention to this passage, I am not suggesting in any way that a person who loses a loved one should stop grieving after only thirty days. I do want you to see, though, that the Old Testament law only permitted the Israelites thirty days to mourn, and then they had to go on. They had to get moving.

The principle behind this verse is important to everyone who suffers loss: Sometimes the best thing you can do when you are hurting is to do something. Get going and keep moving. If you cannot do anything else, just keep moving. Go take a walk. Get outside in the sunshine, and tell God how you feel. Go do something for somebody else. Often, the best way to cooperate with God's healing work in your soul is to go find other hurting people and sow into their lives and be a blessing to them. As you work through your grief, you may have times when you simply need to get your mind off what you're going through because you have done everything you can do about it; there is nothing else you can do, and now you need to wait for the full healing to come.

Sometimes the best thing you can do when you are hurting is to do something. Get going and keep moving.

Whatever you do, don't just sit and think about your loss over and over. You can think yourself right into depression and despair. If you have suffered a loss, perhaps it's time to get up and get moving in a positive direction again.

If you have been through a tragic loss recently, you may not be ready to even think about moving on yet, and that is all right. But the time will come when you will know deep in your heart you must let go of the past and get busy with the future. When that time comes, you will have to make a decision only you can make. When the time does arrive, embrace it and trust the Holy Spirit to guide and comfort you as you move forward.

My uncle's death many years ago was very difficult for my aunt because they enjoyed an amazingly close relationship. It took her a long time to be willing to develop a new lifestyle. She was accustomed to doing everything with him and suddenly he was no longer available. She lived in the home they shared for quite a few years and then reluctantly moved to an assisted-living complex at my suggestion. I wanted her to be in a place with other people and available activities so she would not be lonely.

Even after she moved, she continued to stay by herself most of the time—until about two years ago. Then she decided to get involved in some of the activities available where she lives. Now she is so busy enjoying this new phase of her life I can rarely find her at home. Not only has she gotten involved in activities but she has also become the resident distributor for all my books and CDs. She loves blessing the senior citizens with resources that will help them, and doing so has helped her look forward to each day. She stopped thinking about what she lost and decided to do something fruitful with what she had left. There was plenty of life and joy available to her, but she had to make a decision to take advantage of it.

THE COMFORTER

I believe there are two main things that can heal a broken heart in the aftermath of a loss: time and the comfort of the Holy Spirit. Second Corinthians 1:3 says, "Blessed be the God and Father of our Lord Jesus Christ, the Father of sympathy (pity and mercy) and the God [Who is the Source] of every comfort (consolation and encouragement)." When we have sustained a significant loss of any kind, we must remember: God is the source of every comfort. Other people cannot provide true comfort, so we need to stop getting upset with

> I believe there are two main things that can heal a broken heart in the aftermath of a loss: time and the comfort of the Holy Spirit.

our friends because they cannot make us feel better. If we look to them for the help only God can give, God may not allow them to provide it. He alone is the source of all comfort. He may choose to comfort us *through* people, but that will be because we went to Him first, and He decided to work through them and use them to bless us. When He does, we need to remember to give Him the glory and not to give them the credit—because He is the One working through them to help us.

Referring to the Holy Spirit, 2 Corinthians continues: "Who comforts (consoles and encourages) in every trouble (calamity and affliction), so that we may also be able to comfort (console and encourage) those who are in any kind of trouble *or* distress, with the comfort (consolation and encouragement) with which we ourselves are comforted (consoled and encouraged) by God" (v. 4). I can offer you help concerning grief in this book because God has helped me. Had I not experienced His comfort I would not be able to comfort you. How can I write to you today and tell you God has a great future for you and you do not have to be stuck in the messes from the past? Because He has done that for me. Because of what the Holy Spirit has done in my life, I can comfort you with the comfort with which I myself have been comforted. The same Holy Spirit who has comforted me will comfort you.

A PRAYER FOR YOU

I want to close this chapter with a prayer you can pray if you have suffered a loss. Whatever has happened to you, God cares. He wants to comfort you, help you through the grieving process, and give you the strength to go on.

Father God, I come to You today in Jesus' name. I give You everything that has hurt me. I give You every loss and the pain I have felt over each one. I give You injustice, every unfair situation, everything I don't understand. I give You the people who have hurt me. I give You my past. I give it all to You, and I let it go right now.

I ask for the comfort of the Holy Spirit to come into my life. Comfort me, oh God, the way only You can. Forgive me for running to people and getting angry at them because they could not make me feel better. You are the only One who can make me better.

I thank You, Lord, for healing. I ask that the grieving process take its proper course in me and You would show me when it is time to go on and how to do so. I pray for my joy to return and for my life to return. I commit to You to get up and go on. In Jesus' name, amen.

CHAPTER

11

Put Possessions in Perspective

"Money often costs too much."

—RALPH WALDO EMERSON

Without a healthy attitude toward money and possessions, everyday life can be miserable. People who think too highly of finances and material goods often live in pursuit of luxuries that leave them unsatisfied. They find themselves with full bank accounts and empty hearts, or end up spending more than they make and struggling under the weight of debt. This story, entitled "And This Too Shall Pass," powerfully illustrates the need to have our money and possessions in perspective.

> One day Solomon decided to humble Benaiah ben Yehoyada, his most trusted minister. He said to him, "Benaiah, there is a certain ring that I want you to bring to me. I wish to wear it for Sukkot which gives you six months to find it."
>
> "If it exists anywhere on earth, your majesty," replied Benaiah, "I will find it and bring it to you, but what makes the ring so special?"
>
> "It has magic powers," answered the king. "If a happy man looks at it, he becomes sad, and if a sad man looks at it, he becomes happy." Solomon knew that no such ring existed in the world, but he wished to give his minister a little taste of humility.

Spring passed and then summer, and still Benaiah had no idea where he could find the ring. On the night before Sukkot, he decided to take a walk in one of the poorest quarters of Jerusalem. He passed by a merchant who had begun to set out the day's wares on a shabby carpet. "Have you by any chance heard of a magic ring that makes the happy wearer forget his joy and the broken-hearted wearer forget his sorrows?" asked Benaiah.

He watched the grandfather take a plain gold ring from his carpet and engrave something on it. When Benaiah read the words on the ring, his face broke out in a wide smile.

That night the entire city welcomed in the holiday of Sukkot with great festivity. "Well, my friend," said Solomon, "have you found what I sent you after?" All the ministers laughed and Solomon himself smiled.

To everyone's surprise, Benaiah held up a small gold ring and declared, "Here it is, your majesty!" As soon as Solomon read the inscription, the smile vanished from his face. The jeweler had written three Hebrew letters on the gold band: "gimel, zayin, yud," which began the words "Gam zeh ya'avor"—"This too shall pass."

At that moment Solomon realized that all his wisdom and fabulous wealth and tremendous power were but fleeting things, for one day he would be nothing but dust.[1]

YOU CAN'T TAKE IT WITH YOU

In many cultures around the world today, we place heavy emphasis on money, designer clothes and accessories, high-end electronics, luxury cars, and other material goods. Many aspects of everyday life have fallen prey to commercialization, and societies assign great value to worldly success and provisions, and everywhere we look the message is to earn more, buy more, and have more.

But I am not sure "more" is all it's cracked up to be; I do not believe more money or more possessions are a solution to people's problems. Everywhere I go, I notice men and women, even boys and girls, are so busy trying to acquire more—more money, more "stuff," more anything. People rarely have time for each other anymore—and that does not seem to bother them as much as it bothered people years ago. Life has become so complicated and so driven, often by the pursuit of money and possessions—a pursuit that will leave us empty and unfulfilled if we are not careful.

First Timothy 6:7 says, "For we brought nothing into the world, and *obviously* we cannot take anything out of the world." As we develop a healthy perspective on possessions and finances, we must understand we will not be able to carry anything with us when we pass away. The money and things we have on earth are for us to enjoy and use to bless others. They are not to make us feel superior to someone else, to hoard and protect, or to show off. We are not to love, treasure, or serve *things*; we are to love and serve God. We are not to seek *things* above all; we are to seek God's kingdom first and foremost—and *things* will be added to us (see Matthew 6:33).

The money and things we have on earth are for us to enjoy and use to bless others.

I have no problem whatsoever with people who have nice things. I have some nice things and I enjoy them, but I am determined not to love them. In this day and age, if any of us are going to resist the temptation to love material possessions, we must resist it on purpose because we are surrounded by greed. I often overhear people making comments such as, "Well, I just can't be happy if I don't have a bigger house" or "I just *have* to have those new designer jeans." I have even heard people say, "Oh, that (house, car, outfit) is to die for." These statements represent the values of our culture, but they do not reflect the values of God's kingdom.

CONTENT AND SATISFIED

God's Word has much to say to us about money and physical provisions. In 1 Timothy 6:8, Paul writes, "But if we have food and clothing, with these we shall be content (satisfied). Our modern minds can hardly comprehend this statement. We ask, "How in the world could anybody be satisfied with only food and clothing?" I believe Paul's point here is more than literal food and clothes. He is referring to the basic needs of life. If our basic needs are met, we need to be happy!

> We are to be content with the things we really need, without feeling driven to keep acquiring more.

We are to be content with the things we really need, without feeling driven to keep acquiring more. If we focus on being thankful to God for meeting our needs and if we keep our minds on Him, we will be blessed. Many times, we will end up with more and better things than we can provide for ourselves if we will simply love Him, love people and try to help them, stay humble before God, worship Him, and trust Him. When He knows our hearts truly belong to Him, He knows He can count on us to be good stewards of the things He gives us and not to love them excessively or allow ourselves to have an unbalanced attitude toward them.

RUN!

The passage in 1 Timothy continues: "But those who crave to be rich fall into temptation and a snare and into many foolish (useless, godless) and hurtful desires that plunge men into ruin and destruction and miserable perishing. For the love of money is a root of all evils; it is through this craving that some have been led astray and have wandered from the faith and pierced themselves through with many acute [mental] pangs. But as for you, O man of God, *flee* from all these things" (vv. 9–11, emphasis mine).

Here, Paul encourages Timothy as a man of God to run from the mentality that craves to be rich and loves money. Really, he is speaking to all of us concerning financial greed and saying, "Do not let that get a hold on you." Once again, I want to assure you that God delights in your prosperity and Deuteronomy 8:18 states that God gives us the power to get wealth, but greed is dangerous and steals the life of its possessor (see Proverbs 1:19).

We need to pay attention to what is going on in our minds and with our desires. When we begin to be unhappy because we do not have "one of these" and "one of those" and "another one of that," we are headed toward an unbalanced approach to money and possessions. God does not mind our having things as long as things do not "have" us. He is not opposed to our having money; it is the love of money that gets us into trouble, and is, in fact, "a root of all evils."

God does not mind our having things as long as things do not "have" us.

GREEDY GEHAZI

I want you to know the story of a man named Gehazi, an Old Testament character who loved money to the point it literally kept him from reaching his destiny.

Gehazi was a servant of the prophet Elisha, and one day a military official named Naaman, who had leprosy, went to Elisha for healing. After he was healed, he tried and tried to give Elisha a gift, but Elisha refused to receive anything from him.

In 2 Kings 5, we read about the decision that changed Gehazi's life:

> "But Gehazi, the servant of Elisha the man of God, said, Behold, my master spared this Naaman the Syrian, in not

> receiving from his hands what he brought. But as the Lord lives, I will run after him and get something from him. So Gehazi followed after Naaman. When Naaman saw one running after him, he lighted down from the chariot to meet him and said, Is all well? And he said, All is well. My master has sent me to say, There have just come to me from the hill country of Ephraim two young men of the sons of the prophets. I pray you, give them a talent of silver and two changes of garments" (vv. 20–22).

Naaman gave Gehazi the money and the clothes, and even sent two of his servants to take them to Gehazi's house. When Elisha later asked Gehazi, "Where have you been?" Gehazi told another lie and responded, "Nowhere" (see v. 25). But Elisha knew better and said, "Did not my spirit go with you when the man turned from his chariot to meet you? Was it a time to accept money, garments, olive orchards, vineyards, sheep, oxen, menservants, and maidservants?" (v. 26). As a result of Gehazi's behavior, Elisha said: "Therefore the leprosy of Naaman shall cleave to you and to your offspring forever. And Gehazi went from his presence a leper as white as snow" (v. 27).

I wonder how many times in his life Gehazi sat around with leprosy, looked at other people who were successful, and thought about the man he could have been.

I wonder how many times in his life Gehazi sat around with leprosy, looked at other people who were successful, and thought about the man he could have been.

Gehazi allowed the love of money to change his destiny. How many people today lose their families because of the love of money? How many men work so much their children don't want to be around them anymore or their wives are so lonely they get involved with other men? How many women fail to develop deep, healthy relationships with friends or meaningful relationships with their husbands, but have the respect and admiration of an office full of co-workers they really don't know? This happens more than we like to admit—and it's all because they want money and things! That's the love of money, and it leads to all kinds of trouble.

Sometimes, people have to work extra hard, get a second job, or put in overtime for a season in order to pay off debt, afford a major purchase, or meet unusual needs. Working hard for those reasons for a period of time is admirable. But working frantically for the sole purpose of keeping up with or outdoing other people is ungodly. They need to understand that another boat, another car, or a larger house will not make them happy. Happiness and the ability to enjoy life come from good relationships with God, family, and friends. Happiness also comes from the peace of knowing you are not in debt!

BE TRANSFORMED

I urge you to not be caught up by the world system and its values. Romans 12:2 makes clear God's instructions to believers: "Do not be conformed to this world (this age), [fashioned after and adapted to its external, superficial customs], but be transformed (changed) by the [entire] renewal of your mind [by its new ideals and its new attitude], so that you may prove [for yourselves] what is the good and acceptable and perfect will of God, *even* the thing which is good and acceptable and perfect [in His sight for you]."

I hope you will apply this verse to your life, especially where money and possessions are concerned. Live by the truth of God's Word in these areas, and ask the Holy Spirit to guide you in your decisions. Do not let your friends or co-workers lead you, but live within your means and be secure in your identity in Christ, not seeking affirmation or acceptance in money or things. Make wise financial decisions and purchases so you can live a blessed life.

> Make wise financial decisions and purchases so you can live a blessed life.

GIVE GOD YOUR WHOLE HEART

In Mark 10, we read the story of a man who asked Jesus, "Teacher, [You are essentially and perfectly morally] good, what must I do to inherit eternal life [that is, to partake of eternal salvation]?" (v. 17).

Jesus responded, "Why do you call Me [essentially and perfectly morally] good? There is no one [essentially and perfectly morally] good—except God alone. You know the commandments: Do not kill, do not commit adultery, do not steal, do not bear false witness, do not defraud, honor your father and mother" (vv. 18, 19).

The man replied to Jesus that he had obeyed all the commandments, for as long as he could remember. Notice what happened next: "And Jesus, looking upon him, *loved him.*" (v. 21, emphasis mine). Jesus is about to give this man an instruction *because He loved him:* "You lack one thing; go and sell all you have and give [the money] to the poor, and you will have treasure in heaven; and come [and] accompany Me [walking the same road that I walk]" (v. 21).

This is not the most popular scripture in the Bible. Many people do not like it, often because they do not understand the heart of love behind it. They wonder, "Does God want me to sell everything I have and give the proceeds to the poor in order to serve Him?" No, not at all. The point of this parable is that we have to love Jesus first. We must love Him more than we love our "stuff," which was not the case with the man in the story. We need to get rid of anything keeping us from loving and serving God with all of our hearts.

We need to get rid of anything keeping us from loving and serving God with all of our hearts.

If you have a job that keeps you from serving God, find another job. If you have a boyfriend or a girlfriend who does not want you to love God first, find someone else. If you have a hobby or an interest that takes you away from serving God, find another way to spend your time. In practical terms, these are the kinds of lessons Jesus was teaching the wealthy young man. If you really want a deeper walk with God, you may have to sacrifice some things that are keeping you from it. Many times in God's economy, we have to let go of something lower to take hold of something higher.

Pay attention to Jesus' next words, which He spoke to His disciples: "With what difficulty will those who possess wealth *and keep on holding it* enter the kingdom of God!" (v. 23, emphasis mine). Jesus did not say there was anything wrong with the man's having wealth; He simply said it would be difficult for people to enter the kingdom of God if they have wealth and they *keep on holding it.*

Where our resources are concerned, we are supposed to be channels, not reservoirs. We are supposed to receive from God, be blessed, and use what He gives us to bless other people. We need to view our finances as a stream with a constant flow. Anytime you dam up water, it gets stagnant—and greed has the same effect on us. It can make us want to hold on to everything we have and not share our blessings with others.

We are supposed to receive from God, be blessed, and use what He gives us to bless other people.

Let me encourage you to be a giver. Do not become enamored with the world's value system and its attempts to lure you into "more and more and more." Pay attention to your thoughts and desires so you do not become a lover of money. Study God's Word to find out what He says about having money and being a good steward, and keep your resources flowing by using them to serve God and bless other people.

CHAPTER 12

Be Fruitful

"Beware the barrenness of a busy life."
—SOCRATES

Everyone today seems to be busy. So often, when I ask people how they are, they reply, "Busy," or when I say, "How are things going?" they answer, "Busy." People seem to wear their busyness like a badge, as though it is something to be proud of. But if we look into God's Word, we never once find Him telling us to be busy, frustrated, overworked, or stressed. He does, however, tell us to be fruitful. In Genesis 1:28, after God created the first man and woman on earth, He "blessed them and said to them, *Be fruitful,* multiply, and fill the earth, and subdue it [using all its vast resources in the service of God and man]; and have dominion over the fish of the sea, the birds of the air, and over every living creature that moves upon the earth" (emphasis mine).

There is a difference between being busy and being fruitful. When we are busy, we simply accomplish what we need or want to do, sometimes with no feeling of satisfaction or long-term benefits. When we are fruitful, though, we can sense God's grace on what we do; we feel satisfied and fulfilled; and we know that it will produce lasting results and make an impact greater than we can make in our natural strength.

When we are fruitful, we take the dominion God instructs us

to take in Genesis 1:28. From the very beginning, God gives man authority, saying basically, "You are not to be ruled; you are to rule. If you don't rule and reign, if you don't take authority over things, if you don't have dominion, everything else will rule you and you will never get around to being fruitful and multiplying." So, how do we take authority over the situations demanding our time and attention and become fruitful instead of busy in our lives? Read on.

JUST SAY NO

The number one way to take authority over your time and energy is to learn when to say yes and when to say no. If you are not willing to say no when necessary, activities and commitments will draw you into busyness, whittle away your time, and steal your ability to be fruitful. Saying no when necessary has the same effect on your time and productivity pruning has on a tree. It does not always feel good when you do it, but after a while, you become fuller, stronger, and more productive than before. I spent a large portion of my life "doing" things, but I have now learned to enjoy "being." That doesn't mean I no longer do anything, but I have worked hard to have balance between doing and being. This is why we are called human beings, not "human doings."

The number one way to take authority over your time and energy is to learn when to say yes and when to say no.

I often have to say no to invitations and opportunities. People don't always like or understand that, but I have come to a place in my life where I know what I need to do and not do in order to fulfill the things I am called to do and enjoy my life at the same time. I can't attend every party or go to every dinner to which I am invited. If people want to eat with me, they will probably have to eat early. I don't want to go out and eat at 9:00 p.m. and not be able to sleep all night because I am full. If I do that, I will be tired and unfruitful the following day.

What about you? Do you feel pushed and pulled by saying too many yeses and not enough nos? Are you overcommitted and undersatisfied? I encourage you today to say no when you need to and to seek to be fulfilled and fruitful rather than merely busy. Running an international ministry may not be your challenge; it could be raising three children or running a business. We are not all called to do the same thing, but we all do need to make sure we are not spending our time unwisely or letting people, circumstances, or the world system manipulate us and steal our time to the point we cannot find any time to do the things we really want to do or feel we are supposed to be doing.

EXAMINE YOUR MOTIVES, EVALUATE YOUR PRODUCTIVITY

In John 15:16, Jesus says, "You have not chosen Me, but I have chosen you and I have appointed you [I have planted you], that you might go and bear fruit *and* keep on bearing, and that your fruit may be lasting [that it may remain, abide], so that whatever you ask the Father in My Name [as presenting all that I AM], He may give it to you." Notice in this verse God Himself chose you and called you into relationship with Him, and He did it for a reason. Yes, God wants you to enjoy your life, but He also wants you to be productive and bear good fruit. In fact, that is the purpose for which He chose and appointed you.

Yes, God wants you to enjoy your life, but He also wants you to be productive and bear good fruit. In fact, that is the purpose for which He chose and appointed you.

One way to start getting your busyness under control and begin to be fruitful is to write down all the things you put your time into and then go back and ask yourself, "Why am I doing that?" "Why am I on that committee?" "Why am I going to that party?" "Why am I going to that luncheon?" "Why did I commit to that?"

If you will assess what you are doing and ask yourself why you are doing it, you will discover that much of it is not even for right reasons. You may find you are doing some things to impress someone you don't even like, or to feel accepted, or to keep people from becoming upset. You may also be doing things because you think you should—out of a false sense of obligation.

In addition to examining your motives, another important step toward greater fruitfulness in your life is to evaluate your current level of productivity. Are you being fruitful in some ways, but not in others? Or, are you extremely busy, but not very fruitful at all? Ask yourself these questions and let your answers help you move toward a more fruitful, productive life:

- Are you spending your time in ways that help you fulfill your purpose?
- Are you doing what you really desire to do, or are you merely being controlled and pressured by circumstances and the expectations of other people?
- Are you being productive with your time and energy?
- What are you doing to help somebody else?
- Do you see tangible results from your busyness, or are you just busy?
- What specific changes do you need to make in your commitments if you are going to be fruitful instead of busy?
- How do you need to reorder or reprioritize the way you spend your time so you can be more fruitful?

Let me encourage you to follow the leading of the Holy Spirit as He shows you the changes you need to make to be more fruitful. If you are not willing to change, then nothing will change; your life will stay exactly as it is. You must understand that when you start making changes, some people will be unhappy. If you have been catering to a particular person and you decide to change the amount of time

> Let me encourage you to follow the leading of the Holy Spirit as He shows you the changes you need to make to be more fruitful.

you spend with or doing things for him or her, your decision may not be received well. When that happens, just give the person time to adjust. If they are unwilling to make that adjustment, then perhaps they were not real friends at all. If being controlled by someone is the only way to keep a relationship, then that is a relationship you do not want. Determine that you are not going to stand before God someday and have to explain why you did not use your time wisely. Determine that you are going to bear fruit. Choose every day to do something worth doing.

IT'S YOUR RESPONSIBILITY

You can live an awesome life, but if you are not being fruitful, you will be frustrated. The reason for this is God created you to be productive. He made you to accomplish the plans and purposes He has for your life, and when you are doing so, you feel fulfilled. You know you are using your time wisely; you sense you are walking in God's will for your life; you believe what you are doing is important. You have to make sure you put your time into your purpose; anything less will leave you longing for something more. It has been said that we should put 80 percent of our time into our top two priorities in life. We can so easily "major in minors" and by doing so end up never fulfilling our main goals.

> God created you to be productive. He made you to accomplish the plans and purposes He has for your life, and when you are doing so, you feel fulfilled.

When God called Joshua to finish what He called Moses to start by leading the Israelites into the Promised Land, He said to him: "This

Book of the Law shall not depart out of your mouth, but you shall meditate on it day and night, that you may observe and do according to all that is written in it. For then you shall make your way prosperous, and then you shall deal wisely *and* have good success" (Joshua 1:8). Just as He did for Joshua, God has a prosperous, blessed, wonderful, joy-filled, fruitful life for you! You do not have to sit on the sidelines and listen to other people talk about the great lives they have. You can have good success and a great life too.

There were many years when my life was not wonderful, but that was not God's fault. Even my circumstances were not to blame; it was my fault. Until I took responsibility for my life, nothing changed. If you want change in your life, don't sit around and just wish you were more productive; make the adjustments necessary for greater fruitfulness and productivity in your life. Realize you have many of the same opportunities everyone else does. God is no respecter of persons. What He does for someone else, He will do for you if you take responsibility for your choices in life.

God is no respecter of persons. What He does for someone else, He will do for you if you take responsibility for your choices in life.

If you decide you are no longer going to be busy but fruitful, you will have to make some changes. Some of those changes will be unpopular with people around you, but you are the only one who will stand before God and give an account for your life. Nobody else can do that for you. You have a God-given right to follow the leadership of the Holy Spirit and to fulfill your destiny, but if you don't make the decision to do it and take responsibility for it, the enemy will steal your destiny and rob you of your dreams. And he will do it through simple little things like getting you overcommitted and entangled in activities that keep you busy and wear you out but are not productive and have no lasting value. One of Satan's main goals is to distract us. He knows he will keep us from being fruitful if he can prevent us from focusing on what is important. Your destiny is important; you only have one life to live for God. Be determined to take responsibility for it and do the things He created and called you to do.

STRIKE A BALANCE

Remember what God said in Genesis 1:28: "Be fruitful, multiply, and fill the earth, and subdue it [using all its vast resources in the service of God and man]; and have dominion over the fish of the sea, the birds of the air, and over every living creature that moves upon the earth." What are you doing with what you have? Stop putting off until some other time in life what you feel God has called you to do. Perhaps you intend to obey God at some other time, but good intentions do not equal obedience and they bring no reward. Procrastination deceives people and often steals their destiny.

Notice God was saying, essentially, "Everything I've given you, I want you to use to serve Me and to help people." One of the best ways I know to enjoy life is to do things for other people, and I encourage you to be a blessing to everyone you can in every way you can. But do not allow yourself to become so busy helping everyone else that you neglect yourself, your time with God, or your purpose in life. You do need to live sacrificially and to serve other people, but remember: there's a "you" too. You have desires. There are things you want to do, experience, and enjoy. If God has put a deep desire for something in you, then you will be denying Him if you stay so busy doing other activities that you never pursue what He wants you to do. When it comes to your destiny, you are the only one who can fulfill it. No one else can do it for you. So do what you

If God has put a deep desire for something in you, then you will be denying Him if you stay so busy doing other activities that you never pursue what He wants you to do.

can for other people, but do not allow yourself to be consumed by them to the point that you stop spending time with God or walking in His destiny for your life. If you are too busy for God, then you are definitely too busy!

MAKE THE MOST OF EVERY MINUTE

When we speak of busyness and fruitfulness, we are primarily addressing the way we use our time. Time is a resource God gives us, and we must use our time to be fruitful. Two of the phrases we should avoid, both verbally and in our attitudes, are: "I just have a little time to kill" and "I am just passing the time." Time is not a commodity to kill or to "pass"; it is a gift to steward.

I am not one to waste time. I like to be productive with every minute. In my daily life, I make a diligent effort to keep everything on schedule. Sometimes that gets me in trouble because circumstances sometimes cause me to fall behind, and then I have to rush. I do not like to hurry, so I am learning to put a little more margin in my life—to allow more time between appointments and scheduled activities—and that relieves a good bit of frustration.

There are times when you do not have enough minutes or hours to complete a task or do something you want to do, but it's too early to do the next thing you need to do. When you have five, ten, or fifteen minutes, don't just "kill" your time. Use it to bear fruit. Keep a book or a Bible with you and use those few minutes to read something. Listen to worship music or part of a sermon. Pray. Write someone a note of encouragement. When you have a few minutes, make them count.

I don't mean to suggest that we should be doing something with every minute of every day. Taking time to reflect and just drink in the quiet and silence is also very valuable during those moments between scheduled events. Silence restores the soul and helps prepare us for the next thing we need to do.

Learn to discern your needs emotionally, mentally, physically, and spiritually, and use your time accordingly. Sometimes reading is best and at other times sitting quietly and doing absolutely nothing is best. Just remember that once time goes by you cannot ever get it back, so use it wisely.

To me, one of the worst things that can happen to people is to grow old and look back upon their lives and realize they never took time to do what they thought they were supposed to do or what they wanted to do or to feel they wasted their lives. I do not want you to look back in your latter years and be filled with regret. No matter your age, it is not too late to start using your time wisely and bearing good fruit.

As Christians, we do not mourn over the past; we let go of it and we go on. I believe God can take the years you have left on earth and make them count. He can make up for lost time and redeem days or even years you may have wasted. Your latter years can be even more fruitful than your former years if you determine today not to waste another minute, but to take dominion over every unproductive thing in your life and be fruitful every day.

CHAPTER 13

Wise Up!

"Never mistake knowledge for wisdom. One helps you make a living; the other helps you make a life."

—SANDRA CAREY

A wise woman who was traveling in the mountains found a precious stone in a stream. The next day she met another traveler who was hungry, and the wise woman opened her bag to share her food. The hungry traveler saw the precious stone and asked the woman to give it to him. She did so without hesitation. The traveler left, rejoicing in his good fortune. He knew the stone was worth enough to give him security for a lifetime. But a few days later he came back to return the stone to the wise woman.

"I've been thinking," he said, "I know how valuable the stone is, but I give it back in the hope that you can give me something even more precious. Give me what you have within you that enabled you to give me something more precious. Give me what you have within you that enabled you to give me the stone."[1]

All of us desperately need what was inside the woman with the precious stone: wisdom. If you want to build your life upon a firm foundation of wisdom, one of the best ways to do so is to read and study the book of Proverbs. It will teach you to make good decisions and to use wisdom in your work, relationships, finances, and time management, as well as in other areas of your practical, everyday life.

I like to define using wisdom as "choosing to do right now what you will be satisfied with later on." Wisdom is not the intellectual knowledge you experience; rather, it is knowing in your heart the right way to think, speak, and act in any situation. Wisdom is not reserved for highly educated people, naturally smart people, or those who separate themselves from other people to seek the mysteries of life. No, wisdom is God-given insight and understanding everyone can apply to the circumstances, challenges, and decisions we face in our everyday lives. The more wisdom we use today, the better our tomorrow will be.

Wisdom is God-given insight and understanding everyone can apply to the circumstances, challenges, and decisions we face in our everyday lives.

If you are a believer who knows the Word of God, you have wisdom. The Bible says you have the mind of Christ (see 1 Corinthians 2:16). It also says Christ is made unto us wisdom (see 1 Corinthians 1:30), and "the Lord gives skillful *and* godly wisdom" to those who walk uprightly by faith in Him (see Proverbs 2:6, 7). Wisdom is available to you in the Word of God. If you study the Word you are well equipped to know what to do in any situation and to make good decisions. When you need to make a decision, stop and listen to your heart before taking action. This will prevent you from making emotional decisions that end up badly. Ask God to reveal His wisdom to you and then make decisions accordingly.

WISDOM CRIES OUT

God wants us to use wisdom, and the Holy Spirit will lead us into wisdom if we will simply ask Him to do so. Proverbs 1:20 teaches us, "Wisdom cries aloud in the street, she raises her voice in the markets." In other words, wisdom is not difficult to obtain. God wants to reveal it to us; we simply need to pay attention.

For example, have you ever needed to make a decision and had your head (your intellectual abilities) try to lead you one way while your heart was leading you another? Have you ever had a situation in which your flesh (your natural thoughts and feelings) seemed to be guiding you in one direction, but something inside you kept nagging you to go another direction? For example, have there been times when you stayed up late at night watching television, even though you knew you needed a good night's sleep to be strong and alert for an important meeting the next day—and you kept resisting the knowing in your heart that you really *should* go to bed? Have you purchased something you were excited about on an emotional level, but knew in your heart you could not really afford and didn't even need?

What is happening in the kinds of circumstances I have just described? Chances are, wisdom is crying out to you. Many times, it cries out in the form of the things you find yourself thinking you should or should not do—you *should* eat healthily, you *should* be kind to other people, you *should* not spend money you do not have. These are all practical examples of using wisdom in everyday life. When you sense such leadings, the Holy Spirit, who speaks to your heart, is trying to help you make a wise decision, even though it may not be the choice you want to make or it may not seem to make much sense in your present circumstances.

The Spirit is at war against our flesh, and vice versa (see Galatians 5:17). When we know the wise choice to make and don't make it, the reason is often that we are allowing our flesh to lead us and to see if we can get away with unwise decisions—which are also known as "foolishness." The flesh leads us to foolishness, but God wants us to walk in wisdom and make choices now that we will be happy with later.

God wants us to walk in wisdom and make choices now that we will be happy with later.

SEEK WISDOM

Proverbs 2:1–5 gives us great insight into the way wisdom works and into the value of making the effort to seek wisdom in life:

> My Son, if you will receive my words and treasure up my commandments within you, making your ear attentive to skillful *and* godly Wisdom *and* inclining and directing your heart *and* mind to understanding [applying all your powers to the quest for it]. Yes, if you cry out for insight and raise your voice for understanding, if you seek [Wisdom] as for silver and search for skillful *and* godly Wisdom as for hidden treasures, then you will understand the reverent *and* worshipful fear of the Lord and find the knowledge of [our omniscient] God.

This passage encourages us to seek wisdom as diligently as we pursue other things in life and to understand that the fear of the Lord is essential to living a wise life. In fact, Psalm 111:10 says, "The reverent fear *and* worship of the Lord is the beginning of Wisdom." If we would seek wisdom with as much passion as we seek education, money, good looks, profitable jobs, or fulfilling relationships, our lives would be much better.

Verse 5 of this passage reveals that many people have horrible messes in their lives because they do not understand the "reverential fear" of God. This kind of awe toward God is the first step toward wisdom; without it, we will never be wise. When I use the words "reverential fear," I do not mean we should be afraid of God, but rather that we should have great respect for Him and treat Him with honor. The reverential fear and awe of God means we know God is mighty and He means what He says. God is all-knowing, all-seeing, all-powerful, and everywhere all the time. We should respect His awesomeness and be respectfully afraid to disobey Him.

Many people treat God merely as their buddy, one who is too kind and merciful to discipline them, ask them to sacrifice for Him, or require them to adjust attitudes or behaviors. I believe they have adopted this view simply because they do not want to change their lifestyles and be obedient to God's Word. This approach to God is not biblical. If we are going to relate to Him in reverential fear, as the Bible instructs, we will understand we need to honor and obey Him—because our lives will be in shambles if we don't. God does love us unconditionally, but He loves us too much to leave us in our sins.

WISDOM WILL PROMOTE YOU

Wisdom is one of the keys to promotion and increase in any area of life. Proverbs 4:8 urges us, "Prize Wisdom highly *and* exalt her, and she will exalt *and* promote you; she will bring you to honor when you embrace her."

Wisdom is one of the keys to promotion and increase in any area of life.

I believe many people fail to receive promotions they might otherwise be granted in their professions simply because they do not act wisely on their jobs. Have you ever noticed that sometimes the people who seem smartest or most intellectual are not promoted? That's because brainpower alone is not enough; wisdom and common sense are also important.

I have had some extremely bright people with very good minds on my staff over the years. Some of them, however, did not use wisdom at work. Maybe they were unkind to co-workers. Maybe they talked too much while others were trying to work. Maybe they seemed unable to get back to their desks on time after lunch or spent too much time on personal phone calls during working hours. Their skills were excellent, but they did not demonstrate wisdom in other ways, so I did not promote them. Skills are important, but if a person can type at lightning speed and not manage to be friendly and respectful in the office, he or she will not be promoted in our organization. A wise person who also has good skills, on the other hand, can expect to advance anywhere he or she goes, because wisdom is what promotes us and exalts us.

Similarly, a person can have the best educational credentials on earth and not have any wisdom whatsoever. In modern times, we have almost emphasized education to a fault. We not only need people who are educated and trained, and who operate in significant natural knowledge, but we also need to emphasize the value of wisdom, spiritual understanding, and discernment.

WISDOM AND THE WAYS OF GOD

The Amplified Bible teaches us that part of walking in wisdom includes a deep understanding of God's ways and purposes—not simply who He is or what He does, but how He works in our lives. Proverbs 4:11 reads, "I have taught you in the way of skillful *and* godly Wisdom [which is comprehensive insight into the ways and purposes of God.]"

You see, true Christianity goes far beyond sound doctrine. We certainly need to know the principles of our faith in the form of doctrine, but real Christianity is so much more than a set of beliefs; it is a way of daily, practical living that comes from understanding the ways and purposes of God. I like to say being a Christian begins with a decision to receive Jesus Christ as your Savior and Lord and is walked out in a daily lifestyle that adheres to His principles.

> Real Christianity is so much more than a set of beliefs; it is a way of daily, practical living that comes from understanding the ways and purposes of God.

When we approach everyday situations from the perspective of God's ways and purposes, we ask questions such as: "How would Jesus talk to that person?" "How would Jesus handle this situation?" "How would Jesus act in these circumstances?" "Would Jesus be gossiping now?" "How would Jesus deal with that person's obvious need? Would He walk away from it and not care, or would He try to do something about it?" When we begin to think along these lines, we are learning to be wise because we are seeking to understand the ways and purposes of God.

Moses was a very wise man, one who understood the importance of knowing God's ways. In Exodus 33:13, he cried out to God, "If I have found favor in Your sight, show me now Your way, that I may know You [progressively become more deeply and intimately acquainted with You, perceiving and recognizing and understanding more strongly and clearly.]" God answered Moses' prayer, as we read in Psalm 103:7: "He made known His ways . . . to Moses, His acts to the children of Israel."

Notice the distinction between what God made known to Moses (His ways) and what He made known to the children of Israel (His acts). Some people are only interested in God's acts—what He will do for them. But wise people are like Moses; they hunger for a deep understanding of His ways. Let me encourage you to cry out to God as Moses did. Ask Him to show you His ways and help you understand His purposes. As He reveals them to you, you will grow in wisdom.

MEET WISDOM AT THE INTERSECTIONS

Almost everywhere you travel, you are likely to come to a point where two roads intersect and you must choose whether to turn or to go straight.

We all face intersections in our lives. They are our turning points, the places where we must make decisions. Though Proverbs 8:1–3 does not use the word *intersection,* this passage speaks of the intersections we all encounter: "Does not skillful *and* godly Wisdom cry out, and understanding raise her voice [in contrast to the loose woman]? On the top of the heights beside the way, where the paths meet, stands Wisdom [skillful and godly]. At the gates at the entrance of the town, at the coming in at the doors, she cries out."

Notice that "where the paths meet, stands Wisdom." In other words, wisdom is standing at every intersection of your life. It is waiting for you at every point of decision in your life, and it is crying out, "Listen to me! Don't just *do* what you feel like doing. Don't just *say* whatever you feel like saying. Don't just *buy* whatever you feel like buying. Don't make your own decisions. Follow God! Obey His Word!"

If you are standing at a point of decision in your life right now, let me urge you to follow wisdom.

If you are standing at a point of decision in your life right now, let me urge you to follow wisdom. Seek God with all your heart instead of running to your friends, a talk-show host, a Web site, or books and magazines for advice. Go to God and His Word first, and don't automatically turn to the people and resources around you and ask them what you ought to do. God may lead you to a person for advice or He may answer your prayer by speaking through someone, but it is best to honor Him by seeking Him first.

Recently, I was with an acquaintance who had serious back problems. After an unsuccessful surgery, she continued to have terrible pain. Her doctor released her, saying there was nothing more anyone could do, and suggested she go to a pain-management clinic and learn to live with the pain.

I have a chiropractor who is an expert in muscle work and has helped me over the years. He recently added to his practice a full gymnasium with strength coaches and personal trainers. I told my distraught friend I really thought this doctor could help her. She lived in Arizona and my doctor is in Missouri, but she decided to make the trip and see if he could help her. After one visit, her pain diminished greatly. The chiropractor put her on a rehabilitation strength program and after she returned to him a few more times she was soon completely pain free. Wow!

She did not run to me and ignore God; rather, in seeking God, He gave her advice through me. As I said, God may use a person to speak words of wisdom to us, but it is important that we seek Him because all true wisdom comes from Him. He deserves the credit, no matter what vessel He uses.

Think about this common scenario. Often, when one person goes on a diet and loses weight, everyone around that person wants to know how he or she was so successful. Then we try the same diet but do not get the same results. Wouldn't we be better off to pray and ask God to give us wisdom about our own unique bodies, our appetites, and our nutritional needs, and let Him guide us in a plan that will be effective for each of us individually? That's what I mean by seeking God instead of looking to other people for counsel. God is the source of all wisdom. What works for someone you know will not work for you unless God blesses it, so make sure you don't leave Him out of your plans.

God is the source of all wisdom. What works for someone you know will not work for you unless God blesses it, so make sure you don't leave Him out of your plans.

When you have a decision to make, seek Him diligently, obey His leading, and follow His wisdom. Wisdom is your friend, and she will never mislead you.

WISDOM FOR EVERY DAY

At the beginning of this chapter, I mentioned 1 Corinthians 1:30, which tells us God made Jesus Christ our wisdom, our righteousness, our consecration, and our redemption. In other words, if we have a personal relationship with Jesus Christ, if He lives within us, we have access to the wisdom of God.

Remember: Wisdom is choosing to do right now what we will be satisfied with later. It is taking a long view toward our lives and making decisions now that will benefit us in the future.

The Holy Spirit is the Spirit of wisdom (see Isaiah 11:2); He will lead you to make wise decisions. I cannot encourage you strongly enough to do what God leads you to do. Do not procrastinate, but act when He speaks to your heart. When God tells you to do something, there is an anointing (power) on it at that time. If you will do it when God speaks, it will be easy because you will have grace (God's ability and favor) to do it. If you wait until you think you're ready, or until you think everything is perfectly in place, it may be difficult and you may find yourself striving. But if you will act in faith when God says act, you will find His grace to do whatever He asks of you.

Many times, God will lead you to walk in wisdom by simply helping you use common sense; often, plain ol' common sense *is* wisdom. Use some common sense in the way you act, the way you work, the way you relate to your spouse and children, the way you manage your time, and the way you handle your finances. For instance, don't spend more money than you make; don't eat foods that make you sick; and don't agree to time commitments that will stretch you beyond your limits and cause you stress.

Let me remind you: the enemy wants to kill, steal, and destroy everything in our lives, but Jesus came that we might have and enjoy our lives (see John 10:10). God's plan has never changed. He has a good plan for your life. Do not be foolish and miss out on the blessings He has for you, but be wise. If you do foolish things, you will have problems; but if you use wisdom, your flesh may be uncomfortable for a while, but in the end, you will enjoy victory. Make a commitment today to live wisely and to do now what you will be satisfied with later.

CHAPTER 14

Raise the Standard

"Let us be about setting high standards for life, love, creativity, and wisdom. If our expectations in these areas are low, we are not likely to experience wellness. Setting high standards makes every day and every decade worth looking forward to."

—GREG ANDERSON

All over the world today, societies are decaying, families are falling apart, and individuals are growing increasingly frustrated and miserable. I believe one of the primary reasons for this is that people have stopped setting high standards for themselves, their marriages, their children, their businesses, and their social institutions. We see evidence of widespread moral decline in rising crime statistics, escalating divorce rates, shocking information about sexual behavior in teenagers, and growing problems with drug and alcohol abuse. We also see it in events such as school shootings, suicides, and newborn infants left in garbage containers.

These problems are not what God wants, and they do not reflect the abundant life Jesus died to give the world. But as I have mentioned previously in this book, one of God's great gifts to mankind is the power of choice. If we want to enjoy the blessings He has for us, we need to make lifestyle choices that align with His Word and are consistent with the values of His Word, not choices reflecting the constantly eroding values of the world.

LIVE THE HIGH LIFE

During the days of the prophet Elijah, God's people became fickle. They said they followed Him, but they were not deeply committed to Him. We would say today, "They had one foot in the kingdom of God and one foot in the world." We would also call them "carnal Christians," those who seem very godly on Sunday and just like nonbelievers during the rest of the week.

They enjoy the same types of entertainment popular in the secular community. They watch the same movies and the same television programs as nonbelievers. They dress, speak, act, and think the same way worldly people do; they laugh at the same dirty jokes; and they engage in the same unwholesome conversations. But because they wear Christian jewelry, have bumper stickers with scripture on them, own Bibles, and attend church on Sundays, they think they are Christians. The Bible says, if we are hearers of the word and not doers, then we are deceiving our own selves through reasoning contrary to the truth (see James 1:22). Christianity is not merely a weekly trip to church; it is receiving Jesus as our Savior and then learning to live a lifestyle consistent with His principles.

Christianity is not merely a weekly trip to church; it is receiving Jesus as our Savior and then learning to live a lifestyle consistent with His principles.

People have not changed much since Elijah's time, and he had some strong words for the carnal believers of his day: "How long will you halt *and* limp between two opinions? If the Lord is God, follow Him! But if Baal, then follow him. And the people did not answer him a word" (1 Kings 18:21).

My sentiments exactly! To modern-day believers, I say we must make stronger commitments to God. As Christians, we must raise the standards in our lives to reflect the holiness and excellence of the God we serve. No matter how much our culture deteriorates, we must continue to live on a higher plane—not in the sense of being "above" other people so we can look down on them, but in the sense of refusing to join in with those who enjoy "low living" which keeps them from enjoying God's presence and blessings. Having high standards that reflect the holiness of God does not mean we can never have fun or enjoy anything the world offers. For example, I do not believe it is wrong to watch television, but I do believe we should be selective about what we watch. It is not wrong to tell a joke, but it should be one filled with wholesome humor, not immorality. We live in the world and we cannot ignore the things around us, but we must have high standards that prevent us from becoming "worldly." We should regularly ask God if we have begun to compromise in any area of our lives. If we have, we need to ask Him to forgive us and immediately choose to make a change for the better.

Living above the standards of the world has to do with the choices we make regarding the quality of our conversations, the way we dress, the content and images in the books and magazines we read and in the television shows and movies we watch. It also has to do with the level of integrity with which we live our personal lives, interact with other people, and conduct ourselves in our businesses or professions.

COME TO THE KINGDOM

As Christians, we need to encourage one another to live by godly standards and to resist the pull of the world. We need to be holding each other accountable for the words, images, and information we allow into our minds. A well-known quotation instructs us: "Watch your thoughts, for they become words. Watch your words, for they become actions. Watch your actions, for they become habits. Watch your habits, for they become character. Watch your character, for it becomes your destiny" (Anonymous).

You may be thinking, *Joyce, the music I hear and the movies I watch*

> Setting high standards and living a godly lifestyle will bring peace, joy, stability, and blessings to your life today and set you on a good path toward your future.

are really none of your business. True, but I have a great desire to help you enjoy your life more than you ever have before, and I know that setting high standards and living a godly lifestyle will bring peace, joy, stability, and blessings to your life today and set you on a good path toward your future. I don't believe watching excessive violence, listening to filthy language, or seeing images of people without many clothes on will help you grow in God.

One of my favorite ways to relax is with a good movie. I understand how difficult it is to find something to watch that is both clean and of good quality, but it is possible. I think the important point is for each of us to pay attention to how the things we watch affect our spirits. If we feel grieved inside or convicted by what we are seeing or hearing, then we simply need to choose to watch or listen to something else.

Different things bother different people. My father used a lot of filthy language while I was growing up; therefore I am especially sensitive to dirty language. Romans 14:22 makes clear that we should not do things we feel guilty about and states we should not try to make others live by our convictions: "Your personal convictions [on such matters]—exercise [them] as in God's presence, keeping them to yourself [striving only to know the truth and obey His will]. Blessed (happy, to be envied) is he who has no reason to judge himself for what he approves [who does not convict himself by what he chooses to do]."

THE POWER OF INFLUENCE

God is interested in the influences we allow in our lives. In addition to what we see and hear, we need to be very careful about the people with whom we choose to spend our time. The Bible teaches us not

Christopher Matthews

BOOKS·MUSIC·GIFTS

SEE STORE FOR COMPLETE RETURN POLICY:
REFUND/EXCHGE UP TO 14 DAYS W/RECEIPT.
CREDIT/EXCHGE UP TO 30 DAYS W/RECEIPT.
SALES FINAL ON ALL CODED MERCHANDISE,
OPENED CD/DVD, AND ALL CLEARANCE ITEMS.

1 0446531995
SECRET TO TRUE HAPPINES 25.99
PROMOTIONAL Discount 3.02-
Sub Total 20.97
Sales Tax 1.26
Total Due 22.23

Cash Paid 22.25

Change .02-

Saved with Discounts & Coupons 3.02

This Transaction # 2017064

This Transaction #

2017064

MAY 1, 2008 11:21 2 - 88

THANK YOU!

COOKIE BARTFELD

FESTIVAL AT BEL AIR 410-569-0690
WWW.CHRISTOPHERMATTHEWS.ORG

Christopher Matthew's

BOOKS • MUSIC • GIFTS

SEE STORE FOR COMPLETE RETURN POLICY.
REFUND/EXCHGE UP TO 14 DAYS W/RECEIPT.
CREDIT/EXCHGE UP TO 30 DAYS W/RECEIPT.
SALES FINAL ON ALL CODED MERCHANDISE,
OPENED CD/DVD, AND ALL CLEARANCE ITEMS.

1	0446531995	
	SECRET TO TRUE HAPPINES	23.99
	PROMOTIONAL Discount	3.02-
	Sub Total	20.97
	Sales Tax	1.26
	Total Due	22.23
	Cash Paid	22.25
	Change	.02-

Saved with Discounts & Coupons 3.02

This Transaction # 2017064

This Transaction #

2017064

MAY 1, 2008 11:21 2 - BB

THANK YOU!

COOKIE BARTFELD

FESTIVAL AT BEL AIR 410-569-0690
WWW.CHRISTOPHERMATTHEWS.ORG

to sit passively and inactively in the pathway of sinners, nor to relax and rest in the presence of the scornful and mockers (see Psalm 1:1). Passively going along with whatever other people want to do can be very dangerous. We may not be able to change them, but we do not have to do what they do. It is easy to get into a stream of water and float downstream with the current, but it is more difficult to swim upstream. It is often easier to just go along with other people and do what the majority wants to do, but in the long run doing so can cause us tremendous heartache and misery.

We must set high standards concerning what we wear, what we watch, what we listen to, where we go, how we use our time, how we spend our money, who we associate with, and how we entertain ourselves. We cannot be like the people of Elijah's day, saying basically, "Today I will serve and honor God, but tomorrow I will go along with the people around me!"

I want to say to you what Elijah said to the people around him: "Make up your mind!" Decide whether you are going to dedicate yourself to God or to serve the world and the world system. I urge you to make a decision to serve God wholly and completely, putting Him first in everything you do.

> Decide whether you are going to dedicate yourself to God or to serve the world and the world system.

COMMIT

One of the most important keys to living blessed and godly lives is commitment. If we want to experience God's blessings in our everyday lives, we cannot be half-hearted in our relationships with Him. We must be radically committed, willing to allow Him to rearrange our values and priorities, our schedules, our budgets, and everything else. We must be wholehearted in our devotion to Him and to the principles of His Word.

Let me encourage you to be committed to spending time with God. Be committed to studying and living by the Word. Be committed to prayer. Be committed to a group of people who hold you accountable for your actions. Don't simply attend church when you feel like going, make a commitment to being there, participating, paying attention, and applying the biblical teaching you receive. Become so committed to God and to the things of God you refuse to allow yourself to become lazy or to fail to do what you are supposed to do.

Many people today resist the idea of being committed to anything, because they want to be "free." I want to tell you true freedom is not being able to do whatever you want whenever you want. Real freedom is the ability to make choices that honor God and align with His Word. Being free means we can discipline ourselves to obey God's Word, knowing it will lead to peace and great fulfillment in life.

Do not jeopardize your happiness in life by letting worthless, worldly influences hinder your walk with God. Get committed to Him! Eliminate influences that are bad for you, dishonoring to God, or simply draining the life out of you, and give your time and energy to people and activities that will fill you with the life of God. Follow Him wholeheartedly!

CHRISTIANITY IS A LIFESTYLE

Many people want their lives to be different but are not willing to change their lifestyles. One of the most important lessons I have learned about Christianity is that it is walked out in a *lifestyle*. An important way your faith becomes a lifestyle is by associating with people who share beliefs and values consistent with yours. To grow spiritually, you need to be around people who will encourage you to be godly. The

To grow spiritually, you need to be around people who will encourage you to be godly.

attitudes and beliefs of the people you're around will influence you. If you spend time with people who complain and grumble all the time, you will begin to do the same. If you surround yourself with people who are angry or disrespectful, you will find yourself expressing anger or being disrespectful too. If you associate with people who are stingy and self-centered, you will begin to view those attitudes as acceptable and incorporate them into your own thoughts and behaviors. If the people you spend time with are bitter, resentful, hateful, prejudiced, and judgmental—you will become as they are. If you do spend time with unbelievers or less-committed Christians, be sure you are *affecting* them and that they are not *infecting* you.

If you surround yourself with people who are positive, you will soon find yourself becoming upbeat and optimistic because every time you say something negative, they will offer a positive response. Their right responses will convict you of your wrong ones and you will eventually become positive yourself. If you spend time with someone who is generous to others, you very likely will become generous too. If you develop relationships with people who are loving and compassionate, you will walk in love too.

PAY THE PRICE

I want you to understand that living by high, godly standards will cost you. You may have to give up some of your friends. You may not be the most popular person at your workplace or at your school, but you will be respected and you will enjoy your life. You will have righteousness, peace, and joy. You will not live under the guilt and torment of sin, but you will have confidence because you will know you are making right choices rather than compromising. If you are willing to walk away from wrong relationships, God will eventually connect you with people with whom you can have wonderful, godly relationships. If you will pay the price for high standards, you will be able to face your future with boldness and confidence.

Jesus said that though we are in the world we are not of the world (see John 17:16). We must resist the pull of the world that is continually tugging on us. We must *refuse* to be like the world and determine to live holy lives. Christianity is not simply attending church or reading a Bible verse each day. It is a lifestyle, a way of living and approaching every area of our lives; and it should affect every decision we make.

Christianity is not simply attending church or reading a Bible verse each day. It is a lifestyle, a way of living and approaching every area of our lives; and it should affect every decision we make.

When Christianity truly becomes a lifestyle for us, we won't think the way we once did. We won't talk the way we once did. We won't dress the way we once did. We won't have the habits we had before we were saved. We will make different choices about how to use our money. We won't watch the same kinds of movies we did before we knew God's Word. We may even find ourselves making better choices relating to physical health, such as eating more healthily or exercising more regularly. We learn everything is for Him, to Him, through Him, and in Him (see Romans 11:36).

Sometimes, I think of things Dave and I enjoyed years ago and now I cannot even imagine doing them. I say that we enjoyed them, but, actually, our lives were filled with misery so perhaps we were not enjoying them as much as we thought we were. We can be easily deceived and become hardened and calloused to the evil around us. We grow accustomed to things that are not godly, and that becomes dangerous because we don't even notice people are making fun of God, or taking His name in vain. The devil wants us to not be shocked by the wickedness in our society, so we need to maintain a tender conscience through prayer and fellowship with God and other committed Christians.

We need to pray for sensitivity in our hearts; we need to ask God to make our consciences tender. We need to pray we will have the ability to set and maintain high standards in our lives. We need to draw some "lines in the sand" of our lives and say, "I am *not* going beyond this! I don't care if I am the only one, I'm going to stand with God!" Make a decision. It will cost you a lot to serve God wholeheartedly, but it will cost you a lot more if you don't. There is a price to pay—yes. But the dividends are high! Oh, and by the way, when you do draw a line of moral principles for your life, don't move the line if honoring it becomes inconvenient. Set your mind and keep it set on things above and not on things of the earth, because you belong to God through Jesus Christ.

There is no way I could describe to you how glad I am I made the decisions I made along the way. I really am enjoying my life. There were times in the past when I was always looking for something else I thought I needed to make me happy, but now I am happy and at peace because God meets my needs and satisfies my soul. Of course, there are many things I enjoy, but God is my portion in life; I need Him more than anything else. I enjoy things, but I can live without them if I have to; however, I cannot live without God and His presence in my life.

I am not consumed by bitterness, resentment, or guilt. I am not tormenting myself by wondering what people think about me. I know how to receive God's forgiveness when I make mistakes, and I am not consumed with guilt and condemnation. I'm not wounded, bruised, and bleeding on the inside, because He has healed my soul. I have paid the price for an intimate relationship with God, and I am living in the blessings of loving and serving Him. I hope you will do the same. God does not play favorites. What is available for one person in Him is available to all. With your whole heart, seek Him and His will for you and you will not only find Him, you'll discover a life worth living.

THE PROTECTION OF A GODLY LIFESTYLE

> A lifestyle of following the principles of God's Word offers many blessings.

A lifestyle of following the principles of God's Word offers many blessings. One of them, which some people do not think of, is protection against the enemy. The things we see and hear can be tools the enemy uses to wage war on the battlefields of our minds. When we see or hear something, it is recorded forever in our subconscious mind. Who do you think is behind ungodly scenes, images, and words in so much of today's music, television, Internet, and printed material? It isn't God; it's the enemy!

If we would commit to higher standards of holiness in our lives, we could eliminate some of the enemy's ammunition and thwart some of his plans against us. Our lifestyle choices would help form shields around us Satan could not penetrate.

If I were to offer you a taste of strychnine or arsenic, I am sure you would refuse it. Well, the world offers us poison all the time. These substances may not harm us physically or make us ill, but they destroy our hearts and minds and steal our enjoyment of everyday life. Think about that the next time you flip through television channels, surf the Internet, choose music, select reading material, or wonder which movie ticket to buy. Satan, working through the world's system, is pouring out poison constantly, and often we just sit by passively taking in whatever is being offered. I know I have said this many times in this book, but let me say one more time: *Make wise choices!*

CHAPTER

15

Be Healthy

"The only way to keep your health is to eat what you don't want, drink what you don't like, and do what you'd rather not."

—MARK TWAIN

Picture this: A young mother and talented business executive groggily reaches to turn off her alarm clock at 5:00 a.m. on a Monday morning. She groans at the thought of another long and busy day, but tells herself it takes two incomes to raise a family these days. After several minutes of wishing she could take the week off, she finally drags herself to the shower, applies part of her makeup, and puts on a stylish new pantsuit, which she bought to impress her clients and co-workers and paid for with a credit card that had an "over limit" fee the previous month.

She rouses her son and daughter, hoping they will get up without having to be called again. They don't. In between making their lunches for school and gathering their scattered books and papers, she makes two more trips to their rooms, finally losing her temper as she barks: "Get out of that bed right this minute and get ready for school!" Her husband suggests she should be more patient with them.

By the time the children arrive in the kitchen, dressed for school, there's no time for a healthy breakfast. "Just give them donuts," advises her husband. "That's what we eat." She tells the children to help themselves to donuts and puts a jug of orange juice on the counter, hoping that will give them a little vitamin C.

She rushes to get them to school, finishing her makeup at stoplights, then screeching to a halt just as the bell rings. On the way to her office, she stops at the drive-through window at a local coffee shop and orders a large cup of coffee and a pastry she can eat while driving, because she didn't have time to eat breakfast at home.

Already tired, she sits down at her desk and wonders where to begin dealing with the mountain of work before her. *After all,* she says to herself, *everything is urgent.* As her co-workers arrive, everyone who passes by her office asks, "How was your weekend?" She feels compelled to answer and to ask the same question in return. Her assistant, who is supposed to be a help and not a hindrance, shows up in tears. She had a terrible break-up with her boyfriend over the weekend. She's preoccupied, unproductive, and wishing she were somewhere else.

Monday-morning phone calls, e-mails, and little "emergencies" interrupt the young executive's attempts to do what desperately needs to be done that day. Her son forgot to ask her to sign his permission slip for a trip to the fire station, so she races to the school to do that. Returning to the office, she discovers that her boss needs a report by noon, but failed to mention it until now. Then her boss's boss calls from a business trip and impatiently asks for information he had requested last week, information she meant to give him—and would have if something else hadn't come up. Last week, she'd even asked her assistant to gather the files she needed and to remind her to get it done, but the assistant forgot because she had become concerned about her boyfriend.

She throws the information together and e-mails it to her boss's boss. It's not the quality of work she is capable of producing. She was too busy to do it right, but tells herself she'll do better next time. Soon, she rushes out the door for a lunch meeting—the weekly downtown gathering of up-and-coming professionals. She doesn't really have time to go and almost doesn't, but then she remembers that she needs to network if she wants to climb the corporate ladder.

After lunch, an overwhelming amount of work still awaits her. She is about to begin working on a project that is due by the end of the day but is called into an "important" meeting where much is said and little is accomplished.

She planned to leave the office promptly at 5:00 p.m. to watch the last part of her daughter's ballgame. But a co-worker wants to discuss an important new client, and before she knows it, 5:00 has come and gone. Racing to her daughter's game, she calls her husband to make sure he is there. He isn't, citing the fact that he scheduled a spur-of-the-moment business dinner because, "You said you were going to be there."

When she arrives at the school, her son and daughter are waiting outside, the only two people in sight. She starts to apologize for missing the game, but realizes her apologies don't mean much anymore. The children climb into the car without a word, and stare out the windows as they drive home.

"Mom, I'm hungry," say both children. So she gets them fast-food meals—and dessert, because she wants to give them a little treat in an attempt to compensate for missing the game.

Once the children are in bed that night, she briefly turns on a news channel to find out what happened in the world that day. *Crises everywhere,* she observes, totally oblivious to the fact that her own life is a crisis of its own.

She takes her laptop to the kitchen table to catch up on the work she didn't get done at her other office that day. Out of the corner of her eye, she sees bills that need paying, a birthday present that should have been sent to her brother last Thursday, and a note to return a call to her best friend, whom she hadn't seen in weeks. *I'll deal with all that tomorrow,* she promises herself.

Just before midnight, she stumbles into bed beside her snoring husband. Five o'clock the next morning seems to come quickly. So she groggily reaches to turn off her alarm clock, and repeats the whole routine all over again.

SOUND FAMILIAR?

Can you relate to anything in the story about this stressed-out woman? Whether you are male or female, married or single, childless or with a house full of children, working outside the home or inside the home, I am sure you can understand the stress in this woman's life. Your stress comes from different sources, but you can certainly "feel the pain" of having too much to do in too little time, being overcommitted, and feeling torn between desires, obligations, and responsibilities.

This woman lacks everything she needs to be able to enjoy her life. She doesn't get enough rest; she is in debt; she does not eat healthily; she is overworked and under stress; she tries to do too much; she does not have a deep, supportive relationship with her spouse; she does not take pleasure in her children; she does not exercise; and she neglects important relationships.

Now, let's think about your life. How are you going to enjoy your life right now and have strength for the years to come if you are living every day at a high-stress level and if you are not physically healthy? Stress and enjoyment are often mutually exclusive, and I can assure you that you will have to reduce your stress and improve your health if you want to enjoy today and be ready to fully embrace tomorrow.

> How are you going to enjoy your life right now and have strength for the years to come if you are living every day at a high-stress level and if you are not physically healthy?

TAKE RESPONSIBILITY

I believe one of the major reasons many people do not enjoy their lives is the simple fact that they do not feel strong, healthy, and vibrant. They are tired, sick, aching, or struggling with some other kind of physical affliction.

Many times in my meetings, someone has asked me to pray for physical healing. I do that as the Lord leads, but often I am aware that what people really need is to take personal responsibility for their health and well-being. Often, their physical problems can be solved by improving their health—eating better, exercising, drinking more water, getting enough sleep at night, or taking time for leisure, recreation, and relaxation.

Personally, I have worked hard for many years. As I grow older, I realize I cannot do everything I could do years ago. For example, I must be very disciplined about eating sweets because they affect my blood sugar, which causes me to feel tired and lethargic. I can eat them occasionally, but certainly not every day.

Eating late at night is another no-no for me. In fact, I have come to despise eating late at night because if I do, I do not sleep well or feel well the next morning. For that reason, I often say no to a get-together with friends if it will mean a late night. Other times, I sit with people while they eat and either just fellowship and eat nothing or have only a small amount of food for myself.

If you and I want to be healthy enough to enjoy our lives, we may not be able to do what everyone else does. There are certainly times when I would enjoy staying up late at night, into the wee hours of the next morning, watching movies or doing something else fun. But I have discovered that not keeping a regular bedtime makes me feel bad. It's not even a matter of getting a certain number of hours of sleep; it's about going to bed at the same time every night. For example, if I went to bed at two o'clock in the morning and slept for eight hours, I still would not feel right. I need to keep a regular bedtime, and perhaps doing that would help you too.

If you and I want to be healthy enough to enjoy our lives, we may not be able to do what everyone else does.

I have also learned that not feeling strong and healthy has a tremendous effect on many areas of my life, one of which is my ability to enjoy my daily life. It sends my "joy level" plummeting. Since I know these things, I am determined not to waste any more days not enjoying them. I want to enjoy my life, just as you want to enjoy yours. If I have to make some changes to feel better so I can enjoy myself more, then I'm willing to do so, because I believe joy is important. I encourage you to do the same and to make a priority of being healthy so you can enjoy the abundant life God wants you to have.

Paul prayed that the Philippians would learn to choose and prize what was excellent and of real value, and that is my prayer for you (see Philippians 1:10). Make choices that help you feel energetic so you can thoroughly enjoy every moment you have left of your time here on earth.

Make choices that help you feel energetic so you can thoroughly enjoy every moment you have left of your time here on earth.

WHAT CAN YOU DO?

The first step toward improving your health is to realize how important it is. After all, you only have one physical body and it has to last a lifetime! More importantly, your body is a gift from God to you; it houses your spirit, which is where the Spirit of God dwells within you; and it is the vehicle that enables you to enjoy everything God has made and to do the things He asks you to do.

The apostle Paul wrote, "Do you not know that your body is the temple (the very sanctuary) of the Holy Spirit Who lives within you, Whom you have received [as a Gift] from God? You are not your own" (1 Corinthians 6:19). Let me urge you to begin taking better care of your "temple" today. "How do I do that?" you wonder. I'm glad you asked. Here are four specific disciplines you can incorporate or improve in your life to get you started down the road to increased physical health and less stress. For more specific information and greater detail on this subject, I recommend my book *Look Great, Feel Great.*

Drink More Water

Do you know water comprises two-thirds of your body? That fact alone should encourage you to increase your water intake! Water is so crucial to physical health because the human body must have adequate fluid to function—fluid that surrounds our cells, fluid within our cells, fluid that facilitates waste elimination, fluid that takes energy to the brain and to our muscles, and fluid that helps our immune systems operate properly.

How much water do you need each day? One simple but proven formula says to take your weight and divide it in half, then drink that many ounces of water per day. A person who weighs 140 pounds should get 70 ounces of water per day, while someone who weighs 180 should drink 90 ounces. To make this easy I suggest getting a glass or a water bottle that holds a certain number of ounces, and filling it as many times as necessary to get the recommended amount of water your body needs each day.

A person who weighs 140 pounds should get 70 ounces of water per day, while someone who weighs 180 should drink 90 ounces.

Eat Healthily

Food is the fuel that helps your body go, so a balanced, nutritious diet is critical to good health. As a general rule, a variety of vibrant colors on your plate at mealtime is a good sign. It should mean you are eating fruits and vegetables, which give your body vitamins and antioxidants and cannot be overestimated for their value to your health. Eat them often!

Do your best to avoid refined carbohydrates (foods made with white flour, potatoes, sugars, or other sweeteners). Make sure the fat in your diet is unsaturated instead of saturated or trans-fat. The way to do this is to reduce your intake of red meat, dairy products, and processed foods prepared with hydrogenated oils, and to eat more fish, chicken or turkey, olive oil (extra-virgin), nuts, and avocados. Also, eat brown rice instead of white, and eat whole-grain or multi-grain breads instead of white breads. Finally, do not overeat by piling large portions of food on your plate. Take smaller portions, eat more slowly, and discipline yourself to stop eating before you have "overdone it."

Exercise

In addition to building strength, increasing endurance, helping you lose weight, and contributing to good form and muscle tone, exercise is probably the best thing a person can do to reduce stress. Experts tell us simply walking about thirty minutes per day produces significant results in our bodies. Working out with weights is excellent, as is using a treadmill or other machines that give you a good cardio workout. There are so many ways to exercise—walking, running, swimming, biking, hiking, tennis, golf, team sports, and other activities—that most people should be able to find something to do and enjoy on a regular basis. The key to exercise is to do it regularly, at least three to four times per week, and to keep yourself challenged so you will continue to reap real benefits.

The key to exercise is to do it regularly, at least three to four times per week, and to keep yourself challenged so you will continue to reap real benefits.

Rest

No one was created to work or function at an intense pace all the time. Our bodies and minds need rest and relaxation. We need to take breaks; we need to have fun; we need to do so on a regular basis. We also need to get enough sleep and to be sure our sleep is high quality, not restless or interrupted.

While we sleep, our minds are "turned off," but our bodies are busy performing important functions that refresh and refuel us for the next day. Sleeping at night is like taking your car to the shop for a tune-up. Like your car, your body will also function better when it gets proper maintenance. Sleep gives your brain an opportunity to unload stress; it enables your body to repair injury; and it allows your blood to deliver a fresh supply of energy to your muscles. Lack of sleep leads to poor coordination, reduced response time, and mistakes. On the other hand, a well-rested person is alert, focused, and able to think clearly. Sometimes, a problem that seems monumental when we are tired can be solved easily after a good night's sleep.

Plenty of water, healthy eating, exercise, and adequate rest will combine to reduce your stress and improve your physical health, which will work wonders for your ability to enjoy your life today and be strong and healthy for your future.

In my life, I have felt bad and I have felt good, and I can tell you good is much better!

CHAPTER

16

Keep It Simple

"In character, in manner, in style, in all things, the supreme excellence is simplicity."

—HENRY WADSWORTH LONGFELLOW

Years ago, I lived a very complicated life. For example, there were many times I wanted to have people to our home on the weekends for times of recreation, relaxation, and enjoying each other's company. More often than not, though, when these get-togethers were over, I ended up exhausted! Why? Because I did not know how to live a simple life. I say my life was complicated, but the truth is, I complicated my life. My approach to life needed to change so I could enjoy it.

The ideas I had started out simple. Dave and I would ask one or two couples over for a simple outdoor barbecue. But then I added others to the invitation list because I did not want anyone's feelings to be hurt. Before the group arrived, I decided the house had to be immaculate, so I cleaned everything in sight. I thought the lawn needed to be perfectly manicured, so I made sure it was. Then I wanted new patio furniture—or at least a fresh coat of paint on the old furniture. Then I made sure all the children looked as though they had just stepped off the pages of a magazine. Of course, I also felt I needed to be wearing just the right outfit and to have every hair in place.

When it came to preparing the food, I started with an easy menu—something like hamburgers on the grill, a bowl of baked beans, some potato chips, and a store-bought dessert. But I always changed my plans, because I wanted to impress my guests. I bought steaks instead of hamburgers and spent considerable time making homemade potato salad and enough additional side dishes to feed a small army. Where drinks were concerned, I did not believe iced tea, water, coffee, and lemonade were sufficient, so I made sure we also offered four or five different kinds of soda pop. By the time my guests arrived, I was too tired to enjoy them and at times found myself resenting them for being there!

Even during their visit, I kept working. If they walked into my kitchen, I practically followed them with a broom to make sure they did not track crumbs onto my carpets. If they put down a glass, I snatched it up and washed it. Then I had the nerve to resent everyone else because I was working so hard and they were enjoying themselves! I ended up hosting parties I didn't enjoy, for people we were not even close to, and with food we couldn't afford. I was an expert when it came to complicating simple things.

After many experiences such as the one I just described, I came to a point in my life where I knew God was dealing with me about simplicity. I began to realize more and more how complicated my life was—and that it was my fault. I also realized life was not likely to change. If I wanted things to be different and life to be simpler so I could enjoy it, *I* would have to do the changing.

> If I want things to be different and life to be simpler so I can enjoy it, *I* will have to do the changing.

Not only were my actions and activities complicated, my thought processes were complicated. My relationship with God was complicated because I was trying to earn His love and acceptance instead of simply receiving it by faith. Everything about my life was complicated. I thought I had a lot of complex problems, but I was actually complicating things for myself with my approach to life, people, and everyday situations. I was complicated on the inside, so naturally, everything about my life externally seemed complicated too.

THE GOOD PORTION

You may be familiar with the biblical story of Mary and Martha. These two women were sisters—and complete opposites. One day, Jesus went to visit them at their house. The Bible tells us Mary stopped everything and sat at Jesus' feet, listening to His every word. In contrast, "Martha [overly occupied and too busy] was distracted with much serving" (Luke 10:40).

She was so busy running around the house doing things she actually said to Jesus, "Lord, is it nothing to You that my sister has left me to serve alone? Tell her then to help me [to lend a hand and do her part along with me]!" (v. 40).

Jesus responded, "Martha, Martha, you are anxious and troubled about many things; there is need of only one or *but a few things*. Mary has chosen the good portion [that which is to her advantage], which shall not be taken away from her" (vv. 41, 42).

As Jesus noted, Martha was worried, anxious, and unable to relax in His presence. Mary, on the other hand, was perfectly content sitting and listening to Him. Mary took a simple, relaxed, focused approach to Jesus' visit, while Martha insisted upon complicating things and trying to do too much.

When I read this story, I think about how similar to Martha I used to be. I ran around anxiously, trying to impress God and everyone else with my diligence and my accomplishments. During that time, I was excessively concerned about what other people thought of me. I did not have the security I have now, so I felt better about myself when I was working—as though I had worth as a person only when I was accomplishing something. Like Martha, I resented people like Mary, who enjoyed themselves.

I had never been taught the value of relaxation and fun. As a child, I was abused by my father, and I did not really have the opportunity to enjoy the freedom of being a child. Everything in my life was serious and difficult for as long as I could remember, and because I felt all of life was hard, I thought everyone should be responsible, serious, and working as hard as I worked.

Certainly, there are times we need to work. The Bible is clear about the virtues and rewards of honest work (see Proverbs 10:4; 14:23). We also know that when we do things that bear fruit, God is glorified. But we must not work so much that our lives become unbalanced and stop being enjoyable.

We must not work so much that our lives become unbalanced and stop being enjoyable.

Martha's attitude has its virtues, but so does Mary's. In their respective responses to Jesus' visit to their home, Mary made a better choice than Martha. In my life, I had "too much Martha and not enough Mary." I loved Jesus, but I had not learned He is not impressed by our running around trying to accomplish what we think needs to be done. He is looking for hearts that want to stop for a moment, be at peace, sit at His feet, and enjoy His presence.

IT'S EASY

One of the best ways to define the word *simple* is with the word *easy.* In many cases, these words are synonyms. Sometimes when we say something is simple, we mean it is easy to do. During my "complicated days," nothing about me or about my life was easy. Dave, however, was a different story. Everything about his life seemed easy. As a person, he was simple, straightforward, and uncomplicated. He truly enjoyed his life, while I was miserable. Dave is still this way, and over time, I have become this way too.

One of Dave's secrets was he learned to "cast his care" upon the

Lord (see 1 Peter 5:7), while I always held on to my concerns and let them churn inside me like a brewing storm. I felt "responsible" to fix everything and had not yet learned the secret of trusting God. While Dave did what he needed to do and was "calm, cool, and collected," I fretted and fumed all the time, and stayed constantly upset and worried. I felt crushed by the weight of all the responsibility I thought I carried. Being responsible is an admirable and godly quality, but I had a false sense of responsibility. I did what I could do and then wore myself out trying to do what I could not do. I not only tried to do my part, but to do God's part too.

At times, I resented Dave because life seemed so easy for him, while it was so difficult for me. He was free, and I felt stuck on a hamster wheel—running as fast as I could, using all my energy but never getting anywhere. I was stressed and striving, never seeming to be able to make any real progress in my life even though I tried very hard. When God first began dealing with me about simplifying my life, I was unaware of just how complicated I had made things. As I mentioned earlier in this chapter, most of the habits that kept me complicated were in my mind, in the way I thought about things and approached the situations I faced. These thought patterns developed over time, so I had many bad habits to break, many new ones to develop, and much to learn.

Are you possibly complicating things in your life by the way you approach them? Could you simplify your life by trusting God more? Are you a perfectionist who stresses out over little details nobody notices but you? Do you have a false sense of responsibility, as I did? Are you trying to solve problems that are not yours to solve? If your answer to any of these questions is yes, you can begin today to simplify your life.

A SIMPLE RELATIONSHIP

The Bible does not include many scriptures or much direct teaching about simplicity. As I pondered this, I finally realized the entire New Covenant—the relationship we have with God through Jesus

Christ—is very simple. It is so beautiful and simple that those with complicated minds often have difficulty believing it. God sent Jesus to earth to live as a man and to understand people. Jesus died for our sins, taking upon Himself the punishment our sins demand. He paid the debt of our sins. He rose from the dead and has provided a way for us to live wonderful, joyful, peaceful, fruitful, amazing lives. He did all of this freely and willingly, because of His awesome love for us.

> The entire New Covenant—the relationship we have with God through Jesus Christ—is very simple.

I could elaborate extensively about what Jesus has done for us, but the point is that His work is not complicated. It's profound, it's beautiful, it's amazing, but it's simple. Even a child can understand and believe it: "Jesus loves me, this I know, for the Bible tells me so." All of life in Christ is simple. It requires simple faith, simple prayer, and a simple, faith-filled approach to every situation.

> All of life in Christ is simple. It requires simple faith, simple prayer, and a simple, faith-filled approach to every situation.

The enemy tries to complicate the gospel and the Christian life in believers' minds in order to keep us separated from God. When we return to the simplicity of the gospel and seek to walk in it, we are working *with* God and *against* the enemy, who hates simplicity, because he knows the power and joy it brings. If you pay close attention, you will recognize how the devil tries to complicate your life. Resist him by embracing simplicity.

Years ago, as I studied simplicity, I looked for books on the subject and could not find many. As a result, I had to rely on the Holy Spirit to teach me what I needed to know. He led me to pay attention to what was going on in my life and inside me when I found myself anxious or unhappy. Many times, the reason was that I was complicating a situation.

For example, Dave and I once had an argument not long before we needed to go to sleep. As I have noted, Dave is an easygoing person who has no trouble "forgiving and forgetting" things and moving past them. We both said what we felt we needed to say, and from Dave's perspective, the matter was closed. He lay down and went to sleep.

I, however, went into my home office to stew over what had happened. "How did we get into this argument?" I asked. "And how can I make sure we never argue again?" With my questions and reasoning, I began to complicate a situation Dave had already forgotten.

Replaying our argument in my mind and asking questions about it was not helpful or realistic. A realistic approach would have been to acknowledge the fact that Dave and I are two different people with different opinions. Realism would admit we were not likely to have years and years of married life without ever having another disagreement.

Instead of assessing the situation honestly, I was being idealistic. I wanted to make sure we never argued again; I wanted our relationship to be perfect. People who are idealistic usually do not enjoy life. They want everything to be perfect, and when it does not turn out that way, they become disappointed.

The night of the argument, I was determined to find answers to my questions. The longer I stayed up, supposedly "seeking God," the more frustrated I became. Finally, about one o'clock in the morning, I said, "Lord, what am I going to do?"

I heard clearly in my heart, *Why don't you just go to bed?*

That was exactly what Dave did! He spoke his mind and then let go of the issue. Not me. I thought about it, wrestled with it, questioned, and worried about it for hours. The next morning, Dave was fine, and I was exhausted. Dave's simple approach brought him much better results than my complicated approach yielded me.

SIMPLIFY YOUR DESIRES

One of the dynamics that really complicates our lives, often without our realizing it, is the fact we can be so driven and consumed by our desires.

Unfulfilled desires can even torment us—and that certainly keeps us from enjoying our lives. Most of us can list many things we would like and if we are not careful, we will begin striving to attain them in a way that is out of balance. When we cannot reach them, we will begin to lose our peace and our joy, and become frustrated, disappointed, and upset. We would be much better off if we would choose to simplify or adjust our desires instead of continuing to struggle to get things only God can provide. I am not suggesting we should not be aggressive in trying to reach our goals, but when we lose our joy and peace because we cannot make something happen, then it is time to pray and cast our care on the Lord.

We would be much better off if we would choose to simplify or adjust our desires instead of continuing to struggle to get things only God can provide.

James 4:2 states, "You do not have, because you do not ask." We need to ask God for what we want, and trust Him to give it to us in His timing, in His way. In the meantime, we need to be content with what we do have.

There are two ways to handle our unfulfilled desires. One is by working to acquire what we want; the other is to ask ourselves if what we want is that important after all. "More" is not always better because the more we acquire, the more we must maintain and care for. Sometimes, with many possessions, we can lose our joy because we are so "caught up in keeping up" our belongings and these things begin to have us instead of our having them.

Occasionally, I go through my house and give away some of my possessions. I do not enjoy my home when I collect too many things I don't really need. I don't like to feel that I am living in the midst of clutter, and I can always find someone who can make good use of things that are no longer blessing me. I'm sure the same is true for you. The more cluttered your home is, the more time it will take and the more difficult it will be to keep it clean. Clean it *out* on a regular basis and you will find cleaning it *up* is much easier!

In Psalm 37:4, David wrote, "Delight yourself also in the Lord, and He will give you the desires and secret petitions of your heart." Seek God first; desire Him more than anything else; and you will find He will bless you with what is right for you to have at the right time.

If you are unhappy and are not enjoying life because of something you want but do not have, I encourage you to not allow that desire to dominate you. Trust God to hear your requests and answer them in ways that exceed your best desires and expectations.

Trust God to hear your requests and answer them in ways that exceed your best desires and expectations.

SIMPLIFY YOUR DECISIONS

Life can become complicated when people do not know how to make decisions and stick with them. James 5:12 reads, "But above all [things], my brethren, do not swear, either by heaven or by earth or by any other oath; but let your yes be [a simple] yes, and your no be [a simple] no, so that you may not sin *and* fall under condemnation." In this verse, James is basically saying, "Make a decision. Just say yes or no; and don't keep changing your mind."

We often labor over the choices and options before us when, actually, we just need to make a decision and let it stand. For example, when you stand in front of your closet in the morning looking at all of your clothes, just choose something and put it on. Don't go back and forth until you make yourself late for work!

When you get ready to go out to eat, pick a restaurant and go. Don't become so confused that you feel there is no one place that will satisfy you. Sometimes I would like the coffee from restaurant A, the salad from restaurant B, my favorite chicken dish from restaurant C, and dessert from restaurant D. Obviously, I cannot have everything I want at the same time, so I need to pick one of those places and eat there. I can go to the others later.

Let me encourage you to start making decisions without second-guessing yourself or worrying about the choices you make. Don't be double-minded or wishy-washy, because doubting your decisions after you make them will steal the enjoyment from everything you do. Make the best decisions you can, and trust God with the results. Don't be anxious or afraid of being wrong. If your heart is right and you make a decision not in accordance with God's will, He will forgive you and help you move on.

Be decisive. Whatever you need to do in life, just do it—and keep it simple.

CHAPTER 17

Be Creative

"Be brave enough to live creatively."
—ALAN ALDA

As the old saying goes, "Variety is the spice of life." One way to be sure to enjoy today and look forward to the future is to add a healthy dose of creativity and variety to your daily life. I realize the pressures of work, family, and other commitments often pull you toward a routine in which you simply try to "get it all done," but I want to encourage you not to let the routine become too routine. Too many days of doing the same things the same way at the same time can drain the joy from your life and lead to monotony.

You only live once, so don't be drawn into a mundane, ordinary existence. Add some spice to your life by being creative and do all you can to keep your life fresh, vibrant, and fun. Live life passionately because life without passion is not much life at all. I have written extensively on this subject, and I encourage you to read more about it in my book *I Dare You*.

YOU ARE CREATIVE

All of us know people we would refer to as "creative." They can paint, draw, write, take beautiful photographs, compose or play music, or decorate. Usually, when we think of creative people, we think of those who are artistically gifted.

But I believe everyone is creative in some way. We may not all know what to do with a piano or a paintbrush, but God has given each of us a measure of creativity. For example, a businessman's creativity may express itself through unusual distribution systems or the ability to form successful strategic partnerships that never occurred to anyone else. A graduate student's creativity may lie in the ability to analyze a work of literature or a historical event from a perspective not explored before. A salesperson may demonstrate creativity by thinking of new and different ways people can use the product he sells. A teacher's creativity will be seen as she helps one student learn by listening to stories, while realizing another will learn better by looking at pictures.

Creativity expresses itself in many wonderful ways from one person to the next. God is infinitely creative, and He designed every person on earth with some level of creativity. We all have a need, a desire, and an ability to be creative and to enjoy freshness and variety.

God is infinitely creative, and He designed every person on earth with some level of creativity.

WE CRAVE CREATIVITY

Our God-given need and desire for creativity is the reason we become restless, frustrated, or bored when we have too much "sameness" in our activities, relationships, work, or surroundings. There is nothing wrong with sometimes feeling we just need a change. In fact, most of us fight boredom at times; we simply grow weary of doing "the same old thing" day after day, week after week. We often get into ruts and routines and become stuck in these patterns. We want something new and fresh, but then again, we also feel safe with what is familiar or comfortable.

Some of us are brave enough to make changes in our lives readily and we really enjoy trying something new, while others want to do something different but struggle to identify what they should do or hesitate to do it out of fear. They would rather be safe, comfortable, and bored than excited and living on the edge.

Some people keep the same job, live in the same house, or socialize with the same friends all of their lives not because they really want to, but because it is comfortable and familiar. They may hate their jobs and feel completely unfulfilled, but the thought of doing anything else is extremely frightening. Their needs in a home may have changed, but they are reluctant to move because they are comfortable in their old house, even if they do not need the full basement they remodeled for their teenagers twenty-five years ago or if they need to have a bedroom on the first floor instead of having all bedrooms upstairs. They may think they would enjoy some new acquaintances but do not pursue any out of fear of rejection. They may have dreams about all kinds of changes they wish they could incorporate in their lives, but they do not fully embrace or embark upon the dreams because they fear failure.

No matter what holds people back from making creative, new decisions in their lives, I have never met anyone who *enjoys* being bored. Some people *choose* boredom, but they do not take pleasure in it. We all hunger for newness and diversity, and the reason for this is that God created us for variety. We are made to require freshness in our lives. I do not advocate jumping out in the middle of every opportunity or idea that comes along, but I do believe there are times when we need

We all hunger for newness and diversity, and the reason for this is that God created us for variety. We are made to require freshness in our lives.

to step out of the ordinary, out of the routine, out of the comfort zone, and into new things.

There are times when we don't need to make major changes; we simply need to add a little spice to what we are doing—just as we sometimes want to add a little seasoning to food that is otherwise bland and tasteless. Sometimes something as simple as trying a new hairstyle can make a difference.

I believe God gives us warning signs that may manifest as mild boredom. This is His way of letting us know we need to change things up a little. There are times when I simply feel I want to sit in a different place in my home to drink my morning coffee. A different view is refreshing for a while, and after a couple of days I am ready to go back to my usual place. If we will pay attention to this need for change, we can avoid serious trouble. Our emotional makeup *needs* change. Denying ourselves necessary variety because of laziness, fear, or insecurity—or for any other reason—is dangerous. If we do so, we are headed for a great loss of enjoyment. But if we will be creative and incorporate some variety in our lives, we will find ourselves able to enjoy today and look forward to tomorrow.

DON'T OVERDO IT

While our desires for new experiences and opportunities is healthy and stems from our God-given desire for variety and diversity, we must remember God's Word also encourages us to be content (see Philippians 4:11; Hebrews 13:5). We need to find a way to balance being satisfied with longing for something different, because balance is the key to an enjoyable life full of both creativity and contentment.

First Peter 5:8 encourages us: "Be well balanced (temperate, sober of mind), be vigilant *and* cautious at all times; for that enemy of yours, the devil, roams around like a lion roaring [in fierce hunger], seeking someone to seize upon *and* devour." In this verse, we see that balance is very important in our lives. When we throw ourselves off balance by doing too much of one thing and not enough of another, we open a door for the enemy.

The Word of God instructs us to do all things in moderation (see 1 Corinthians 9:25). This is another way of encouraging us to be balanced. Without balance, we can end up in trouble. Physical sickness, mental and emotional pressure, relational problems, and certainly loss of joy can all be the result of unbalanced living.

Physical sickness, mental and emotional pressure, relational problems, and certainly loss of joy can all be the result of unbalanced living.

Any good thing can become bad if allowed to get out of balance. For example, a friend heard that vitamin E was good for the human body, so she took it by the handful. But she did not take it in moderation and she became ill because it thinned her blood excessively. Another friend discovered she loved the taste of Balance protein bars, and ate so many she became allergic to them. We joked that she got out-of-balance with her Balance bars. Our flesh gravitates toward extremes, and, left unrestrained, it will cause problems. The flesh cannot be allowed to have or do everything it wants.

When I find a restaurant I like, one that has a certain menu item I really enjoy, my natural temptation is to go to that restaurant and eat that dish until I grow tired of it and never want to eat there again. But if I will discipline myself to some variety, and eat that particular dish occasionally instead of several days in a row, I can enjoy that restaurant indefinitely.

Sameness ushers us into staleness. When we do the same things too often, we stop enjoying activities we once thoroughly enjoyed. But variety ensures our continued, long-term ability to enjoy the things that give us pleasure because it keeps them fresh. Even when we prefer one thing over several others, we are wise to incorporate them all, just for the sake of variety and the benefits it brings to our lives.

This is true in many areas of life. I find if I spend too much time with people I really enjoy and delight in, and don't spend enough time with others, a staleness eventually comes into our relationship. After we have been together too long, we reach a point where we do not enjoy each other's company as much as we once did. We travel with a specific crew when we do conferences and crusades in third-world countries. These trips are long, and the team may be together for as long as three weeks. We are in the airplane together; we eat our meals together; and we ride in the car together as we travel to our appointments. We all really like each other, but by the time a trip is over none of us wants to get together for quite a while!

Dave and I really love each other, and we have a great relationship. We are comfortable with one another, and that is good, because we spend a lot of time together. We not only live together, we also work together, so we spend much more time together than the average married couple. As much as we enjoy each other, we also need time apart—time for ourselves and time with other people. He needs to get out and play golf with his friends, and I need to fellowship and have lunch with some of my friends. This kind of variety is good for both of us as individuals and for our marriage.

> We need diversity in life. It keeps the ordinary fresh!

We need diversity in life. It keeps the ordinary fresh!

GIVE YOURSELF SOME OPTIONS

Years ago, one of the first ways in which God began to deal with me regarding boredom and sameness dealt with the color of my pantyhose. That may make you chuckle, but you see, I had worn "suntan" pantyhose for years. I never wore any other kind—always the same brand and the same color.

When I noticed other ladies wearing black, navy blue, cream, or even light pink pantyhose or nylons, I liked them, but I still kept buying suntan. God used this very ordinary and simple example to show me I was sticking with what I thought was safe, even though I really wanted to venture out and wear something different once in a while.

"Suntan" probably did look better than any other color with most of my clothes, but a little variety occasionally would have added some spice to my life and kept me from being bored with my outfits.

God uses many of the simple things we deal with in everyday life to teach us vital lessons about ourselves if we will only listen to Him. I began to realize through this one little incident how stuck in sameness I was. In my heart, I wanted to venture out, but the safety of sameness was holding me in boredom. The pantyhose situation caused me to begin looking at other areas of my life and helped me to break into new expressions of creativity and freedom in many ways.

Even science recognizes the benefits of variety. Medicine has proven many people are allergic to the foods they eat most often.

Even science recognizes the benefits of variety. Medicine has proven many people are allergic to the foods they eat most often. Part of their cure is to vary their food choices and introduce new foods into their diets.

A friend of mine once dealt with this condition. To rid her body of allergens, doctors instructed her to eliminate from her diet for twenty-one days the foods to which she was allergic. After three weeks, she could try adding them back into her diet, but only occasionally, in some instances, only once every four days, depending on the severity of her allergies to each food.

God has created even our bodies to demand variety. If we don't give them the variety they need and crave, then they rebel. In essence they say, "I can't handle this. You're giving me too much of this thing, therefore, I'm going to get sick or have some kind of negative reaction every time you feed it to me." Sickness, pain, or other adverse physical reactions are a body's way of saying, "Something's not right." Many times, all that is wrong is that we are out of balance—eating too much of one food and not enough of another.

Perhaps you are not resting enough or laughing enough. Maybe you are working too hard. Too much stress, frequent emotional upset, and a lack of variety can affect your health adversely.

Where creativity and variety are concerned, God used some very simple things like pantyhose and eating habits to get my attention, but the principle of balance, moderation, creativity, variety, and diversity can be applied in many aspects of life. Once you understand how important these things are, you can apply them to relationships, spending, eating, work habits, dress standards, entertainment, and any other part of your life in which you may begin to feel the need for a change.

EASY VARIETY

Adding variety and creativity to your life does not have to be expensive or complicated. If you want to do something different in the evening, take your family for an outing. If you have young children, they might enjoy riding in the car and seeing the sights outside their windows. Just thirty minutes may be all you need. Or, go out and get a cup of coffee. Yes, you could make it at home, but you might not have as much fun and you would not be able to enjoy the atmosphere of the coffeehouse. Go for a walk. Ride a bicycle or watch children play at a park. During the holidays, take a ride around your neighborhood and look at the colorful Christmas lights on various houses.

If you have a big, all-day project in front of you, plan to take a few short breaks as you work toward its completion. Walk outside for a few minutes if the weather is nice, then have a glass of lemonade or iced tea. If you see your neighbors, strike up a conversation

> If you have a big, all-day project in front of you, plan to take a few short breaks as you work toward its completion.

with them, or at least say a friendly, "Hello." Take a mental break by getting away from the project at hand for a short time. You must never lose sight of your goal, but short breaks, which I call "mini-vacations," can make all the difference in your productivity and in how you feel about the project.

GO AHEAD AND TRY

As you have read this chapter, maybe you have been inspired to make some changes in your life. Perhaps you even have a great desire to do so, but you are hesitant to undertake them because of fear. Let me encourage you to not be afraid to act on the God-given desires in your heart. Go ahead, give them a try. If you make a mistake, it won't be the end of the world. If you fail, it's no problem; at least you tried.

Let me encourage you to not grow older and wish you made different decisions, embraced opportunities for change, or allowed yourself new experiences. I do not want you to look back and be sad, wondering what could have been. I can promise you, you will not enjoy everything you try, but at least you will have the personal experience of knowing. You won't have to live your whole life hearing about what everyone else is doing and wondering what it would be like.

For years one of my favorite eating places was an Oriental restaurant a friend and I found one day. We heard it was very good, but we were not able to find any specific information about its location. We even discussed trying to locate it several times previously, but each time, we decided not to.

Then one day, we were feeling adventurous, so we took the sketchy information we had and decided to risk getting lost in order to find the place. We tried—and we found it! As a result of our willingness to make the effort, we enjoyed eating there for years.

I am not advocating foolishness, but I do encourage you to find the balance between living in fear and living with wisdom. I would have been unwise to start out after dark by myself looking for that restaurant with no phone in my car. But it was daytime; I had a friend with me; and we had a cell phone. Basically, the only danger we faced was the possibility of getting lost and having to ask someone how to get home.

Let me encourage you to be creative and adventurous in your life. Do not become trapped in routines or allow yourself to become "stale." In matters big and small, be creative, be adventurous, stay fresh and vibrant, and add a little variety—the spice of life—to every day.

In matters big and small, be creative, be adventurous, stay fresh and vibrant, and add a little variety—the spice of life—to every day.

CHAPTER

18

Have a Seat

"Patience is not passive; on the contrary, it is active; it is concentrated strength."

—EDWARD G. BULWER-LYTTON

One of the secrets of enjoying today and embracing tomorrow is learning how to wait. I do not mean simply passing time or wasting time; I mean learning to wait well. There will be many times in your life when you feel you are in a "waiting room." You know you have an appointment with destiny, but it seems to be a long time coming. You wait and you wait, but no one calls your name; you do not move to the next step or make any progress toward your dream. You simply wait.

How you handle this time of waiting, even though it may be difficult, is critical to your current life and to your future. In fact, you will probably spend more of your time waiting on the fulfillment of the dreams God has given you for your life than you will receiving them, so developing the ability to wait patiently and expectantly is very important. The culmination of our dreams and goals can occur in a moment, but we often wait for them for years. The attitude with which we wait determines our level of enjoyment.

James 5:7, 8 gives us valuable instruction about waiting well: "So be patient, brethren, [as you wait] till the coming of the Lord. See how the farmer waits expectantly for the precious harvest from the land. [See how] he keeps up his patient [vigil] over it until it receives the early and late rains. So you also must be patient." Just as a farmer has to wait for a harvest after he plants a seed, you will also have times of waiting after God plants seeds of dreams or desires in your heart.

When we are waiting for the fulfillment of a promise, there is a purifying work that must be done in our lives to equip us for what God has put in our hearts. We must be prepared, and preparation is a process that requires time. It cannot happen any other way, so we need to learn to wait well. Learning to wait well simply means learning to wait with a good attitude that trusts God. True patience is not merely the ability to wait; it is the way we think and act while we are waiting.

When we are waiting for the fulfillment of a promise, there is a purifying work that must be done in our lives to equip us for what God has put in our hearts.

Many times, the reasons we must wait are connected to our attitudes. If we tend to become jealous of others who already have what we are waiting for, if we have "pity parties" and focus excessively on ourselves and our lives, if we allow ourselves extreme emotional ups and downs, or if we complain about how long we have to wait—then we are not demonstrating godly attitudes. These attitudes and similar ones are the very things that must be dealt with and worked out of us before we can receive God's promises and handle His blessings with maturity. I have realized that my attitude is more important to God than my getting what I want. He knows if I have a good attitude, I can be joyful no matter my circumstances. That kind of stability is His will for each of us.

If we understand that waiting is an important discipline and learn to wait with positive attitudes, we can actually enjoy waiting periods and learn the lessons we need to learn during times of delay. Good attitudes can even make our waiting periods shorter. The sooner we learn the valuable lessons God wants to teach us, the earlier we may graduate and begin enjoying what we have waited for.

The inability to wait well is one of the major reasons people do not enjoy their everyday lives. They are so focused on where they are going that they do not enjoy the journey that gets them there. They allow themselves to become so consumed with tomorrow they completely miss today. Many of these people never enter the fullness of what God has for them. They never see the fulfillment of their dreams and visions simply because they don't understand the importance of waiting well and enjoying their journeys.

I want you to make the most of today as you move toward a great tomorrow. One of the best ways to do that is to learn to wait well.

I don't want you to be one of these people. I want you to make the most of today as you move toward a great tomorrow. One of the best ways to do that is to learn to wait well.

WE HAD TO WAIT

When God called us to begin a television ministry in 1993, we accepted the call and the responsibility that went with it. We knew we were to go on television, but we had absolutely no idea how to go about it, so before we could take even the first tiny step, we had to wait on God for more specific direction.

As we began to investigate the process of televising our ministry, we discovered we needed a producer—and we had to wait for God to bring the right person to us. He reminded us of a job application we received just a few months earlier. A man who was producing a television program for another ministry submitted an application to us, and at the time, we said, "File it. We aren't on television. What would we need with a television producer?" But God knew what we did not, and He was providing a producer for us before we even knew we needed one. We hired the producer, and he began to research the equipment we would need for a broadcast. We then had to wait for all that information to be collected so we could make wise and informed decisions about purchasing what we needed.

In the meantime, we shared with our partners and friends what God was leading us to do. We asked them to give financially toward our television ministry, and then we waited for the money to come in. We finally purchased our equipment, and then realized we needed cameramen to travel with us and film our conferences, so we waited for God to provide them.

Finally, it was time for us to begin approaching television stations with the idea of airing our programs. The station managers told us we needed a pilot program before they could make any commitments to us, so we waited for that to be finished and then we waited to see if they liked it!

At last, after *much* waiting, we went on television. In the early days, only a few stations carried our broadcasts—and we had to wait to see what kind of response we would receive before we knew whether we could continue the television ministry or not.

God has since expanded our television ministry to the point we broadcast all over the world. It started with His speaking to our hearts His plan and desire for us—and then it required a lot of diligence and an enormous amount of patience. But we have seen God's faithfulness through it all; we have seen the value of the waiting periods we endured; and we have come to understand that without the wait, we would not have been prepared to handle everything that comes along with a television ministry.

> Waiting is a fact of life—and it is a necessary ingredient of success.

I hope you can see from this story that each phase of life and of the fulfillment of dreams requires waiting. Remember, James 5:7 exhorts us, "So be patient, brethren, [as you wait.]" This verse does not say, "Be patient *if* you have to wait," but "Be patient as you wait." Waiting is a fact of life—and it is a necessary ingredient of success.

GIVE IT TIME

God rarely places dreams in our hearts one day and fulfills them the next. He begins by giving us a desire for something, but He rarely gives us the exact timing for when that desire will be fulfilled. There is always a preparation period, and it is different for different people. We should trust God's timing and enjoy the journey.

Genesis 15:1–5 tells the story of Abram (later called Abraham) and a promise he received from God. Abram had a very clear, definite word from God about his future. Speaking of a son for very old Abram and his very old wife, God said, "He who shall come from your own body shall be your heir" (v. 4). Abram knew what God promised, and he knew his time was short as he considered his age and the fact his wife was past her childbearing years and was barren all her life. He had a promise from God, but no word from God regarding when it would take place. He had no choice but to have a seat in God's waiting room.

The same is often true for us. Once God speaks to us or shows us something, we can become consumed with it. If we are not careful, we can focus on it to the point we do not carry out our other responsibilities well or we become preoccupied and distracted by our dreams. Instead of becoming obsessed with the future and missing out on the blessings of every day between your promise and its fulfillment, just relax and give it time to come to pass.

CLOUDS OF CONFIRMATION

Have you ever become frustrated because you feel you have waited so long and so patiently for something that seems it will never come to pass? You know intellectually you have not waited forever, but you feel you have. You become weary, and you feel you simply cannot wait any longer.

This happens to all of us; it is often part of the process we go through as we walk with God through seasons of waiting and as we hold fast to the promises we believe He wants to fulfill in our lives. Since biblical times, God's people have had to learn to wait, and through the centuries, He has sent messages of encouragement at just the right moment.

Since biblical times, God's people have had to learn to wait, and through the centuries, He has sent messages of encouragement at just the right moment.

First Kings 18 tells the story of a man who had to wait and stay faithful when it seemed nothing was happening for him. In verse 1, God said to Elijah, "Go, show yourself to Ahab, and I will send rain upon the earth." This was during a time of severe famine in the land, a time when crops and animals desperately needed water, but no water was available.

Shortly after Elijah received the promise of rain from God, he encountered the prophets of Baal, and a showdown ensued between these false prophets and Elijah, a prophet of the God of Israel. After God revealed Himself as the one, true God and Elijah did away with the prophets of Baal, he told King Ahab, "Go up, eat and drink, for there is the sound of abundance of rain" (v. 41).

Elijah must have seemed silly with his declaration that it was going to rain, because the sky was perfectly clear. He sent his servant to look for storm clouds *six times,* and each time, the sky remained blue and sunny—not a rain cloud in sight. Elijah must have been tempted to doubt God's promise of rain. Surely he became discouraged over having to wait so long! But when he sent his servant to survey the sky a seventh time, the servant returned with good news: "A cloud as small as a man's hand is arising out of the sea" (v. 44). If you think about the size of a man's hand against the enormity of the sky, it is tiny. But this miniscule sign gave Elijah the encouragement he needed.

I watched God send "clouds" into my life for years as I prepared for ministry. I had such a big vision, and I was "pregnant" with a dream. The longer I waited for opportunities, the more I was tempted to wonder if I had really heard from God or if I had made it up. Just when I was about ready to quit believing in God's promise, He would do something to keep my hope alive. It may have been a small thing like Elijah's cloud, which was only the size of a man's hand, but it was enough to help me to not give up. I encourage you to start looking for your clouds of confirmation.

Those years of waiting were very difficult, but very necessary. I was growing, gaining wisdom and experience, learning how to come under authority, learning the Word I was called to preach. I was being prepared for my promise, and God knew the preparation time could not be cut short.

> Having a promise from God or a dream He has placed in our hearts is like being pregnant with what God has said.

Having a promise from God or a dream He has placed in our hearts is like being pregnant with what God has said. He has planted a seed in us, and we must enter a time of preparation. This time prepares us to handle the thing God has promised to give us or do for us. It is very much like the birth of a child. First the seed is planted in the womb, then come nine months of waiting, and finally, a baby is born. During those nine months, so much takes place. The seed is growing into maturity. The mother's body goes through many changes in preparation to give birth. The parents accumulate the equipment necessary to properly care for a child and prepare their home for the baby's arrival.

Most of the activity inside an expectant mother is not visible to the natural eye. Of course, her growing belly is evident to all, but many other important developments are taking place within her, changes no one can see. A similar dynamic takes place for us spiritually concerning God's promises to us. Just because we cannot see or feel anything happening does not mean He is not busy preparing us to receive what He wants to give us. God does some of His best work in secret, and He delights in surprising His children.

I want to encourage you today to be on the lookout for the "clouds of confirmation" in your life. Whatever you are waiting for, don't give up. Be patient; stay faithful; and when you feel you simply cannot wait any longer, look for a cloud. It may be very small, but God wants to help you as you wait for the fulfillment of His promises, which will come in His perfect timing.

GOD'S TIMING, GOD'S PERSPECTIVE

One of the biggest mistakes we make as believers is failing to remember that God's timing rarely matches our timing. We think and plan in temporal terms, and God thinks and plans in eternal terms. What this means is we are very interested in right now, and God is much more interested in the long term. We want what feels good right now, what produces immediate results, but God is willing to be patient and deliberate as He invests in us over a period of time to produce results far better and longer lasting than we can imagine.

Just as our children try to talk us into giving them what they want right away, we often try to talk God into immediately giving us what we want. He loves us even more than we love our children, and He loves us too much to give in to our pleadings. He knows something born prematurely might struggle to survive, so He waits until He knows everything is properly prepared for the arrival of our dream.

God sees and understands what we do not see and understand. He asks us to put aside our natural tendencies to want to figure out what should happen in our lives and when it should happen. He wants us to resist the urge to "help" Him accomplish His divine purposes with our human reasoning and with fleshly efforts. He also desires us to stop being frustrated because things do not go according to our plan, and instead to relax, enjoy the ride, and trust He is working everything out according to His timing and the wisdom of His plan.

Without true trust in God, we will never experience satisfaction and enjoyment in life; we will always be striving to "make things happen" when we think they should happen. We must remember God not only has plans for our lives, He also knows the perfect timing for each aspect of those plans. Many times we fail to realize that being out of God's timing is the same as being out of His will. Fighting and resisting the timing of God is equivalent to fighting and resisting His will for our lives.

> We must remember God not only has plans for our lives, He also knows the perfect timing for each aspect of those plans.

Psalm 31:15 assures us our times are in His hands. He is working, often in ways we cannot see, to bring His plans to pass in our lives in the best possible ways, to bring us the greatest possible joy. He sees the big picture of our lives, from start to finish; He knows what needs to happen and when. We simply need to trust Him and remember His perspective is far superior to ours and that His timing is perfect.

If you are waiting for the fulfillment of a dream or plan God has placed in your heart, be encouraged. God is working on it; He is preparing it for you and you for it. Just have a seat (enter God's rest), and when the time is precisely right, He'll call your name.

CHAPTER

19

Follow Directions

"Your word is a lamp to my feet and a light to my path."

—PSALM 119:105

One sure way to add lightheartedness to your life is to be around children. They are carefree, resilient, and, often, very funny. I once read a list of children's comments about the Bible. I want to share a few of them with you, and I hope they will add a little humor to your day. (The original spelling errors have been left to add to the humor.)

- Joshua led the Hebrews in the battle of Geritol.
- Lot's wife was a pillar of salt by day, but a ball of fire by night.
- The Egyptians were all drowned in the dessert. Afterward, Moses went up on Mount Cyanide to get the Ten Amendments.
- The Fifth Commandment is humor thy father and mother.
- Noah's wife was called Joan of Ark.
- Moses died before he ever reached Canada.
- Solomon, one of David's sons, had 300 wives and 700 porcupines.
- The greatest miracle in the Bible is when Joshua told his son to stand still and he obeyed him.[1]

Obviously, these children knew something about their Bible stories. They did not have all their words exactly right, but I applaud their efforts because knowing the Bible is vitally important. We need to know, honor, and obey God's Word if we want to enjoy our lives today and embrace our futures tomorrow. Every subject we can imagine is covered in the Bible, and it contains all the directions we need to follow to live our lives with peace, joy, power, and a sense of fulfillment.

I want you to understand something about the Word of God: the words in the Bible are not ordinary words. They are words inspired by God Himself through His Spirit, and they are full of life-changing power. They are a written record of God's thoughts (see John 5:38); they teach us how to live, what to believe, how to think, and how to relate to God and to other people.

We cannot truly know God without knowing His Word. To know Him and to enjoy an intimate, personal relationship with Him, we must have a deep, intimate relationship with His Word. His Word reveals His thoughts, attitudes, behavior, character, wisdom, and heart for you and me. It is absolute truth and it makes truth known to us.

God's Word not only teaches us truth, it also has the power to help, encourage, and strengthen us to do what it says—if we make it a priority in our lives. It is a book of wisdom, teaching us not only *what* to do but *how* to do it. The power of God's truth, revealed through His Word, totally transformed my life and continues to change me day by day—and it can do the same for you.

MEDITATE, OBSERVE, AND OBEY

When I first began to love and live by God's Word, one of the first scriptures I learned to really study, pay attention to, and meditate on was Joshua 1:8: "This Book of the Law shall not depart out of your mouth, but you shall meditate on it day and night, that you may observe *and* do according to all that is written in it. For then you shall make your way prosperous, and then you shall deal wisely *and* have good success."

We need to understand the meaning of this phrase: "This Book of the Law shall not depart out of your mouth, but you shall meditate on it day and night." These words teach us the importance of meditating on God's Word. To meditate is to murmur, mumble, and roll over and over in our minds the truths we read in the Bible. We are to focus on God's Word, to think about it, and to speak it quietly to ourselves. When we need to make decisions, we are to make them in accordance with God's Word. In this way, the Word does not "depart out of" our mouths; it stays with us every day.

When we keep the Word on our tongues and meditate on it, Joshua 1:8 says we will "observe and do" (see and obey) what is written in the Word. Then, this verse promises we will make our ways prosperous, deal wisely, and have success. We can pray for God to prosper us, but this verse says we make our own ways prosperous by doing what we should do, which only happens as we live by the Word. Furthermore, the Word teaches us to "deal wisely," and we will not be successful unless and until we learn to conduct ourselves with wisdom. If we want to prosper and be wise and successful, we need to know, meditate on, and obey God's Word. Whether we go to sleep at night muttering scripture verses, learn them by playing songs based on scripture, or listen to CDs or downloads of Scripture, we must do whatever it takes to get the Word established in our hearts and minds if we want to enjoy our lives and be successful.

If we want to prosper and be wise and successful, we need to know, meditate on, and obey God's Word.

MAKE THE INVESTMENT

If you have ever tried to operate an electronic device or an appliance without reading the directions, you may have found yourself frustrated and confused, unless you are naturally gifted or experienced in such things. Failure to read directions often leads to assembling things in the wrong order or trying to force parts into places they don't belong. On the other hand, a careful reading of directions often enables a person to build or install things with less frustration and in a way that ensures they will function properly. So why don't more people read directions? Usually, they think they know what they're doing and they simply do not want to take time to look at diagrams and read the instructions.

In the early years of my relationship with God, I did not take time to carefully read His directions for my life in His Word. I tried to live my life as a Christian without really being a student of God's Word. I was faithful in my church attendance; I listened when our preacher preached his sermons on Sunday mornings; and I read one chapter of the Bible every night before I went to bed, as quickly as possible. Most of the time, I did not understand what I read and I rarely paid much attention to the words on the pages of my Bible because I was simply reading in order to meet an obligation. I thought I was *supposed* to read the Bible, so I did. But I cannot say it made much difference in my life because I only did it out of a sense of duty.

Many people go to church and call themselves Christians without being students of the Word, and they experience little transformation in their lives because they do not obey the truths and principles of God. I believe we can fall in love with God's Word, that we can hunger for it, gain understanding of it, find life in it, and live in it. When I use the term "live in the Word," I mean studying it and then doing what it says in every situation we face. Once again, the Word is full of wisdom and guidance for every circumstance. It teaches us about our attitudes, desires, emotions, minds, finances, relationships, motives, and the purposes for which God created us. To enjoy our lives today and embrace our futures tomorrow, we need to invest time in the Word. We need to set apart time in our daily schedules to read, study, meditate, and pray about the things we read in the Bible. Then we need to apply these lessons and principles in practical ways. That's the only way the Word will change our lives.

You and I put our time into what we value, and if we value God's Word, we will be happy to allot time for it, because we will see the use of our time as an investment, not as some kind of religious duty. Reading and studying the Bible is something we do for ourselves, not for God. Certainly, God is pleased when we spend time in His Word, but sometimes we approach reading the Word as something we are doing for *Him*. In reality, our investment in the Word is something we do for *ourselves*. The best way we can possibly use our time is to invest it in God's Word.

I challenge you to dedicate a certain amount of time each day to reading and studying God's Word. Make an appointment with God and don't break it. You will begin to make better choices, and that means you will reap on the investment of time you have made. I always thank God for what I know. I have studied His Word for more than thirty years and I can honestly say without hesitation that I am a transformed person. Of course I am still growing and changing and have not arrived at perfection, but I have definitely experienced great progress.

THE POWER TO CHANGE YOUR LIFE

God's Word is powerful, more powerful than any other book or writing on earth, and it has something to say about every area of our lives (some of the specific areas the Word addresses are listed for you in chapter 2, "Start with God"). By now, you have read several times that I believe God's Word can change your life. But how? On a practical, personal level, how do the words of Scripture work in our lives?

All through the Bible, we can read how its truths work in us. Jeremiah 23:29 says it is like a hammer that can break even the most stubborn rocks into pieces. Ephesians 5:26 tells us it is like water that washes the filth of the world off of us. Psalm 119:105 teaches us the Word shows us which way to go because it is "a lamp to my feet and a light to my path." Hebrews 4:12 tells us the Word of God is sharp and powerful and quick like a two-edged sword, dividing issues, exposing motives and purposes, and revealing our hearts. As we see the truth expressed in God's Word, we recognize that many of our ways are wrong and we see why we are not being successful in life. John 8:31, 32 teaches us that as we continue in God's Word we will know the truth and the truth will set us free.

As we see the truth expressed in God's Word, we recognize that many of our ways are wrong and we see why we are not being successful in life.

The Word exposes true motives and thereby shows us the reality of ourselves. As the truth reveals our hearts, we may realize we are doing certain things because we are proud, jealous, angry, or seeking revenge against someone. We may discover we are doing things to impress others or because of the fear of man. Once we understand our motives, we can repent, be cleansed, and experience the joy of forgiveness and freedom.

According to 2 Timothy, as we read the Word and apply it to our lives, we will be convinced, rebuked, corrected, warned, urged and encouraged to do the right thing, taught, convicted of sin, disciplined, and trained in righteousness.

Psalm 107:20 is a scripture I have loved for many years. It says, "He sends forth His word and heals them and rescues them from the pit *and* destruction." I believe this happens when we read the Word and allow it to work in our hearts and lives. God sends forth His Word and we can be healed—spiritually, physically, mentally, emotionally, financially, and relationally. When God's Word gets rooted in our hearts, our minds are renewed; we are healed in many ways; and we are delivered from various "pits" or difficulties we encounter in life.

The Word of God also exposes lies because it teaches us truth and renews our minds (see Romans 12:2). The enemy lies to us, and when we believe lies, those lies become truth to us, and that's deception. Many people are trapped in deception, but the more we study and live in the Word, the more those lies will be exposed, and the more we will know the truth.

Studying God's Word actually teaches us the proper way to think. If we don't know the truth, the devil can fill our minds with all sorts of wrong thoughts that produce terrible results. Our thoughts might depress or discourage us. They might cause us to distrust people or be resentful. They can evoke fear and prevent us from enjoying a creative and passionate life. But studying God's Word will teach us the proper way to think, which opens the door for God's perfect will in our lives. The Bible says in Proverbs 23:7 that as a man thinks in his heart, so does he become.

The Bible also strengthens us when we face difficulties. When we have trouble, or when we are afraid or discouraged, all we need to do is read Psalm 23: "The Lord is my Shepherd [to feed, guide, and shield me], I shall not lack. . . . Yes, though I walk through the [deep, sunless] valley of the shadow of death, I will fear *or* dread no evil, for You are with me. . . . You prepare a table before me in the presence of my enemies. . . . My cup runs over." Those are not words the enemy wants to hear when he is trying to cause us to fear or be depressed! The Word will make us strong in our hearts when we face trials or adversity.

Another way the Word works in our lives is by helping us make good decisions. Psalm 119:11 also says, "Your word have I laid up in my heart, that I might not sin against You." The King James Version of this verse speaks of having God's Word "hidden" in our hearts, and if we hide His Word in our hearts, then when we are about to make a wrong decision, the truth of the Word will arise within us and keep us from sinning if we obey it.

We must remember God's Word has the power to change our lives, and it always accomplishes its purpose. In Isaiah 55:11, God says, "So shall My word be that goes forth out

We must remember God's Word has the power to change our lives, and it always accomplishes its purpose.

of My mouth; it shall not return to me void [without producing any effect, useless], but it shall accomplish that which I please *and* purpose, and it shall prosper in the thing for which I sent it." Our lives will not change significantly or for long if we do not love the Word. Let me encourage you to give God's Word a place of priority in your daily life and to be diligent to learn and apply its truths in every situation, because that will empower you to enjoy today and embrace tomorrow.

CHAPTER

20

Give Them a Break!

"Be kind, for everyone you meet is fighting a hard battle."

—PLATO

You've heard it before: Nobody's perfect. All of us make mistakes; we all have personality quirks; and we need help in certain areas. None of us have "arrived"; we are all works in progress. I like to say, "I'm okay and I'm on my way," and this is true for everyone. If we are sincerely seeking God's will, then we are getting better every day; we are continuing to develop as individuals, becoming wiser, and gaining maturity. But we still have shortcomings and faults. We will never reach a place in our lives where we no longer need the mercy of God. We know we have faults but we must not focus excessively on our weaknesses, feel guilty about them, or allow them to stunt our personal growth. To enjoy our everyday lives, we need to take a gracious, merciful approach to ourselves and to others. We need to receive God's mercy and then let it flow through us to other people. We need to give ourselves—and the people around us—a break.

We need to receive God's mercy and then let it flow through us to other people. We need to give ourselves—and the people around us—a break.

Have you noticed how terribly some people treat others these days? Sometimes I am shocked as I walk through a grocery store, a coffee shop, or a restaurant by the way people treat each other. Their comments and interactions are often full of judgment, criticism, and very strong opinions. I rarely observe or overhear people encouraging, forgiving, or complimenting each other anymore. People with a short fuse are abundant, but long-suffering (patience), a fruit of the Holy Spirit (see Galatians 5:22), seems to be in short supply in our society.

I believe a lot of this criticism and lack of grace and mercy comes from the fact we want ourselves and others to be perfect, and we want our relationships to be perfect. We often have unrealistic expectations that set us up for disappointment. Where personal interactions are concerned, the prevailing message of our day seems to go something like this: "If you suit me perfectly; if you never make mistakes; if you always treat me just right; if you do everything just the way I want you to, then I will applaud you and receive you into my life. I will like you, love you, and accept you. But if you make mistakes, even if I let you stay in my life, the very least I will do is let you know you made a mistake, because I certainly wouldn't want you to think you're getting away with anything. I cannot let anything slide without giving you a warning or, at the very least, a little dose of rejection because if I let anything slide you might think you can just do it again and again."

The problem with the attitude I just described is it's completely unbiblical. If we want to enjoy life and relationships, we need to live by the truths and principles in God's Word. His Word does not teach us to be hard and demanding toward others, but to be kind, compassionate, patient, and gracious. God is extremely merciful toward us. In fact, He has fresh mercies for us every morning of our lives (see Lamentations 3:23); and He wants us to be merciful toward others.

All of us need mercy every day—probably more than we even realize. Sometimes I wonder how many times God shows mercy to us without our ever knowing it or how often He overlooks our faults and mistakes—and doesn't even call it to our attention. More than we realize, He blesses us when we don't deserve to be blessed and gets us out of trouble or saves our lives. I am sure He thinks on a regular basis, *I understand why you did that; I understand where you came from and what you've been through. I'm going to give you some mercy; I'm going to give you some space; I'm going to give you some time. I'm going to give you another chance.*

God is merciful. Mercy is part of His nature. He continually offers it to us; and we need to continually extend it to others.

GIVE IT TO GET IT

Jesus said in Matthew 7:1, "Do not judge *and* criticize *and* condemn others, so that you may not be judged *and* criticized *and* condemned yourselves." This is a clear example of the biblical principle of sowing and reaping, of experiencing in our own lives what we plant in the lives of others.

We do reap a harvest from the seeds we sow (see Galatians 6:7). If we sow mercy, we will reap mercy. We all need mercy, and the way to get it is to give it away. If we want people to give us a break—to extend grace and mercy to us—we need to extend grace and mercy to them.

God does not ask us to give away what we do not have. However, once we have received a gift from Him, He does expect us to freely share that gift with others. We know from God's Word He has given us forgiveness; He expects us to now forgive others. He has also shown us mercy; He now asks us to be merciful to others. God loves us unconditionally; He now wants us to love others unconditionally, without judging them or trying to make them earn everything we give them. The way God treats us shows us how He wants us to treat others.

> The way God treats us shows us how He wants us to treat others.

MERCY OVER JUDGMENT

Abraham Lincoln once said, "I have always found that mercy bears richer fruits than strict justice." His observation is based in Scripture. James 2:13 says, "For to him who has shown no mercy the judgment [will be] merciless, but mercy [full of glad confidence] exults victoriously over judgment."

When people around us are struggling or making mistakes, we need to help them, not judge them and criticize them. Isn't this the way we want to be treated when we don't do everything right?

In God's eyes, mercy is much greater than judgment, and we should always choose to be merciful instead of judgmental or critical. This does not mean we should never, ever correct or confront people or that we should allow people to walk all over us, or abuse and mistreat us. It simply means we refrain from pointing out and criticizing every wrong thing a person does. True mercy does not cower in the face of deliberate or blatant wrongdoing or sin; it confronts in love, with the goal of helping people live in the blessings of obedience to God's Word. But when people are doing the best they can with pure motives, mercy does not call attention to faults and flaws.

I believe many relationships are in serious trouble today because people simply do not exhibit grace and mercy toward one another. People are tired of being nitpicked and criticized for their mistakes and imperfections—and this has endangered countless relationships. If you are in this situation—you know you are being too hard on someone—let me urge you to develop a merciful attitude toward people's failures and mistakes. This simple attitude adjustment could save an important relationship and turn a miserable situation into a relationship you really enjoy.

A LONG FUSE

Philippians 4:5 encourages us: "Let all men know *and* perceive *and* recognize your unselfishness (your considerateness, your forbearing spirit)." What is a "forbearing spirit"? A person with a forbearing spirit is one who can put up with a lot from people without being judgmental or losing his or her temper. To be forbearing is, in common terms, to have "a long fuse," to be patient with others and to give them grace when they make mistakes or do annoying things. We can choose to let things go or point them out. I spent many years not enjoying my life because I was not willing to practice this principle. I made a big deal out of every little mistake people made. The longer I walked with God, the more I realized He was not pleased with my behavior in this area and I asked Him to change me and help me extend mercy as often as wisdom allowed. As I already mentioned, there are times when not confronting an issue would be unwise, but the truth is most of the time the things that upset us are rather petty.

To be forbearing is, in common terms, to have "a long fuse," to be patient with others and to give them grace when they make mistakes or do annoying things.

We should be the kind of people who must be pushed and pushed and pushed and pushed before we become angry. We do not want to be quick-tempered, easily frustrated people who get upset over innocent, insignificant infringements of the rules and regulations we impose upon others.

Whether we realize it or not, we all have rules or codes of behavior in our relationships with others, and other people have rules they want to apply to us. Each person in our lives has a set of expectations for us, just as we have for them. This is why relationships become complicated. One person wants a specific behavior from us, while the next person wants the opposite response. One person wants us to talk; another person wants us to be quiet. One person wants to know what we think; another becomes angry if we offer our opinions.

Over time, we all begin to feel we must become relational geniuses to keep everyone happy. Trying to deal with different people and

> Trying to deal with different people and different types of personalities can be trying, so we must develop an attitude of patience and forbearance toward everyone.

different types of personalities can be trying, so we must develop an attitude of patience and forbearance toward everyone. This way, we can begin to build honest, healthy, long-term relationships that will enrich our lives and the lives of those with whom we interact. I encourage you to pray in this area, because merely trying won't work. We need divine help on a regular basis if we want to go through life at peace with people.

COVER IT

Sometimes, the best way to deal with an offense or with something that gets on our nerves is simply to overlook it. If we insist upon calling every little mistake to people's attention (this is called "nit-picking"), we are *not* being gracious and merciful. You have probably heard the saying "Love is blind," which means we often overlook people's faults when we love them. Another way to say this is, "Love covers a multitude of sins" (1 Peter 4:8).

Let me repeat: Nobody's perfect. Every member of every household on earth has bad habits. In our home, I have habits Dave wishes I didn't have and he has habits I wish he didn't have. For instance, Dave does not always close his closet door. In our closets, the lights stay on if the doors are open. For years, I had a hard time simply closing the closet door for him; I always wanted to make sure Dave *knew* he left the door open and I had to close it again!

Our fleshly natures really enjoy telling people what they have done wrong and how we have fixed it. The best way for me to handle Dave's open closet door is to close it and go on about my day, not to say, "You left your light on again" every time he does it. There are similar things Dave needs to do for me. There are plenty of times when I am not perfect and I want him to cover my mistakes.

In adult relationships, both in marriage and in other relationships, we need to cover each other's mistakes. While there are times when situations need to be confronted and resolved, there are other times when people are busy or rushed and they simply need us to step in and do what they have unintentionally left undone. We need to do these things without feeling we must mention the fact we saved the day!

People do not want to hear about every little mistake they make. Remember, the Bible says, "Love covers all transgressions" (Proverbs 10:12). When we speak of being merciful and gracious to others, we are speaking of demonstrating love—and love *covers* those irritating little things people do.

I encourage you to apply this verse to your everyday life. Before you point out what someone has done wrong, remember love covers transgressions. When you want to say, "You left your socks on the floor again!" or "I had to let your water out of the bathtub again!" remember, *love covers*.

> Before you point out what someone has done wrong, remember love covers transgressions.

I really appreciate the times people cover my mistakes; I believe you do too. Sow a little mercy into someone's life today, and when that person does something that would normally frustrate you, simply cover it.

DON'T BE A NAG

No matter what people do, how thoroughly they frustrate you, or how desperately you wish they would change, you are absolutely powerless to change them. You can cover them with prayer, but you cannot change them. Only God can work within the human heart and change the nature of a person.

Philippians 4:6 says, "Do not fret *or* have any anxiety about anything, but in every circumstance *and* in everything, by prayer and petition (definite requests), with thanksgiving, continue to make your wants known to God." We have to ask God to change people, and we need to do so with thankful hearts, not with murmuring, grumbling, and complaining.

We can try to prescribe rules and regulations for people to live by, but if their *hearts* are not changed, they will break our rules and resent us for making them.

In relationships, we should clearly communicate our needs, desires, and preferences; we may tell people what we don't like and what makes us unhappy. But we must not continue to tell them and tell them and tell them. That's called nagging; and no one likes a nag!

As an example, I think of Dave's lifelong affinity for high-powered cars. He gets a real thrill out of stomping on the gas pedal and hearing the *vroooom!* of the engine. Sometimes, when I ride with him, he floors the gas when I least expect it. I don't like that, and I have said to him many times, "I would prefer not to end up with a sore neck just from riding in the car with you."

Then I'll say, "You do not have to drive this way."

Dave typically responds, "Yes, I do, honey! Do you realize that other car would have hit us if I hadn't gotten out of his way?" Or, he might say, "I had to do that to get ahead of the traffic."

"That is not true," I reply. "You just want to drive fast. You drive this way because you want to, not because you have to!"

Dave has done this as long as I have known him. I do not like it; I have never liked it; but I have accepted the fact that nagging him is not going to change it.

My point is we must stop nagging people and begin to pray for them to change. We can't try to manipulate them with prayer; we must pray out of genuine love for them and then we need to thank God for working in the situation and the person's heart. We can't pray sometimes and nag sometimes because nagging can negate our prayers.

I know—keeping our mouths shut is difficult. But we must learn to do so. Most of the time, the things people do that make us want to scream are quite insignificant in the grand scheme of things; they simply get on our nerves. This is where we have to realize and admit we are being selfish. What they are doing makes *us* uncomfortable or is inconvenient to *us*.

THE ROOT OF UNHAPPINESS

The heart of the gospel—and the heart of love—is dying to self. If we are really going to love others, we have to resist self-centeredness in every form. Self-centeredness means being completely focused on ourselves, our wants, our needs, our interests, our priorities. When we are self-centered, we expect people around us to exist for our benefit. We think they should work to keep us happy, do what we want, and put us first. And by all means, they should never do anything to irritate us, frustrate us, or inconvenience us.

The heart of the gospel—and the heart of love—is dying to self.

William Gladstone, a man who served four times as prime minister of Great Britain, said, "Selfishness is the greatest curse of the human race." I agree with him. I also believe selfishness is the root of most unhappiness and the inability to enjoy life. The overwhelming majority of the unhappiness, upset, and frustration we feel comes from not having things we want or from having to deal with situations we don't want. When our personal desires are not being met, we fall into discontent—and this is selfish.

I have heard so many single women say, "I want to get married. If I can just get married, I will be happy." I want to say, "No, you won't. While marriage can be wonderful, simply being married will not make you happy. Being married means another person is present in your life all the time—a person with his or her own wants, needs, interests, and issues. It means having to consult someone else on matters you could handle on your own while you were single." I have also heard married women say, "Oh! If I just had some freedom I would be happy!" I have heard some women comment, "If I could just have a baby, I would be so happy," while others say, "I will be so glad when these kids grow up!" I also hear countless people say they will be happy when they make more money, buy a boat, live in a bigger house, or retire.

All of this never-ending wanting keeps us focused on ourselves; it breeds selfishness, which keeps us from being thankful for what we do have and from truly loving others. We must learn to be content. We need to be satisfied with what we have and with what we do not have. Happiness, after all, has nothing to do with possessions; it has to do with the condition of our hearts. A selfish heart is never happy; it is constantly demanding. Ask God for your want or need, and then go on enjoying the life you have right now. Learn how to enjoy where you are on the way to where you are going!

Learning to love unselfishly will enable you to enjoy life and to enjoy the people around you. The Bible says, "[And it is, indeed, a source of immense profit, for] godliness accompanied with contentment (that contentment which is a sense of inward sufficiency) is great *and* abundant gain" (1 Timothy 6:6). I want to encourage you to put aside any selfish thoughts and behaviors you may have, and to seek to be content with yourself, your possessions, and the people with whom you have relationships. Be satisfied and content with who they are without demanding they change to make you happy. Be gracious; be merciful; and give people a break—and you'll find yourself enjoying life and people more than ever.

Learning to love unselfishly will enable you to enjoy life and to enjoy the people around you.

CHAPTER 21

Stay Positive

"The pessimist sees the difficulty in every opportunity; the optimist sees the opportunity in every difficulty."

—WINSTON CHURCHILL

Holocaust survivor and famous author Viktor Frankl wrote:

> We who lived in concentration camps can remember the men who walked through the huts comforting others, giving away their last piece of bread. They may have been few in number, but they offer sufficient proof that everything can be taken from a man but one thing: the last of the human freedoms—to choose one's attitude in any given set of circumstances.[1]

I believe one of the great privileges of life is being able to choose our attitudes. If we choose to be positive, life will go well for us; and if we choose to be negative, it will not. A positive attitude is absolutely necessary if we are to enjoy our lives today and look forward to tomorrow.

FOR YOUR HEALTH

I believe the most important mental attitude a person can have is a positive approach to life. A positive attitude helps us deal with stress, makes

I believe the most important mental attitude a person can have is a positive approach to life.

us fun for others to be around, and can keep us healthy. In an article in *Newsweek* magazine, Dr. Howard LeWine of Harvard University writes about the health benefits of a positive attitude:

> What does it mean to have a "positive attitude"? The image of a bubbly, fun-loving individual may spring to mind. But such an outgoing, social person may be inclined to engage in riskier behaviors that cause injury and poor health.
>
> Instead, there are several features of a positive attitude that research has found to be associated with healthier aging. If you have a positive attitude, you see relatively few of life's challenges as overwhelming. You feel in control most of the time. You believe you can strongly influence, if not completely determine, your health. For example, you believe that your lifestyle choices—healthy eating, regular exercise, and avoiding dangerous habits—really can affect your health. Indeed, you take pleasure in controlling your life through your choices, while understanding that there are no guarantees.
>
> Finally, you are flexible. You know that life will sometimes make it hard to follow your agenda for health, but that if things happen that don't allow you to follow your exact program, you go with the flow. There is time later that day or the next to get back on track.[2]

Dr. LeWine goes on to rank a positive attitude as the number one contributing factor to healthy aging, even over exercise and a healthy diet, and cites a Yale University study which determined that optimistic people live an average of 7.5 years longer than those who have a negative outlook on life.[3]

While some people are naturally more optimistic than others, anyone can develop a positive attitude by simply choosing to do so. As a result, life will be not only healthier, but much more enjoyable.

POSITIVE ATTITUDE, POSITIVE LIFE

A true positive attitude is not ecstatic and upbeat one day, then doubtful the next, then discouraged, then hopeful again. A real positive attitude is a matter of choice. We must choose to take an optimistic approach toward life every day, to set our minds—and keep them set—in positive directions.

Many times I quote the scripture "This is the day which the Lord has brought about; we will rejoice and be glad in it" (Psalm 118:24). Quoting these words from my heart and making them personal is one way I develop a positive mind-set every day. I *choose* to rejoice, to enjoy life, and to be glad. I am of the opinion that no matter how negative people might be, they can change if they really want to. I was actually taught by my father to be negative. I remember his making comments such as, "You can't trust anybody. Everybody is merely using you to get what they want." The interesting point is he saw people that way because he was that way. He used people to get what he wanted and cared nothing for them, so he assumed the entire world was the same way. He taught me to be suspicious, so it was not easy for me to learn to trust. But with God's help I have been transformed from being extremely negative about almost everything, to being very positive. Since I have lived both ways, I am qualified to tell you that approaching life in a positive way is better.

We must choose to take an optimistic approach toward life every day, to set our minds—and keep them set—in positive directions.

Proverbs 23:7 says, "For as he thinks in his heart, so is he." What this means is, we become whatever we think about. What goes on in our minds directly affects what happens in our lives. Whether it's a hot fudge sundae, the completion of a big project,

Whether it's a hot fudge sundae, the completion of a big project, or a closer walk with God, if we focus our thoughts on it, we will direct our actions toward it.

or a closer walk with God, if we focus our thoughts on it, we will direct our actions toward it. The same is true for our overall lives. If we think positive thoughts toward life, we will pursue and ultimately enjoy happy, confident, fulfilled lives.

DON'T DEPEND ON CIRCUMSTANCES

Martha Washington, the wife of America's first president, made an observation with which I wholeheartedly agree: "The greatest part of our happiness depends on our dispositions, not our circumstances." Many people allow circumstances to determine their attitudes. If their circumstances are favorable, they look at life through a positive lens. If their circumstances are negative, they see every situation from a negative point of view. We must be more mature than that; we must develop a positive outlook on life, no matter what happens. We need to be as positive when the car breaks down or when we need a root canal as we are when we receive a raise or promotion. We cannot wait until circumstances change to decide to adjust our attitudes. We need to be stable and consistent in our upbeat approach toward every situation.

To develop the stability we need, we have to eliminate the mindset that says, "I will enjoy life *when* I don't have this problem anymore." "I will enjoy myself *when* this situation is resolved." "I will enjoy my family *when* my children behave better." "I'll be glad *when* I finally pay all of my debts." "I will relax *when* I finish this stressful assignment at work."

The fact is, "when" rarely comes. When the issue you see as a hindrance to your enjoyment of life finally goes away, something else will arise. If you are like most people, you will have a little reprieve, and then something else will come up. I'm not being negative; I'm just telling you how life is. It's not perfect; *something* always needs to be addressed, fixed, resolved, or confronted.

We never know what we will have to face or when unexpected situations will demand our attention. Life is full of surprises; sometimes they are wonderful and sometimes they are unpleasant or even heartbreaking. Whatever unexpected events and surprises come our way, we need to meet them with a predetermined, positive mind-set. Having a positive mind-set doesn't mean our disappointments don't hurt. We can feel hurt and still decide not to let our feelings rule us. Being able to decide how we will behave apart from how we feel is one of the greatest privileges we have as human beings. The ability to choose is a gift from God and we should use it to our benefit. When all is said and done, life is relatively short and we should not waste even one day being negative and downcast.

BE GLAD TODAY

As we move beyond saying, "I'll be glad when . . ." we need to begin saying, "I am glad now. I am going to be happy and positive today. My life may not be exactly what I want it to be, but I choose to be glad today." I am still working with the Holy Spirit to break the habit of saying, "I'll be glad when . . ." I have made a lot of progress, but still find myself making that comment even in little things. The other day I heard myself say, "I'll be glad when the weather gets warmer." Then I quickly added, "But, I am also glad right now!" I am fighting the good fight of faith in this area and trusting God to cause me to hear myself every time I say, "I'll be glad when . . ." I am determined to be glad *now!*

Why is it important to be positive today? Because a positive attitude gives us the strength not only to endure the situations we face, but also to overcome them. Anyone can go through a difficult time with a bad attitude; it takes a positive person to endure it victoriously.

To encourage us in this, the Bible is full of scriptures such as these:

- "Yet amid all these things we are more than conquerors *and* gain a surpassing victory through Him Who loved us" (Romans 8:37).
- "He Who lives in you is greater (mightier) than he who is in the world" (1 John 4:4).
- "I have strength for all things in Christ Who empowers me" (Philippians 4:13).

These verses and others remind us to meet every situation with strength and the joy that accompanies certain victory. God is on our side—and that's all the reason we need to have a positive attitude in the face of challenges and difficulties.

To have a positive attitude is not to deny pain, hardship, suffering, or grief. It does not protect us from being hurt, keep us from crying, shield us from difficult situations, or prevent "bad days" once in a while. It simply means we trust God, keep our emotions under control, and refuse to allow our feelings to determine our attitudes and actions.

The apostle Paul, who suffered many hardships during his ministry, writes,

> "I have learned how to be content (satisfied to the point where I am not disturbed or disquieted) in whatever state I am. I know how to be abased *and* live humbly in straitened circumstances, and I know also how to enjoy plenty *and* live in abundance. I have learned in any and all circumstances the secret of facing every situation, whether well-fed or going hungry, having a sufficiency *and* enough to spare or going without *and* being in want."
>
> *(Philippians 4:11, 12)*

Paul's attitude, reflected in these words, is tremendous to me. It gives me great hope, as it shows us he learned the secret of contentment. If he learned it, so can you and I. We may not have been perfected in this area, but we can keep pressing toward being positive and satisfied, no matter what our circumstances may be.

ALL THINGS WORK TOGETHER FOR GOOD

My husband is a very happy man; he is consistently joyful and peaceful. Over the years we have been married, he has enjoyed his life much more than I have enjoyed mine, and he has not spent (wasted) nearly as much time as I have being angry, upset, and frustrated. Most of the time, I was the one who stewed over situations and allowed things to bother me, while Dave went on his merry way and enjoyed each day.

When certain problems arise, Dave says, "If you can do something about this, do it. If you can't, go on about your business, trust God, and let Him take care of it." That always sounded good to me, but it used to take me longer to "let go and let God" than it did him, but now I am catching up.

Recently, we were riding in the car together and Dave received a phone call about a change in one of our television air times. This happened to be on one of our best stations and he did not like the change. He started getting upset and I heard myself say, "Don't let it bug you. God will make it work out for the best if we pray." I didn't even have to try to be positive; it was my first response. I am continually amazed at how much God can change us if we continue praying and letting Him work in our lives. Here I was actually encouraging Mr. Positive, when most of my life it had been the other way around. That felt good!

One way to stay peaceful, content, and unruffled is to know how to "cast your care on the Lord" (see 1 Peter 5:7) and respond to every challenging situation with a scripture such

One way to stay peaceful, content, and unruffled is to know how to "cast your care on the Lord" (see 1 Peter 5:7).

as Romans 8:28: "We are assured *and* know that . . . all things work together *and* are [fitting into a plan] for good to *and* for those who love God and are called according to [His] design *and* purpose."

This verse teaches us how to approach everything we face in life. It means that, if we really love God and want to do His will, then we must believe—no matter what happens in our lives—that God is in control and He will take everything that happens and make it work out for our good. Certain circumstances may not always feel good or appear to be good, but God will cause them to work together with other things in your life to bring about good. God is a good God, and He can take even the worst situations and bring something positive out of them.

I believe Romans 8:28 is a key to enjoying life today and facing tomorrow with confidence. I cannot promise you circumstances will always be pleasant or comfortable. Challenge is part of life. I do believe, however, that regardless of the circumstance you face, if you will say from your heart, "I believe this will work out for my good. I don't like the way it feels right now, God, but I do know I love You; I do know I want Your will; and therefore, I believe this is going to work out for my good," then that's exactly what will happen.

God wants us to stay positive and joyful, no matter what we encounter, because the joy of the Lord is our strength (see Nehemiah 8:10). The reason it is so important to be joyful in trials is that trials and difficulties drain our strength, but joy restores it. A good, hearty laugh makes everyone feel better. If we allow ourselves to be drained without being restored, the enemy can defeat us. But if we fight back with that fruit of joy, we will be strengthened to endure hardships and emerge victoriously.

If we allow ourselves to be drained without being restored, the enemy can defeat us. But if we fight back with that fruit of joy, we will be strengthened to endure hardships and emerge victoriously.

If we take an honest, realistic approach to life, we must accept that we will have trouble at times. In John 16:33, Jesus says, "In the world you have tribulation *and* trials *and* distress *and* frustration; but be of good cheer [take courage; be confident, certain, undaunted]! For I have overcome the world. [I have deprived it of power to harm you and have conquered it for you.]"

In other words, we can count on difficulties in our lives, but we can also "be of good cheer," which is another way of saying, "stay positive," because Jesus has deprived hardship of the power to harm us. I don't think this verse means we never hurt or grieve, but that painful situations cannot do us any permanent harm. Remember, all things work together for our good. We must believe that, and base our positive attitudes toward life on that truth.

OUR WORDS AFFECT OUR JOY

Just as a positive mental attitude helps us enjoy our lives, the words we speak also affect the levels of joy we experience. Matthew 12:34 explains why this is true: "Out of the fullness (the overflow, the superabundance) of the heart the mouth speaks." When we are filled with joy, peace, and optimism, we will speak words reflecting those attitudes. If we listen to what we say, we will be able to stay in touch with what is going on in our hearts.

Our words are powerful. They not only reveal the conditions of our hearts, they also influence our ability to enjoy life. Proverbs 18:20, 21 makes this point clearly: "A man's [moral] self shall be filled with the fruit of his mouth; and with the consequence of his words he must be satisfied [whether good or evil]. Death and life are in the power of the tongue, and they who indulge in it shall eat the fruit of it [for death or life]."

Our words are powerful. They not only reveal the conditions of our hearts, they also influence our ability to enjoy life.

If we speak negatively, we will have negative experiences. On the other hand, if we speak positively, we will see good, positive things happen in our lives. If we talk about our problems, our problems will seem to grow and become more difficult to deal with—and we will be depressed and discouraged. But if we talk about our ability to endure and overcome our problems, we will find ourselves discovering solutions, feeling strong and confident, and able to work through those problems to achieve positive results. Why are these principles true? Because we eat the fruit of our words, according to Proverbs 18:21. We can poison our own joy by the thoughts we think and the words we speak.

If we want to enjoy our lives, we have to watch what we say and choose our words carefully. First Peter 3:10 says, "For let him who wants to enjoy life and see good days [good—whether apparent or not] keep his tongue free from evil and his lips from guile (treachery, deceit)." The connection between enjoying our everyday lives and the words we speak could not be clearer. We need to speak positively, talk about things that make us happy, use our words to encourage others, and refuse to speak evil of people or negatively about circumstances.

Look also at Proverbs 15:23: "A man has joy in making an apt answer, and a word spoken at the right moment—how good it is!" Not only can we bring ourselves joy with the words we speak, we can use our words for positive purposes in other people's lives. If you have ever had someone speak just the right words to you at just the right moment, you know that can change your perspective, encourage you to keep going, or even affect the course of your life. Because we reap what we sow, the more joy we give to others through the words we speak, the more joy we experience personally.

BE DETERMINED TO ENJOY LIFE

Let me encourage you to be determined to enjoy every day of your life by keeping a positive attitude. Use your mind to think positive thoughts and your mouth to speak positive words.

Use your mind to think positive thoughts and your mouth to speak positive words.

You will have to be diligent to stay positive, but you can do it. The minute you feel yourself becoming negative, stop and make an attitude adjustment. The best way to do this is to spend time with God.

Even if you need to lock yourself in the bathroom to get a moment's peace and quiet in your busy household or sit in your car during your lunch break at work, take time to get with God and say, "Okay, God, I'm starting to think negative thoughts. I'm starting to feel discouraged. I am tempted to give up. Show me what the problem is. Strengthen me right now, Lord. If there's something I need to see, let me see it. If there's a change I need to make, help me make it. Otherwise, give me Your strength and Your grace to have a positive attitude and do whatever I need to do and to do it with joy. I wait on You, God, because I know You're the source of every good gift and I believe You are working all things together for good in my life." Don't merely "try" to have a better attitude, pray about it!

As you spend time with God, He may reveal to you why you have stopped enjoying life at that moment or why you have become negative. For example, He could show you the reason you have lost your positive attitude is that a colleague at work received a promotion you wanted. Maybe you became jealous or bitter and developed a bad attitude because you wanted to move up but now have to continue in your old job.

When God shows you something like that, you can say, "You're right, God. I'm sorry. I'm not going to be jealous. Bless that person,

Lord. Give them wisdom and grace to do the new job well. I know You have a plan for my life, and I know nothing can keep me from the good things You have purposed for me. I choose to believe this will work out for my good. Since I did not get the promotion I wanted, You must have something better in store for me. I am going to wait on that with a positive attitude."

God also may reveal to you something that is bothering you subconsciously. God once revealed to me that I was angry at my son because he was not as spiritual as I wanted him to be. I knew we had a difficult time getting along with each other, but I honestly was not aware that I was angry with him and certainly not conscious of the fact I was angry because he wasn't handling his spiritual life as I thought he should. I became negative about my son and didn't even know exactly why. I even felt aggravated when I was in the room with him, but in order for me to understand why, God had to reveal to me what the exact problem was. When I saw the truth, I was able to repent to both God and my son, and my joy increased. Things hidden in the dark have power over us, so don't be afraid to ask God to show you what is wrong and to walk in the light of what He reveals.

Things hidden in the dark have power over us, so don't be afraid to ask God to show you what is wrong and to walk in the light of what He reveals.

A friend of mine shared that any time he finds himself in a bad mood he knows it is rooted in something and he immediately proceeds to ask God what it is. Sometimes it is unforgiveness, at other times it is another sin he has not recognized and needs to repent of, it may be worry or even fear, but it is always something. He has learned not to merely be passive about bad moods, but to aggressively find out how he opened the door to them and change whatever is necessary to get back on track with God. A person who has a positive attitude cannot be defeated. He or she will enjoy life, no matter what. I encourage you to decide to eliminate negative thinking and negative speaking from your life right now. As soon as you do, you'll find yourself enjoying today and looking forward to tomorrow in brand-new ways.

CHAPTER

22

Be Out-of-Control

"Him that I love, I wish to be free—even from me."

—ANNE MORROW LINDBERGH

I heard a story about a young lady who received salvation in a church service. After she finished at the altar, she returned to her seat, where her fiancé was waiting for her. She was so excited, and she began to encourage him: "Oh, I feel so wonderful. I just gave my life to the Lord, and He's forgiven me of my sins, and I feel so much peace and joy. It's wonderful! Come and give your life to Jesus! Come on! Go to the altar and pray!

The skeptical young man replied, "I'm not getting into all that emotional stuff."

After she had spent quite some time trying to talk her fiancé into becoming a Christian and he continued to resist and make fun of her, she finally looked at him and said, "Okay. You can choose not to go to heaven with me, but don't ask me to go to hell with you!"

Even though the young woman loved this man enough to marry him, she was not going to allow his decision to determine her destiny. She was her own person, she made her own choice; and she refused to let his thoughts and actions control her.

YOU DECIDE

We will never enjoy our everyday lives if we allow other people to control us. In fact, we will be miserable, confused, and tired as a result of trying to please people who seek to influence us in ways that go against our own hearts. To enjoy life and truly embrace the freedom Jesus died to give us, we must exercise our God-given right to make our own decisions.

Allowing other people to make your decisions for you is not only foolish, it will make you unhappy. You were created to use the free will God has given you. You were made to seek guidance from Him and to know in your heart what you should do in every situation. You alone are responsible before God for your choices, so you need to be the one who makes them.

Far too often, we run from person to person, asking, "What do you think about this? "What should I do?" Many times the reason we do this is we want these people to accept or approve of us, or not to be angry with us. If we do what they say, we reason, they will be pleased with us. This need for acceptance and approval often drives us to ask for advice from people who are not qualified to give advice or who might even give us suggestions that would work for their benefit instead of ours. Bad advice, if followed, leads to bad decisions, and bad decisions make for a miserable life.

Bad advice, if followed, leads to bad decisions, and bad decisions make for a miserable life.

I want to present a balanced approach to this matter and to be clear that there are times we do need wise counsel. Seeking wise advice from a mature, trustworthy person who has our best interest at heart is different than soliciting opinions from people we hardly know, people who do not demonstrate wisdom, or people who simply like to tell us what to do.

Some people can put counsel and suggestions in perspective and not allow it to influence them unduly. Others want to follow advice quickly and thoroughly once they hear it. Depending on the kind of person you are and the way you respond to other people's input in your life, I would say this: If you can listen to someone else's opinion and then step away from it and make your own decisions, fine. But if hearing someone's opinion makes you feel you must act on it, then don't ask for much advice. Do whatever you need to do to be in a position to hear God's voice for yourself and allow Him to guide you, rather than allowing the opinions and advice of other people to lead you.

Years ago, my daughter, Sandy, allowed people's opinions to affect her quite significantly. She was strongly influenced by what the people around her thought. When she needed to make a decision, she asked so many people for their opinions she became confused to the point she hardly knew what to do.

As time passed, I watched Sandy fight her way out of needing so much input for every decision, and I saw her learn to stand her ground. As part of the learning process, she almost became too forceful about saying she was going to do whatever she wanted to do, but people often swing too far in the opposite direction when they are trying to break the power of control in their lives and establish new patterns of thought and behavior. I knew Sandy would end up in a healthy, balanced place—and she did.

Now, Sandy can ask someone, "What do you think about this outfit?" or "How do you like my new hairstyle?" and she can handle an honest response without becoming insecure. If a person does not answer positively, she can say, "Well, I appreciate your opinion, but I like my hairstyle, and I am going to keep it." She can accept other people's opinions without giving in to them, and she is free enough to go ahead and do what she really wants to do. To me, that's balance.

She frequently asks me what I think about certain things, but she does not always take my advice and that does not offend me. I want her to follow her own heart, not mine. She considers what I say as she makes her decision, but she does not let my opinion control her.

I think it is foolish for anyone to never ask for or be willing to take advice, but it is also foolish to be a people pleaser and work so hard trying to keep people happy that you are never happy yourself. All of us need to be balanced when it comes to the input we allow others to have in our lives. We need to realize we have the right to make our own choices. If we are wise, we will ask God to help us and lead us in our decisions, and not be led by the opinions of other people. We need to be smart enough to seek truly wise counsel at strategic times and then take the advice we receive to the Lord and ask Him to give us peace about the decisions He wants us to make.

We need to be smart enough to seek truly wise counsel at strategic times and then take the advice we receive to the Lord and ask Him to give us peace about the decisions He wants us to make.

BE TRUE TO YOU

To really enjoy life and make good personal decisions, an individual must be true to his or her own heart. People have understood this for centuries. In fact, the playwright William Shakespeare, who wrote during the late 1500s and early 1600s, penned these famous words in his play *Hamlet*: "To thine own self be true." You are the one who must live with the consequences of your decisions, and the best way to be happy with them is to follow what is in your heart, not what is in someone else's.

You will be miserable and unfulfilled if you constantly do what others want you to do, especially if you do not want to do it. This does not mean you never do what somebody else wants you to do, because there are times we need to make sacrifices because we love people. It simply means you don't make a habit of allowing others to control you and direct the course of your life.

As the leader of Joyce Meyer Ministries, I am responsible for the conferences we conduct. To be faithful to the call God has placed upon my life and the leadership position He has given me, I determine what happens in our conferences as I am led by the Holy Spirit. I never walk onto the platform and ask the audience what they want to hear that day but I go with a message prepared—one I believe God has led me to share with that particular group. I do what God leads me to do, not what people think I should do. The message God gives may not always be a comfortable one. Quite often, my messages challenge people to come up higher in their behavior. Sometimes, people even ask me to teach on a specific subject that interests them. I always respond that I will keep their requests in mind, but I must be led by the Holy Spirit. I think many ministers get into trouble because they preach what they think people want to hear instead of what God is telling them to preach. Some messages are not easy to hear. Jesus often offended people with His preaching and teaching, and He did so because He was determined to tell them what would really help them and not just what would be easy to hear.

I have to stand before God and give an account of my life and the gift God has put in me, and so do you. God is not going to want to hear that we disobeyed Him because we did not want to make anyone angry. If you would like more teaching on this subject, my book *Approval Addiction* would be an excellent resource for you.

I have to stand before God and give an account of my life and the gift God has put in me, and so do you. God is not going to want to hear that we disobeyed Him because we did not want to make anyone angry.

BUILD SOME BORDERS

I have a strong personality, and Dave is more easygoing. He has no problem with my doing as I please most of the time. For example, when we go out to eat, he usually lets me choose which restaurant we will go to because it really doesn't matter much to him. He is also agreeable to most of the social plans I make; he does not complain about or resist things I want to do. But as pleasant and laid-back as Dave is, he also has limits, and he refuses to let me (or anyone else) control him. In many situations, he will only let me go so far. And do you know what? I respect him for that.

In many relationships, one of the two people—whether friends, work associates, marriage partners—will have a stronger personality than the other. Some people naturally take the "lead roles," and others really thrive as followers. I am a leader, and I will lead no matter where I go or what I do. I don't take charge of situations on purpose; leading is just who I am. Being a strong leader is part of my personality. But remember: It's one thing to be a leader; it's something else altogether to be a controller or a manipulator. Most of us with strong leader-type personalities have to find this out one way or the other. I spent years trying to control everyone and everything and finally realized there was a big difference between control and true godly leadership.

If you have a leader or a person with a strong personality or will in your life, I want you to know something that may surprise you: *Most strong people do not respect those who allow them to be controlling.* These people would really respect you for creating some limits you will not allow them to cross, just as I respect Dave for not allowing my strong personality to control him.

Even though you may be a milder, more peace-loving, more easy-going personality, you must build some borders in your life. If you don't, you will one day look back over your life and feel that people used you, abused you, walked all over you, and generally treated you without respect. You may end up bitter and resentful, and that will not be anyone's fault but yours. You are responsible for standing up for yourself. No

> You are responsible for standing up for yourself. No one else will build the borders you need. If you are tired of feeling controlled, begin to set some limits.

one else will build the borders you need. If you are tired of feeling controlled, begin to set some limits. If you have allowed people to have their way all the time, they may find it difficult when you first establish borders, but you must persist and do so for their sake, as well as for your sake.

CONFRONT CONTROL

I used to be extremely controlling and manipulative. I specifically remember several friends whose personalities were not as strong as mine and who were easygoing and adaptable. I was very strong in my interactions with these people; I bossed them around and controlled them with my anger. They knew they would suffer my rejection and harsh words if they made me angry.

I look back now on those relationships and think, *Why didn't one of them ever say to me, "Shut up, Joyce! Run your own life; and quit telling me what to do with mine!"* I really believe I would have changed a lot sooner, had someone simply confronted me. If someone is controlling you, don't just get angry at that person, but take responsibility and stand up to him or her. People certainly should not be controlling, but you are as guilty as they are if you allow yourself to be controlled. Even though they may get angry when you initially confront them, they will respect you in the end.

Control and manipulation drain the energy, joy, and vitality from us and suffocate our minds, wills, emotions, relational abilities, and other aspects of our lives. If we are going to choose to enjoy our lives, then we must also choose to confront the people who try to control us.

As I mentioned previously, once we have allowed people to control us for a period of time, confronting them can be very difficult. It can be hard on both the one who confronts and the one being confronted. The one confronting is not accustomed to taking a position of strength toward the controller and the controller may not like it! But the goal of confrontation is to expose the truth of the control in the relationship and then to break established relational habits and patterns. New patterns of relating to one another with mutual respect must then be developed; and that takes time and effort. The controller's fleshly nature may throw a few fits before he or she finally decides to understand and accept that the relationship must change.

The goal of confrontation is to expose the truth of the control in the relationship and then to break established relational habits and patterns.

Whether you are being controlled by a child who screams in the grocery store when you won't buy him a piece of candy, an elderly parent who tries to make you feel guilty for not doing more for them, or a boss who requires you to prioritize your job over family, you must be the one to stop the control. The controller will not do it. But with God's help, you can—and when you do, you'll find yourself with more peace, joy, and inner strength than you have ever known.

Don't allow the fear of losing a relationship cause you to submit to being controlled and manipulated. Any relationship worth having must be one of mutual love and respect. If anyone should be in control, it is God, but even He respects our right to free choice. He leads, guides, directs, and suggests, but He never forces, controls, or manipulates.

LIVE TO PLEASE GOD

Pulitzer Prize-winning journalist Herbert B. Swope said, "I cannot give you the formula for success, but I can give you the formula for failure—which is: Try to please everybody." Indeed, trying to please people leads not only to failure but to great frustration. Colossians 3:22 encourages us to seek to serve and please God in everything we do, and not to be "pleasers of men." We cannot live to please God if we seek to please other people by allowing them to control us. We

We cannot please both God and man; we cannot serve two masters.

must choose whether we will serve God or another human being. We cannot please both God and man; we cannot serve two masters. Yet, many people are trying to serve God while also keeping the people around them happy. That will not work!

The Bible addresses this subject in several places. Jesus says in John 12:42, 43,

> And yet [in spite of all this] many even of the leading men (the authorities and the nobles) believed and trusted in Him. But because of the Pharisees they did not confess it, for fear that [if they should acknowledge Him] they would be expelled from the synagogue. *For they loved the approval and the praise and the glory that come from men [instead of and] more than the glory that comes from God. [They valued their credit with men more than their credit with God]* (emphasis mine).

The apostle Paul understood that we cannot please both God and man. He wrote, "Now am I trying to win the favor of men, or of God? . . . If I were still seeking popularity with men, I should not be a bond servant of Christ (the Messiah)" (Galatians 1:10). In this verse, Paul is basically saying, "If I were a man-pleaser, if I were trying to keep everybody around me happy, I would not be an apostle of the Lord Jesus Christ. God would not be using me the way He's using me. I would not have the spiritual insight and understanding I have or be able to help people the way I do." In other words, so much of Paul's destiny would have been stolen had he tried to please people instead of God. I believe the same is true for you. God has a great plan and purpose for your life, but you will have to seek to please Him instead of catering to other people if you want to accomplish and enjoy all He has for you. The Bible does say we should live to please others, and even try to adapt ourselves to them and their opinions, but that in no way means we should disobey God in order to obey man.

I want to encourage you today to break free from people's opinions, judgments, criticisms, expectations, and thoughts of you. Do not allow others to influence your life inappropriately. Seek God, follow Him, and be true to your own heart. Care more about what God thinks than what people think, and want His will more than you want to be popular. Under the leadership of the Holy Spirit, make your own choices and live your own life.

CHAPTER

23

Cultivate Good Habits

"We are what we repeatedly do. Excellence, then, is not an act, but a habit."

—ARISTOTLE

A habit, according to *Webster's Dictionary,* is "an acquired pattern of behavior that has become almost involuntary as a result of frequent repetition." In other words, habits are things we have done so many times we can do them without thinking about them. We can have good habits—such as eating healthily, exercising regularly, paying our bills on time, keeping a clean house, or spending time in God's Word. We can also have bad habits—such as eating too much junk food, biting our fingernails, not taking proper care of our belongings, or watching television shows that promote ungodly values and principles.

Remember, habits are formed through repetition. The old saying is true, "Practice *does* make perfect." When you try to break a bad habit and develop a good one, you will have to commit to repeating your new thoughts or behaviors on a regular basis. At first, it will not be easy because you are not accustomed to it. It will need to be programmed into your attitudes and actions by virtue of doing it over and over again. That takes discipline, of course, but I can assure you, the benefits of breaking bad habits and cultivating good ones are worth the effort.

NINE HABITS OF HIGHLY EFFECTIVE CHRISTIANS

One of our responsibilities as Christians is to live in ways that cause other people to hunger for a relationship with Jesus Christ. When we do this, we are being effective as believers, we are bearing fruit in God's kingdom, and we enjoy our lives. To be successful as Christians, we need to break our bad habits and develop and maintain good ones, so for the remainder of this chapter, I will focus on nine habits of highly effective Christians.

> To be successful as Christians, we need to break our bad habits and develop and maintain good ones.

1. Make a Habit of Spending Time with God. I believe one of the very best habits a person can have is spending time with God on a regular basis. These moments with Him can include praying, reading and studying the Bible, singing or playing worship music, quietly listening for His voice, or other ways of experiencing His presence.

David, whom the Bible calls "a man after God's own heart" (see 1 Samuel 13:14), prayed and communed with God every morning. He wrote, "In the morning You hear my voice, O Lord; in the morning I prepare [a prayer, a sacrifice] for You and watch *and* wait [for You to speak to my heart]" (Psalm 5:3). As we read the book of Psalms, much of which David wrote, we see that he also prayed at noon and at night. He lived a lifestyle of continual prayer and communion with God.

When we think of prayer and spending time with God, we must remember that it is a privilege. It is not a burden or an obligation, but a great honor because it connects mere human hearts with the awesome power of God. The result of our prayers, according to James 5:16, is that "tremendous power" is made available to us.

The enemy knows the dimension of power that is released from heaven to earth when believers pray, so he does everything he can to hinder our spending time with God. He knows we become highly effective as Christians when we pray, so he tries to distract us, keep us too busy to pray, or convince us that God is not listening to our prayers. All these things are lies. Do not believe them, but make a priority of spending time in faith-filled prayer every day.

In addition to praying, we also need to set aside time to read and study the Bible. I have emphasized the importance of God's Word in this book already, so I encourage you to reread the chapters entitled "Start with God" and "Follow Directions" for more insight on the life-changing truth and power of the Word.

I want to call your attention to two specific scriptures that teach us how the Word works in our lives. Second Corinthians 3:18 says, "And all of us, as with unveiled face, [because we] continued to behold [in the Word of God] as in a mirror the glory of the Lord, are constantly being transfigured into His *very own* image in ever increasing splendor *and* from one degree of glory to another; [for this comes] from the Lord [Who is] the Spirit." In other words, because we continue to study the Word, we are constantly being changed and transformed for the better.

I also want you to remember what Jesus said in John 8:31, 32: "If you abide in My word [hold fast to My teachings and live in accordance with them], you are truly My disciples. And you will know the Truth, and the Truth will set you free." Making a habit of living by God's Word will enable you to know the truth, which will set you free from any kind of bondage that affects your life.

I repeat: One of the best habits you can ever develop is to spend time with God. Pray, read His Word, study His Word, and listen for His voice. Guard your fellowship with Him carefully and make sure it becomes a strong habit in your life. Spending time with God will increase your joy and cause you to look hopefully and expectantly at your future. In His Presence is fullness of joy (see Psalm 16:11).

Spending time with God will increase your joy and cause you to look hopefully and expectantly at your future.

2. Make a Habit of Keeping Your Conscience Clear. Nothing will keep us from enjoying life like feeling guilty all the time. In fact, Jesus died to forgive our sins and to cleanse us from guilt and condemnation. Anytime we do anything wrong and then earnestly repent, He forgives us completely and forgets about our sin. Therefore, we have no need or reason to live our lives feeling guilty.

One of the best ways to avoid a guilty conscience is to do our best to do what is right. In Acts 24:16, Paul said, "Therefore I always exercise *and* discipline myself [mortifying my body, deadening my carnal affections, bodily appetites, and worldly desires, endeavoring in all respects] to have a clear (unshaken, blameless) conscience, void of offense toward God and toward men." He did everything he could to make right choices so he did not have to endure a guilty conscience; he disciplined himself so he would not feel guilty later.

> One of the best ways to avoid a guilty conscience is to do our best to do what is right.

No one is perfect; no matter how we try to be blameless, we will sin. When we do, we must remember forgiveness is always available through Jesus Christ. If our conscience is guilty because we know we have not treated a person right, we should admit it without excuse, apologize, and ask God and the person we have offended to forgive us.

For a surefire way to keep from feeling guilty, if you can't do what you are about to do in faith (with confidence), do not do it (see Romans 14:23)! When you are full of guilt and condemnation, you cannot be effective for God, nor can you enjoy your life; but when you are walking in the confidence of forgiveness and a clear conscience, you will feel free and happy, and He will use you in amazing ways.

3. Make a Habit of Living by Faith, One Day at a Time. Some people would question whether or not faith can be a habit. They are the ones who view faith as some spiritual, ethereal dynamic reserved for monks and mystics. I believe faith can definitely be a habit because, far from being mystical, faith is extremely practical and an invaluable habit to cultivate in our everyday lives.

Simply put, faith is confidence and assurance; it is a positive attitude (which can certainly become a habit) and a basic, foundational trust in God for every aspect of life. Faith empowers us to be optimistic and hopeful about what we cannot see (see Hebrews 11:1), and it forms a habit of knowing that what we can see in the world and its circumstances are not nearly as powerful as God, Whom we do not see.

Faith is a positive view of God and His ability and willingness to help us; and faith always expects something good to happen (see Psalm 27:13, 14). Faith believes God's Word is superior to human thoughts, reasoning, or feelings, and clings to the truth of His Word, no matter what. Believing God releases joy and peace in our lives (see Romans 15:13).

Faith is a positive view of God and His ability and willingness to help us; and faith always expects something good to happen.

When we live by faith, we take life one day at a time, trusting God in everything that takes place. I like to say, "Faith today trusts God *with* yesterday and *for* tomorrow." Faith believes it will have grace for tomorrow, tomorrow.

4. Make a Habit of Doing Your Best. Andrew Carnegie, who made a fortune in the steel industry, observed, "People who are unable to motivate themselves must be content with mediocrity, no matter how impressive their other talents." I believe mediocrity is unacceptable for a Christian. We must be motivated to excellence and to our very best in whatever we do. God is an excellent God; everything He does is first-rate, and He never gives less than His best. As His representatives, we should be excellent too. Paul urges us to "learn to sense what is vital, *and* approve *and* prize what is excellent and of real value." (Philippians 1:10). As we press past mediocrity and make excellence a habit in our lives, we will sense God's joy in our lives and be good examples to the world.

One way to ensure we do our best and strive for excellence in everyday situations is to follow Matthew 7:12, which is often called "The Golden Rule": "So then, whatever you desire that others would do to *and* for you, even so do also to *and* for them." In other words, treat others as you would like to be treated. Here are some practical, everyday ways to do that:

- Don't leave messes for other people to clean up.
- Don't take the last of the coffee in the coffee pot, the paper in the copier, or the toilet tissue at home and not replace it.
- Don't park in handicapped spaces if you are not handicapped.
- Don't hit someone's car in a parking lot and fail to leave your contact information.
- Say "please" and "thank you."
- Smile.
- Don't interrupt others when they are talking unless it is an emergency.
- Don't brush crumbs off the table and onto the floor.
- Don't lie about anything.
- Don't be dishonest in any way.
- Don't take office supplies home from your workplace (pens, paper, paper clips, rubber bands, etc.)
- Don't run copies of material for your Bible study or Sunday school class on the copier at work without permission.
- If you are going to clean something, clean it thoroughly.
- Make people feel valuable.

This list could go on and on. I am sure you have a very good sense of how you like to be treated, so just remember that as you interact with other people. Everything we do is a seed we sow. We must be determined to be excellent if we want to reap an excellent harvest, which means we have to resist the temptation to live mediocre lives. If we are excellent in every way, we will be highly effective Christians.

5. Make a Habit of Handling Criticism in a Godly Way. Elbert Hubbard, an American writer, said, "The final proof of greatness lies in being able to endure [criticism] without resentment," and I believe that is true. Everyone who is truly successful in life has to deal with criticism. Sometimes criticism comes from people who do not understand what we are doing, cannot see the vision we see, or are jealous of our success. Whatever the source, criticism can be painful, but learning to deal with it in a godly way is always a great testimony to the people around us.

In Matthew 10:10–14, Jesus tells His disciples how to deal with criticism or with people who will not receive their message. His advice: "Shake it off." He says, "And whoever will not receive *and* accept *and* welcome you nor listen to your message, as you leave that house or town, shake the dust [of it] from your feet" (v. 14).

Jesus Himself was criticized frequently, and He usually ignored it (see Matthew 27:11, 12). Often, the best way to respond to criticism is to say nothing at all. When you must respond, here are a few suggestions for handling criticism in a godly way:

- Don't get defensive. Remember, God is your defense; He is your vindicator.
- Don't get angry or upset. Keep your peace, because peace brings power.
- Don't fall into the trap of pride and say, "How *dare* that person criticize me!"
- Don't retaliate with criticism toward your critic.
- Don't assume your critic is wrong without being willing to examine yourself.
- Don't assume your critic is right and start feeling guilty without consulting God.

- Forgive completely. Make a habit of forgiving quickly, before bad feelings take root in your heart.
- Thank your critics, because they may do more for you in life than those who always agree with you.

Make a habit of trusting God with your reputation. When you are criticized, respond in a way that honors Him. The Bible says only a fool hates correction, and although I believe that is true, I must say that in my life I have only known one person who I can honestly say appreciated it and it wasn't me, although I wish I could say it was. Probably like most of you I am somewhere between hating correction and loving it, but I am striving to have a positive attitude toward correction as well as everything else in life.

6. Make a Habit of Practicing Peace. Thomas á Kempis, a German priest and writer who lived around the turn of the fifteenth century, wrote, "First, keep the peace within yourself, then you can also bring peace to others." All around us, people are upset; they need peace. We need look no further than the Internet, our daily newscasts, or the break room at work to hear about people who are angry or offended. One of the qualities that sets believers apart from the world is the ability to have inner peace. Even when circumstances are difficult or frightening, or when others would feel justified in being furious, we can have peace in our hearts.

> One of the qualities that sets believers apart from the world is the ability to have inner peace.

In John 14:27, Jesus makes it clear peace is available to us: "Peace I leave with you; My [own] peace I now give *and* bequeath to you. Not as the world gives do I give to you. Do not let your hearts be troubled, neither let them be afraid. [Stop allowing yourselves to be agitated and disturbed; and do not permit yourselves to be fearful and intimidated and cowardly and unsettled.]" We see from this verse that peace is a choice. We can either allow ourselves to be "agitated and disturbed" or not. Jesus says we can permit ourselves to be fearful and unsettled—or we can choose to be at peace.

Years ago, I had a habit of getting upset about every little thing that did not go my way. I really threw fits, making myself and everyone around me miserable. Now I have made a habit of staying calm and at peace. Jesus says in Matthew 5:9, "Blessed (enjoying enviable happiness, spiritually prosperous—with life-joy and satisfaction in God's favor and salvation, regardless of their outward conditions) are the makers *and* maintainers of peace, for they shall be called the sons of God!" When we make and keep peace around us, and when we become habitually peaceful, people know we belong to God and we become very effective as believers.

7. Make a Habit of Finishing What You Start. We all need a sense of purpose and accomplishment in life. We need to know we are making progress and actually completing things when we invest our time and energy. We need to be diligent to finish what we start because that makes us trustworthy. When we begin projects or activities and then leave them undone, we end up with a sense of failure and cause other people to feel they cannot depend on us.

> We need to be careful and thoughtful before we commit to anything, making sure that when we start, we can follow through to completion.

The Bible teaches diligence, steadfastness, and determination—all of which have to do with finishing what we start. Jesus gives us great advice in the form of a question when he asks, "Which of you, wishing to build a farm building, does not first sit down and calculate the cost [to see] whether he has sufficient means to finish it?" (Luke 14:28). He goes on to say, "Otherwise, when he has laid the foundation and is unable to complete [the building], all who see it will begin to mock *and* jeer at him, saying, This man began to build and was not able (worth enough) to finish" (vv. 29, 30). Clearly, our ability to finish what we start speaks volumes to those around us. We need to be careful and thoughtful before we commit to anything, making sure that when we start, we can follow through to completion. Finishing what we start is part of being people of excellence, integrity, and effectiveness.

8. Make a Habit of Living by Discernment. There's more to life than meets the eye—especially the natural eye. Things are not always what they appear to be, so we must learn to be discerning. Simply defined, discernment is spiritual understanding, and developing it takes practice. As we grow in our understanding of God's Word and in our relationships with Him, we also grow in our ability to discern.

As we grow in our understanding of God's Word and in our relationships with Him, we also grow in our ability to discern.

To live by discernment, we have to pay attention to our hearts. We have to know when we do not feel right about something in our hearts. For example, let's say a businessman has been looking for a certain kind of business deal for quite some time and an opportunity for such a deal finally presents itself. As he reviews the paperwork, the deal appears to be sound. But when he begins to pray about entering into the deal, he senses he should not do it. Even though everything appears to be in order, he just does not have peace about the deal. The more he prays, the more he feels he should not do business with the people involved in the deal. This man is looking beyond the natural elements of the deal and using his discernment.

The best way for me to help you learn to live by discernment is to offer this simple advice: if you don't feel right about something in your heart do not do it. You may discover later why you didn't feel good about it, but you may not. Either way, you can be at peace knowing you used your discernment instead of making decisions based on your mind, your emotions, or natural circumstances.

Discernment is a precious gift from God that will help us avoid a lot of trouble in life if we pay attention to it.

9. **Make a Habit of Being Generous.** The world is full of selfish, stingy, greedy people. But God wants us to be generous. In fact, 2 Corinthians 9:7 tells us, "God loves (He takes pleasure in, prizes above other things, and is unwilling to abandon or to do without) a cheerful (joyous, 'prompt to do it') giver [whose heart is in his giving]."

Oil magnate John D. Rockefeller was one of the wealthiest men of his day, but he understood the importance of generosity, and urged others, "Think of giving not as a duty, but as a privilege." I heartily agree with that statement, and know it to be good advice. I have found few things in life to be more rewarding than helping and giving to others. Let me encourage you to become a giver and develop the habit of giving in every way you can think of. For example:

- Give help
- Give encouragement
- Give compliments
- Give money
- Give gifts
- Give yourself
- Give time
- Give your talents and abilities
- Give forgiveness

Giving makes the devil mad. He wants us to be selfish, self-centered, stingy, and greedy. People who are self-centered are some of the most miserable, unproductive people on earth, and selfish Christians are useless and unfruitful in God's kingdom. But those who give cheerfully and generously are happy, fulfilled, and highly effective.

CHAPTER 24

Let God Lead

"You don't have to see the whole staircase, just take the first step."
—MARTIN LUTHER KING JR.

I believe one of the secrets of enjoying our lives is to let God lead us instead of trying to make our own way through life. Knowing we are in partnership with God in all we do is extremely rewarding. We are limited in our understanding of what is best for us, but God knows and He will guide us. We are unable to see the future, even into next week or next year, but God can see every day of the rest of our lives. We do not know what experiences, opportunities, or skills we will need to fulfill God's plan for our lives, but He does and He gives them to us. We cannot perceive what will satisfy us and make us truly happy in life, but God knows exactly how to bless us and exactly what we need to live richly rewarding lives and to be deeply satisfied.

Let me ask you: Are you following God or trying to get Him to follow you? If we insist upon trying to make our own way and follow our human reasoning, God will allow us to do so, but we may end up unhappy. If, instead, we determine to let God lead us through every day and every situation, one step at a time, we will enjoy the fruitfulness, blessing, grace, peace, and joy that only come from following Him.

FEELINGS ARE FICKLE

Many people allow their feelings to lead them through each day. They make decisions about what to do, where to go, and who to spend time with based on how they feel. They say things like, "Well, I feel like lying on the couch all day, so that's what I'll do today," or "I don't really feel like going to work today, so I'll call in sick," or "I don't feel like visiting my grandmother in the nursing home today, so maybe I'll go next week if I feel like it." Following our feelings may offer us temporary happiness, but they will never give us permanent joy.

The problem with feelings is that they are fickle; they simply are not trustworthy. Feelings are based on emotions, and they go up and down like a roller coaster. On a Monday morning, a man can feel he will love a woman forever, but by Monday night he feels she is not giving him enough space. One week, a couple can feel they are ready to have a child, but the next week they can feel they don't want responsibility of being parents. A woman can feel she wants to dye her hair bright red when she walks into a beauty salon, but as soon as another client walks by with bright red hair, she can feel she wants to go blonde instead.

The problem with feelings is that they are fickle; they simply are not trustworthy.

Everywhere we look, people are running their lives according to their feelings! All around us, we hear the constant chorus: "I feel happy! I feel sad! I feel depressed! I feel good! I feel bad!"

"I feel, I feel, I feel" is no way to build a successful, enjoyable, productive life. Feelings and emotions are part of the soul of a person, not part of the spirit. The soul seeks to satisfy itself and its fleshly desires, but the spirit of a person longs to please God because it is where the Spirit of God dwells. God speaks to and leads us in our spirits, so we need to build up our spiritual strength instead of feeding our souls by letting our feelings guide us.

Hebrews 4:12 says, "For the Word that God speaks is alive and full of power [making it active, operative, energizing, and effective]; it is sharper than any two-edged sword, penetrating to the dividing line of the breath of life (soul) and [the immortal] spirit, and of joints and marrow [of the deepest parts of our nature], exposing *and* sifting *and* analyzing *and* judging the very thoughts and purposes of the heart." In other words, the Word of God can help us distinguish between what is carnal and fleshly, or "soulish," and what is spiritual. We need to know the difference so we can follow God and not allow our feelings to lead us.

The Word of God can help us distinguish between what is carnal and fleshly, or "soulish," and what is spiritual.

According to Galatians 5:17, "the desires of the flesh are opposed to the [Holy] Spirit, and the [desires of the] Spirit are opposed to the flesh (godless human nature); for these are antagonistic to each other [continually withstanding and in conflict with each other], *so that you are not free but are prevented from doing what you desire to do*" (emphasis mine). Following the flesh may be tempting at times, but in the end, it will actually keep you from doing what you really want to do. As you follow the Spirit of God, though, you will be free to experience and enjoy the things He knows you really long for in the depths of your heart.

Following the flesh may be tempting at times, but in the end, it will actually keep you from doing what you really want to do.

I am certainly not encouraging you to deny your feelings, because that is not healthy. I am simply urging you not to allow them to control your life or dictate your decisions. Instead, acknowledge your feelings, but realize they are merely feelings; and pray, seek God, and allow Him to be your guide.

LISTEN FOR GOD'S VOICE

God promises to lead us and guide us. He says in Isaiah 30:21, "And your ears will hear a word behind you, saying, This is the way: walk in it, when you turn to the right hand and when you turn to the left."

We need to choose to listen to God because He will speak to us. We need to quiet all the noise in our lives and become sensitive to His still, small voice. We will always have to fight the voices trying to compete with God for our obedience. Our feelings and mind-sets try to influence us; our friends and families may want to tell us what to do; the enemy whispers to our minds; the past reminds us not to make the same mistakes we made before; and the rules and regulations of the world try to convince us we must follow them. None of these voices or influences will lead us into truth and life. Only God can be trusted to say, "This is the way; walk in it." We have to tune our ears to His voice by staying in close communion with Him through prayer, Bible study, and worship so we will recognize His voice when He speaks.

Most of the time, God does not speak to us in an audible voice. We hear Him in our hearts. Sometimes He speaks by reminding us of a truth or principle from His Word; sometimes He gives us thoughts or ideas we could not have had on our own; sometimes we simply have a strong sense of knowing what to do.

God does not only speak in the urgent or important matters of life. He also guides us in the most seemingly insignificant situations. He does this because He loves us and wants to lead us in every aspect of our lives.

> God does not only speak in the urgent or important matters of life. He also guides us in the most seemingly insignificant situations.

For example, I was on my way home one day and intended to stop and get a cup of coffee, when I had a strong impression that I should call my secretary and see if she wanted a cup too. When I called, she said, "I was just standing here thinking, *I would love a good cup of coffee right now.*" You see, God wanted to give her the desire of her heart, and He wanted to work through me. I did not hear a loud voice, nor see an angel, nor did I have a vision; I simply had an inner sensing that I should offer her a cup of coffee. As a result, we both experienced great joy in knowing God cares about the smallest details of our lives.

Quite often we ignore little things like this. The more we do, the harder it is to develop sensitivity to the Holy Spirit. Had I ignored the prompting in my heart, the worst thing that could have happened would have been for her to say she did not want any coffee. In that case, she would have had the blessing of knowing I was thinking of her. If someone is on your heart, I encourage you to pray for that person or call him or her and say, "I was just thinking of you." You never know how a seemingly small thing like a phone call can alter a person's day or maybe even change someone's life. Let me encourage you today to keep your heart sensitive to God's voice. He will speak to your heart and lead you in the way you should go. Do not let disobedience, distractions, or the noise and busy pace of the world cause you to miss His voice when He speaks, but stay quiet and peaceful on the inside so you can hear Him when He speaks to you. Remember this: Each time we disobey God, it becomes more difficult to hear Him the next time He speaks; but every time we obey Him, it gets easier to hear and be led by His Spirit.

LOOK FOR GRACE

In the Old Testament, Joshua had the job of leading God's people, the Israelites, into the Promised Land. The priests of that day carried the ark, which carried and represented God's presence, at the head of the procession, and all the people followed it. In Joshua 3:2, 3 we read, "After three days the officers went through the camp, commanding the people: When you see the ark of the covenant of the Lord your God being borne by the Levitical priests, set out from where you are and follow it."

The officers' command to the people to follow the ark is similar to my message to you in this chapter. Just as they encouraged the people to follow God's presence, I encourage you to follow God.

You may have a heart to follow God, but you are not sure how to do it. One way is to listen for Him to speak to your heart, as I have written already. Another way is to follow peace. Only God can give you peace in your heart, so always check your heart when you are trying to make a decision. Don't do anything that leaves you restless or unsure in your heart. Wait until you reach a decision that brings peace, and then you can move forward in confidence.

A third way to follow God is to look for His grace upon a situation, an endeavor, or a decision. When God's grace is upon something, it comes easily to us and we can trust that He approves of it. Grace is God's ability coming to us and enabling us to do something with relative ease. The project we are attempting may require effort on our part, but it is not a great struggle and we are filled with the confidence that it can be done. If God's grace is not present, everything is difficult and frustrating. It is like trying to operate a rusty machine that has not been oiled in years. I remember all the years I tried to change myself and the more I tried the more frustrated I became. I failed to pray and ask God to do it by His grace. He promises to give us more and more grace to help us overcome all of our evil tendencies if we will ask Him instead of striving to do it ourselves (see James 4:6).

Grace is God's ability coming to us and enabling us to do something with relative ease.

Having grace does not remove all the obstacles from our way or cause all the challenges to disappear. We may still need to fight some battles, but we do so with the clear sense that God is on our side, winning the battle for us. When God's grace is on something and we are following Him, the impossible is made possible through the power of the Holy Spirit.

After many years, I have learned when God's grace is present and when it is not. I am finished trying to accomplish anything without God's grace. I do not want to struggle anymore, and I am sure you don't either.

Sometimes we want other people to do things God has not given them grace to do. Just because we think people should do certain things does not mean God wants them to do those things. When I try to force Dave to do something he does not have God's grace to do, all it does is cause strife between us. The right thing for me to do is pray, "God, if this is what You want, I ask You to convince Dave and give him grace for it."

Sometimes, everything about a situation seems right to me, but there does not seem to be the grace—the supernatural ability—to accomplish it at that time. Part of following God is to work with His timing and to sense not only His grace to accomplish something, but His grace for the right moment in which to do it. In these situations, I pray, "God, I believe this is the right thing to do, but the timing just isn't working out. Show me when the time is right."

I used to do everything in my own timing, whenever I felt it was right. If I felt like making a comment to someone, I made it. If I wanted to talk about a matter with Dave at a particular time, I forced the conversation right that minute.

But I have learned now to be more sensitive to the Holy Spirit's leading. I look for His grace not only in situations but also in timing. Sometimes I can sense in my heart to simply wait a few moments, hours, days, or weeks. I do not always understand why I need to wait; I simply know in my heart I need to delay my words or actions until I feel free to speak or act.

Learn to follow God by looking for His grace in the matters of your everyday life. Watch to see where He is helping you, speaking to you, fighting for you, and making things easy for you.

Learn to follow God by looking for His grace in the matters of your everyday life. Watch to see where He is helping you, speaking to you, fighting for you, and making things easy for you. Wherever He makes the impossible possible, wherever His supernatural abilities are evident in your natural circumstances, His grace is there.

CHOOSE TO FOLLOW

Psalm 32:8, 9 issues a clear call for us to choose to follow God: "I [the Lord] will instruct you and teach you in the way you should go; I will counsel you with My eye upon you. Be not like the horse or the mule, which lack understanding, which must have their mouths held firm with bit and bridle, or else they will not come with you." In these verses, God makes plain His desire to lead and guide us, but He also tells us not to be stubborn. We need to follow Him willingly and joyfully.

We read a similar scripture in Isaiah 30:15, 16: "For thus said the Lord God, the Holy One of Israel: In returning [to Me] . . . you shall be saved; in quietness and in [trusting] confidence shall be your strength. But you would not, and you said, No! We will speed [our own course] on horses! Therefore you will speed [in flight from your enemies]! You said, We will ride upon swift steeds [doing our own way]! Therefore will they who pursue you be swift." Here, God is saying, basically, "I tried to lead you. I told you which way to go. I told you what to do—and you would not do it. You insisted upon going your own way!" As a result, the people's enemies pursued them swiftly. That's what happens when we choose to go our own way instead of following God.

I worked at a church in St. Louis for five years. I really liked my job there, but the time came when God wanted me to move on to something new. He said to me, *Now I want you to take this ministry and go north, south, east, and west. I don't need you here anymore. I want you to leave this place.*

Now that place was where my ministry started. I had a fulfilling job, a regular paycheck, and my name on my office door. But God said, *I'm finished with you here.*

How can that be? I wondered. *After all, I'm a pillar of this church. How can the place run without me?*

I continued to work at the church for a full year after God told me to leave, and that year was absolutely miserable. I did not understand why I was so unhappy, why there seemed to be no grace to do what I had had great grace to do in previous years.

Finally, one morning, I cried out to God, "God, what is wrong?"

He spoke to my heart, *Joyce, I told you a year ago to leave and you're still here.* That was all He said.

God will not force us to follow Him. He gives us the gift of choice, so we can decide whether or not we will obey His leading. He will speak; He will lead; He will guide: He will make His plans and desires clear. But He will not force His will on us; we must consciously and deliberately choose to follow Him.

God will not force us to follow Him. He gives us the gift of choice, so we can decide whether or not we will obey His leading.

CHAPTER

25

Expect Abundance

"Not what we have, but what we enjoy, constitutes our abundance."

—JOHN PETIT-SENN

God is a God of abundance. According to Ephesians 3:20, He "is able to [carry out His purpose and] do superabundantly, far over *and* above all that we [dare] ask or think [infinitely beyond our highest prayers, desires, thoughts, hopes, or dreams]." Remember, one of the reasons Jesus came to earth was for us to "have and enjoy life, *and have it in abundance* (to the full, till it overflows)" (John 10:10, emphasis mine). We receive the promises of God through believing them, so make sure you believe for abundance in your life.

One of the keys to enjoying life is understanding that God loves us unconditionally and wants to bless us abundantly. We will never enjoy our lives if we try to earn His affection and favor. His goodness simply isn't for sale; it only comes to us as a gift—free and undeserved. We cannot earn God's love, grace, forgiveness, provision, or kindness; these gifts can only be received by faith. Perhaps you have heard the old saying, "Grace is God's riches at Christ's expense." It's true; Jesus, through His death on the cross, paid every debt we could ever owe. We do not have to struggle, strive, or try to earn or "buy" anything from God. His gifts are free. Salvation is free. Grace is free. Favor is free. Mercy is free. Forgiveness is free. We simply have to learn to receive what has already been purchased for us and now belongs to us.

GETTING OR RECEIVING?

We often ask people if they "got" something, particularly when we speak of spiritual matters. "Did you 'get' a breakthrough?" we want to know, or "Did you 'get' your blessing?" I don't believe the idea of "getting" from God is biblical. Let me explain.

The Bible teaches us about *receiving*, not about getting. "What's the difference?" you wonder. Well, the difference between getting and receiving is significant. To "get" means "to obtain by struggle and effort." I assure you, if the things you have came to you through struggle and an effort, then you are not enjoying life.

When everything in your life requires effort, life becomes frustrating and exhausting—and that's not the kind of abundant life Jesus came to give us. No, God wants us to live with a holy ease, a grace that keeps us from striving and struggling through life. That doesn't mean everything will be easy, but it means even difficult things can be done with a sense of God's presence and help.

When everything in your life requires effort, life becomes frustrating and exhausting—and that's not the kind of abundant life Jesus came to give us.

"Getting" puts the burden on us to have to figure out things, to manipulate circumstances, and to try to force situations to work out a certain way. Receiving, on the other hand, means we act as receptacles and simply take in what is being offered freely. We don't strive; we simply relax and enjoy what comes to us.

I usually take time in my conferences to teach people how to "receive" from God rather than struggling to "get" their needs met. I tell them to relax and take time to take in by faith what they have asked God for and then believe they have it—and it will manifest in their lives. Many people do not know how to receive from other people or how to receive from God. I'm sure you know people who struggle with receiving. They refuse help; they do not want anyone to do anything nice for them; and they are embarrassed when people try to help or extend kindness to them.

The inability to receive is often rooted in insecurity and a poor self-image. The other day, I offered something to eat to a teenager who was visiting with someone else and invited him to sit down and watch a television program with me. I knew he was hungry and would enjoy the time with me, yet he responded by saying, "No, I'm all right." I had to tell him at least three times that he was welcome to eat and sit with me and that I would enjoy his company. Finally he said, "Well, I am a little hungry and I'll probably come in after a while and watch television."

This particular young man has a history of insecurity and is therefore unable to readily believe people would want to do something nice for him. He does not want to appear needy and prefers to act as if he has no needs and requires no help.

God wants to give us so much more than we can imagine. He is waiting to pour out blessings in our lives, and we need to know how to receive—both from Him and from others. Sometimes God works miraculously to meet our needs, but He frequently works through other people. If we pray for help, then we must let God choose how and through whom He will send it. We should not be embarrassed to be needy, because we are all needy in some way or another. God did not intend for us to be so independent that we would never need help.

> God wants to give us so much more than we can imagine.

BEGGARS OR BELIEVERS?

One way to learn to receive is to simply believe God wants to bless us abundantly, not because we think we deserve to be blessed, but because He is a good, generous, loving God. Many times, we relate to Him as beggars instead of believers. Instead of believing He is good and wants to bless us, we start begging Him to give us something or do something for us. God's Word says we should come boldly to His throne of grace and receive the help we need (see Hebrews 4:16).

Many times, God wants to give us exactly what we are asking for and more, but it does not happen because we do not know how to receive it. I have known many people who ask God to forgive them and then never receive the forgiveness He so freely offers. Sometimes they go on for years saying, "Oh God, forgive me. God, forgive me. God, please forgive me. Forgive me, God. Forgive me. Forgive me." The truth is they are forgiven! Forgiveness belongs to every believer. Jesus paid for our forgiveness with His life. We do not have to beg for it; we simply have to trust the work of the Cross, believe it belongs to us, and begin to say from our hearts, "Lord, I thank You for Your forgiveness. I receive Your forgiveness as a gift."

Many times, God wants to give us exactly what we are asking for and more, but it does not happen because we do not know how to receive it.

Learning to receive from God was one of the keys that released joy in my own life. Jesus said, "Ask and receive that your joy might be full" (see John 16:24). Years ago, I realized I was asking God for so much I was not receiving because I had fearfully developed the attitude of a beggar instead of the attitude of a believer. The world teaches us, "There's no such thing as a free lunch." We are trained to believe we must earn, deserve, or pay for everything we want. We realize we are sinners who have been forgiven and restored to fellowship with God through His grace and mercy. We know we do not deserve anything except punishment, but our minds must be renewed to believe that God is merciful and that the very nature of mercy gives blessings when punishment is deserved.

Thinking we must work for or deserve God's blessings is a very religious attitude. It is "stinking thinking" at its best! Legalistic, religious people think we need to earn everything—just as the Pharisees thought in Jesus' day. They did not want anyone to have anything he or she did not deserve. When Jesus healed a man who had been born blind (see John 9), they were furious because they did not think he deserved to be healed. This kind of attitude does not reflect God's heart of grace and compassion; it is religious and offensive to Him.

> Thinking we must work for or deserve God's blessings is a very religious attitude. It is "stinking thinking" at its best!

Many years ago, I had a neighbor friend I did not consider to be nearly as spiritual as I was. In those days, I thought true spirituality consisted of good works, rules, and regulations, and doing everything perfectly. My friend did not attend church as often as I did; she didn't give as much; she didn't pray as much; she didn't do anything I considered "spiritual" as often or as well as I thought I did.

The problem was, I was doing all of my "spiritual" activities with wrong motives. I did them to impress people, not out of pure obedience to God or out of love for Him. I didn't understand that if my neighbor did just one tiny thing out of pure-hearted love and obedience to God, her one little bit meant more to the Lord than the large number of things I did with bad motives.

At that time, I was asking and believing God to give me a fur coat. I prayed and prayed and had my faith worked up for a fur coat. I was sure God would give me one—because, after all, I was extremely spiritual! Please keep in mind, the last thing I really needed was a fur coat, but at that time I usually asked God for material things because I was not mature enough to know what was really important in life.

One day my doorbell rang, and I answered it to see my neighbor standing there brimming with excitement, holding an enormous box in her arms. "You won't *believe* what God gave *me*!" she exclaimed.

She went on to explain that a mutual friend of ours dropped off the box and said to her, "God told me to give this to you."

I wondered what it could possibly be. Then she opened the box, and in it was *my fur coat!*

I clearly remember thinking, *That lady delivered that box to the wrong house. She meant to bring that coat to me!* Of course, I tried to give a "spiritual" response: "Well, praise the Lord," I said. "Glory to God. I'm *so* happy for you!"

In my heart, I was saying, *God, You've got to get her out of my house—now!* I was seething inside with anger and jealousy. I was furious with God, saying silently, *How could You possibly give her that fur coat? With the way she acts, how could You? This is not fair! I am so spiritual and she is not. This is not right! What about me?*

I really thought I deserved a fur coat and my neighbor did not. I did not understand God's love and grace or I did not know that perhaps He was wooing my neighbor into deeper relationship with Him through His kindness. I did not realize He simply wanted to let her know He loved her. For me, it was all about earning His blessings. But that's just not the way it works with the God who loves us. I also firmly believe God gave her the coat to teach me a lesson I had to learn in order to go forward with His plan for my life. I needed an attitude change much more than I needed a fur coat.

When we try to "buy" from God with our good works what He wants to give us freely, He sometimes withholds those things until we learn how to receive by faith. We have to learn how to receive and to receive *freely* from God and to know we do not always have to deserve everything He wants to give us. The Bible tells us God's kindness is what leads us into relationship with Him (see Romans 2:4). He does not have to have a reason to bless us. His love for us is reason enough.

When we try to "buy" from God with our good works what He wants to give us freely, He sometimes withholds those things until we learn how to receive by faith.

LIKE CHILDREN

I believe with all my heart that God wants to do so much more for us than we can even begin to imagine. The reason we do not always experience everything He wants to give us is we really do not know how to receive from Him the way He wants us to receive from Him. Jesus teaches us the secret of receiving properly in Luke 18:17: "Truly I say to you, whoever does not accept *and* receive *and* welcome the kingdom of God like a little child [does] shall not in any way enter it [at all]."

This verse does not say "whoever does not 'get' the kingdom of God." I want to emphasize this because we need to understand how important the difference is between getting and receiving. We need a new mind-set toward God's blessings—one that can relax and receive from Him as little children do, not one that thinks we must strive to earn His goodness.

If I were to walk into a Sunday school class for kindergarteners at my church and start handing one-dollar bills to the children, saying, "This is for you, this is for you, and this is for you," how do you think they would respond? I have done this with children in my conferences before and I guarantee you, they have no problem receiving the money! Their faces break into enormous smiles; some even laugh aloud, but they all keep looking at me expectantly to see if I will give away anything else!

I have never had a child look at me suspiciously or say, "No thanks, Joyce, I don't deserve this dollar." Not one of those children has ever said, "I was not good this week. I can't take that." Giving the children money provokes joy in them. Why? Because I offer them something they didn't earn and they know they don't deserve. They take the bills gladly! I have no good reason for giving children dollar bills, but something happens when I do: I end up with better relationships with those children.

The same dynamic is at work in our relationships with God. He wants to be good to us. More than that, He wants a good relationship with us. He does not want us to try to perform to earn His blessings; He simply wants our love. He does things for us because He loves us, and He wants us to do what we do for Him from the same motive. Never do anything for God except out of pure love and obedience to His Word. We should not love God or even obey Him in order to get Him to do things for us. We love Him because He first loved us, and because His goodness and mercy amaze us. It is the goodness of God that leads men to repentance (see Romans 2:4), and I believe it is His goodness that draws us into a deeper and more intimate relationship with Him than we could ever imagine.

We must be as innocent and trusting as little children are if we want to experience the good life available to us in God's kingdom. We must "welcome and accept" His kindness as little children accept gifts and not feel we have to be good enough to be blessed.

We must be as innocent and trusting as little children are if we want to experience the good life available to us in God's kingdom.

YOU DON'T HAVE TO DO EVERYTHING RIGHT

Many years ago, God kept leading me to read Matthew chapter 12 and I could not understand why. In this chapter, Jesus' disciples were walking through grain fields picking and eating spikes of grain because they were hungry. The Pharisees were outraged, because they said it was illegal to eat from the fields on the Sabbath day. Jesus responded by reminding them that David and his men actually ate bread from God's house when they were hungry and the priests in the temple often violated the Sabbath and were guiltless (see vv. 3–5).

When I read those words, my mind went "tilt." How could someone do something wrong and be guiltless? I just didn't understand. But Jesus went on to say to the Pharisees, "If you had only known what this saying means, I desire mercy [readiness to help, to spare, to forgive] rather than sacrifice *and* sacrificial victims, you would not have condemned the guiltless" (v. 7).

The best way I can explain this principle is to share with you the example God gave me when I was trying to understand it. He reminded me of a time when our youngest son, Danny, was about ten years old. He was a wonderful, fun-loving, affectionate young man, but he was not very disciplined or interested in work; he just wanted to have a good time. He really enjoyed life, and that upset me because I was more inclined toward working all the time.

To help Danny develop discipline, Dave and I made a list of chores we expected him to do and taped it on his bedroom door. When he did his chores, he received check marks and when he had enough check marks he received stars, and when he had enough stars, he could have a present.

During this same period in Danny's life, he was often the target of our neighborhood bully. That mean boy often took Danny's ball away from him and threw it in the sewer, and as a result, Dave and I frequently heard Danny screaming, "Daddy!!"

Dave had no patience for the bully and the way he picked on Danny. One day, Danny called for him and Dave raced out the door and began chasing the bully down our street, yelling, "You leave my son alone!" He scared that bully to the point he never bothered Danny again!

As God was helping me understand what it means to desire mercy instead of sacrifice, He brought this scene to my mind and said to my heart, *What kind of parents would you and Dave be if Dave said, "Joyce, I hear our son screaming for help. Run downstairs and check his chart. See how he's done with his chores this week. If he has enough check marks, I'll help him; if not, he's on his own"?*

The Lord showed me that, of course, Dave would help Danny. If he found out Danny had not done his chores, he would deal with him later, but he certainly would not refuse to help him when he was in trouble. The message God was trying to communicate to me was that when I made mistakes, He didn't want me to try to earn His mercy with good works or "perfect" behavior; He wanted to give me mercy. He would deal with me about my weaknesses later; He would help me and would teach me, and I would grow, but the fact that I had shortcomings would not keep him from loving or helping me.

You see, you don't have to wait until you think you are perfect for God to help you. You don't have to wait until you do everything right for God to be merciful to you or to bless you. Even on your worst days, you can still pray and God will still help you because He is a God of mercy and grace. He wants to give you favor, and favor means He will do things for you when you don't deserve them. He's a good Father, a loving, merciful, gracious God who longs to be good to you if you will just receive it.

> You don't have to wait until you do everything right for God to be merciful to you or to bless you.

RECEIVE AND ENJOY

I really want you to be free to receive and enjoy the abundance God has for you. Jesus says in John 16:24, "Up to this time you have not asked a [single] thing in My name [as presenting all that I AM]; but now ask *and* keep on asking and you will receive, so that your joy (gladness, delight) may be full *and* complete." Notice the progression in this verse: *ask*—in Jesus' name, based on His merits, not your own works; *receive*; *have joy*. It's very simple.

I encourage you to begin living like a "receiver" by approaching God with faith in His goodness and in what He has done for you. You might begin to pray in the following ways: "God, I ask You to forgive my sins, and I receive that forgiveness right now. I believe You have given it to me. You keep Your word, and I take Your forgiveness right now and I call myself free." Or, "God, I need mercy. I don't deserve Your help in this situation, but I'm asking You to be merciful to me,

God, and bless me anyway. Even though I haven't earned it, God, I'm asking You to bless me anyway, and God, I receive it right now. I receive Your help. I receive Your blessings. I receive Your favor. I'm asking You, God, to bless me because You are good, not because I'm good—but because *You* are good."

When you begin to approach God this way, it will provoke you to praise Him like never before. I cannot even count how many times a day I say, "Thank You, Lord, for all Your goodness in my life." Once I learned to receive from God rather than feeling I had to deserve everything I got, my blessings increased dramatically. The increase in blessing has brought an increase in praise. I see so many things for which I can be thankful that it has helped me to stop complaining so much. My heart overflows with the thought, *God, You are soooooooo good!* But in order to say that, I had to experience His goodness in my life, and for that to happen, I had to learn how to receive.

You will see major changes take place in your life as you learn to receive from God. He wants to bless you more than you could ever imagine. You belong to Him; everything He has belongs to you by virtue of your personal relationship with Him through faith in His Son. Everything He has is yours, and Jesus purchased your right to enjoy it when He died on the cross and was resurrected from the dead. He paid the debt you owed as a sinner and opened the way for you to have an unreserved approach to God's throne of grace (see Ephesians 3:12).

> You will see major changes take place in your life as you learn to receive from God. He wants to bless you more than you could ever imagine.

My goal in this book is to help you enjoy your everyday life, and you really cannot enjoy your life the way God wants you to without learning to live in a receiving mode—not with a getting mentality. Unless you learn to receive from Him, you will miss a lot of things He wants you to have and a lot of things He wants to do for you simply because you have a religious mentality that makes you think you have to earn and deserve everything. This kind of thinking is deeply ingrained in people, so you will have to renew your mind on God's Word to develop a godly, faith-filled perspective toward the abundance God wants to give you. From now on when you ask God for anything, I encourage you to follow your request by saying, "I receive it from You now, Father . . . Thank You!"

CHAPTER 26

Practice Discipline

"Discipline is the soul of an army. It makes small numbers formidable, procures success to the weak, and esteem to all."

—GEORGE WASHINGTON

The very thought of being disciplined makes some people cringe, but I believe discipline is one of the most important character traits a person can have. The Bible states that the love of Christ constrains us (see 2 Corinthians 5:14). In other words, we discipline ourselves not to earn God's blessings, but because we love Him. Without discipline, we miss much of the enjoyment life has to offer, but when we discipline ourselves and live disciplined lives, we have the time, energy, and resources to enjoy today and embrace tomorrow. In general, I believe disciplined people feel better about themselves than those who are undisciplined.

When I think of undisciplined people, I think of those who want "the perks without the works." In other words, they want all the benefits life has to offer, but they do not want to do the work or make the effort required to gain those advantages. Then, they often become jealous of those who do enjoy life's blessings, not realizing that they were the ones willing to make the investments and exercise the discipline needed for those perks.

All kinds of blessings are available to you, and I do not want you to miss a single one through lack of discipline. If you consider yourself a disciplined person, this chapter can help you improve and expand your good habits. If you are a person who rolls your eyes at the thought of being disciplined, I challenge you to adopt a new attitude right now. Don't see discipline as difficult, but look at it as a means to blessing, peace, fun, and great enjoyment in life. Don't see discipline as an enemy, but as a good friend who will help you be what God wants you to be and do what He wants you to do. God has actually given us a spirit of discipline (see 2 Timothy 1:7), but we must choose whether to use it or not.

Don't see discipline as an enemy, but as a good friend who will help you be what God wants you to be and do what He wants you to do.

WHAT DO YOU MEAN, "I CAN'T RESIST"?

Let's say you really like ice cream—to the point you have a weakness for it. When asked about ice cream, you respond, "Oh, I love ice cream. I just can't say no to a big scoop of ice cream!"

In that case, I would respond, "Yes, you can."

And you would say, "Oh, no I can't. I love ice cream too much."

I would then proceed to prove to you that you could indeed pass up an opportunity to eat ice cream.

Imagine yourself in the largest ice cream parlor in the world. They have every flavor known to man—even flavors you never even imagined. The clerk behind the counter asks, "What would you like? Just name it and I will make it for you."

You place your order, and soon, the clerk hands you the biggest, creamiest, most delicious-looking ice cream treat you have ever seen.

Now, I ask you again, "Can you put down that ice cream? Can you discipline yourself not to eat it?"

"Heavens no!" you reply. "That would be torture!"

Just as you are about to take your first bite of ice cream bliss, you hear a click. You then feel a cold, metal object touch your head. Out of the corner of your left eye, you see a large hand holding a gun. A deep voice says, "If you eat that ice cream, I will shoot you."

Now, let me ask you again, "Can you pass up that ice cream?"

Of course, my story is fictitious and far-fetched, but I am sure you see my point. You can discipline yourself to say no if you understand the consequences of not doing so.

The consequences of certain actions, or failure to take actions, lead to misery and death, both in this life and in the life to come. For example, Romans 6:23 clearly states that the consequence of sin is death. Romans 8:6 tells us that allowing our minds to be undisciplined also leads to death: "Now the mind of the flesh [which is sense and reason without the Holy Spirit] is death [death that comprises all the miseries arising from sin both here and hereafter]."

Do you believe there are certain temptations in life you cannot resist? First Corinthians 10:13 says that's not true: "For no temptation (no trial regarded as enticing to sin, no matter how it comes or where it leads) has overtaken you *and* laid hold on you that is not common to man [that is, no temptation or trial has come to you that is beyond human resistance and that is not adjusted and adapted and belonging to human experience, and such as man can bear]."

> You have the strength to resist and the power to overcome whatever comes your way. You can withstand it and have the discipline needed to bear it patiently.

You have the strength to resist and the power to overcome whatever comes your way. You can withstand it and have the discipline needed to bear it patiently.

CHARACTERISTICS OF THE DISCIPLINED

Over the years, I have observed that the disciplined people I know have a number of characteristics in common. If you will make the effort to incorporate these positive traits in your life, you will become a more disciplined person:

- Disciplined people always go "the extra mile" (see Matthew 25:1–10).
- Disciplined people don't take shortcuts, and they do more than is necessary to "just get by."
- Disciplined people don't expect to reap where they have not sown or hope others will do their work for them.
- Disciplined people are prepared when doors of opportunity open.
- Disciplined people never take the easy way or the path of least resistance. They stay on the narrow path that leads to life and all its perks (see Matthew 7:13, 14). Even though the narrow path is more difficult, they choose to walk it.
- Disciplined people are investors, not gamblers. To gamble, according to the dictionary, is "to play a game of chance; to take a risk hoping to gain an advantage that would be much greater than what was put into the game." To invest, in contrast, is "to commit in order to gain a future profit; to give up something now for future benefits."
- Disciplined people know how to say no to others and to themselves. Jewish theologian and philosopher Abraham J. Heschel said, "Self-respect is the fruit of discipline, the sense of dignity grows with the ability to say no to oneself."

As people who want to enjoy our lives today and be strong and healthy for the future, we need discipline in many areas of our lives. This includes: our eating and exercise habits; our sexual lives; the way we view and handle money and possessions; the way we use our time; our thoughts, words, and emotions; our ability to respond to criticism properly and endure suffering.

DISCIPLINE BEARS GOOD FRUIT

The apostle Paul clearly understood the importance of discipline, and wrote about it in 1 Corinthians 9:24–27:

> Do you not know that in a race all the runners compete, but [only] one receives the prize? So run [your race] that you may lay hold [of the prize] *and* make it yours. Now every athlete who goes into training conducts himself temperately *and* restricts himself in all things. They do it to win a wreath that will soon wither, but we [do it to receive a crown of eternal blessedness] that cannot wither. Therefore I do not run uncertainly (without definite aim). I do not box like one beating the air *and* striking without an adversary. But [like a boxer] I buffet my body [handle it roughly, discipline it by hardships] and subdue it, for fear that after proclaiming to others the Gospel *and* things pertaining to it, I myself should become unfit [not stand the test, be unapproved and rejected as a counterfeit].

I have never heard anyone say discipline is easy, but the point is not ease; it's results. Hebrews 12:11 says, "For the time being no discipline brings joy, but seems grievous *and* painful; but afterwards it yields a peaceable fruit of righteousness to those who have been trained by it [a harvest of fruit which consists in righteousness—in conformity to God's will in purpose, thought, and action, resulting in right living and right standing with God]."

> When discipline is sown, like a good seed, it yields a harvest of things that fulfill and satisfy us—things that make us happy and release peace and joy in our lives.

Discipline is something we do for ourselves; it does not bring immediate joy or results, but later on, it yields good fruit to those who submit to it. As the writer of Hebrews asserts, discipline trains us. It is a tool for us to use for our good—not a taskmaster for us to resent or despise. It produces good fruit and brings about healthy, positive results. When discipline is sown, like a good seed, it yields a harvest of things that fulfill and satisfy us—things that make us happy and release peace and joy in our lives.

DISCIPLINE IS AN ACT OF LOVE

I want you to understand that discipline is a way of demonstrating love. It's a way God expresses His love for us and a way we communicate love to our children. By disciplining ourselves we show love to ourselves and prove our love for God.

Throughout His Word, God plainly states that He disciplines us for one reason: because He loves us. Hebrews 12:6–10 says, "For the Lord corrects *and* disciplines everyone whom He loves. . . . You must submit to *and* endure [correction] for discipline; God is dealing with you as with sons. . . . He disciplines us for our certain good." We need to receive God's discipline as an expression of His love, and according to Revelation 3:19, to actually receive it with enthusiasm: "Those whom I [dearly and tenderly] love, I tell their faults and convict *and* convince *and* reprove and chasten [I discipline and instruct them]. So be enthusiastic *and* in earnest *and* burning with zeal and repent [changing your mind and attitude]."

Just as God disciplines us because we are His children, natural parents need to discipline their sons and daughters. Hebrews 12:7, 8 makes a clear connection between discipline and parenting: "For what son is there whom his father does not [thus] train *and* correct *and* discipline? Now if you are exempt from correction *and* left without discipline in which all [of God's children] share, then you are illegitimate offspring *and* not true sons [at all]." Most child-raising experts say that deep down children really want and need to be disciplined, even though they often resist the process. Parents who want to raise their children in the ways of God will take the effort to discipline their sons and daughters, and their efforts will bring positive results in the days to come. Undisciplined parents raise undisciplined children, but disciplined parents raise disciplined children who will bear good fruit as they continue to grow.

Just as God reveals His love to us in part through His discipline and parents express love by disciplining their children, our willingness to discipline ourselves indicates a healthy love and respect for ourselves. Imposing discipline on ourselves shows we are serious about being the best we can be and meeting our full potential. It also proves we are serious about enjoying every moment of our lives and being prepared for the future. A lack of personal discipline, on the other hand, reveals we are satisfied with mediocrity and willing to be content with whatever we can have without effort or inconvenience.

Finally, I want to point out that one way we demonstrate our love for God is through disciplining ourselves. In John 21:15–17, Jesus asked Peter three times if he really loved Him. Peter answered yes all three times and finally said, "You know that I love You." Then Jesus said, "Feed My sheep." In other words, "If you love Me, then help other people." It requires discipline to choose to live in such a way that we are regularly helping other people.

One way we demonstrate our love for God is through disciplining ourselves.

DISCIPLINE BRINGS FREEDOM

I once read the following definition of *discipline*: "a state of order maintained by training and control; a system of regulations for conduct; systematic training, especially of the mind or character, order, efficiency, or obedience."

Notice that discipline is a state *maintained* by continual diligence. A one-time effort is not discipline. We cannot only gain discipline for a few days or weeks; we must maintain it over the long term. The apostle Paul understood this, and wrote, "Stand fast then, and do not be hampered *and* held ensnared *and* submit again to a yoke of slavery [which you have once put off]" (Galatians 5:1).

At Joyce Meyer Ministries, we want to be excellent in every way, and we set very high standards for our employees. Sometimes, people feel we have too many rules and regulations when they first come to work for us. But, over time, many of our employees have come to me after working for us for a year or so and said, "Thank you for making me an excellent person. I never realized how wonderful it could be to know I am doing my best in everything I do, rather than simply 'getting by.'"

People can exist and be undisciplined, but they will never have the good life Jesus intends for them. Some people will always resist discipline because it imposes restrictions and restraints, but it actually leads to great freedom. I challenge you to find out for yourself! Choose one area of your life in need of discipline and commit yourself to applying it. No matter how difficult it is at first, keep at it. It is not what we do right once that produces good results in our life, but it is what we do consistently. Remember the familiar saying, "No pain, no gain!" Don't be afraid of the discomfort of discipline. No one has ever died from discipline, but through discipline multitudes have learned to truly live.

Some people will always resist discipline because it imposes restrictions and restraints, but it actually leads to great freedom.

DISCIPLINE PAYS DIVIDENDS

Although discipline can be difficult, it also eventually pays dividends. For example, I have always taken good care of my skin. I never go to bed with makeup on. I always cleanse my face and use various lotions and skin products to keep it in good condition. I have done that all of my life and people tell me all the time that my skin looks amazing for my age. I enjoy the compliments, but I also had to be willing to discipline myself.

Another example is how my husband Dave has exercised since he was sixteen years old and has enjoyed good health and an abundance of energy throughout his life. His body is not sagging like those of many people his age, because he paid the price of discipline and is now reaping dividends.

Our ministry has no debt and we have never paid any interest on anything because we save money and pay cash for what we need. That frequently means we have to discipline ourselves to wait to purchase something we would like to have right now. I am not saying it is wrong to borrow money, but I think anyone would agree it is better not to be in debt. A lot of the debt load in our society today could be avoided if people were simply willing to discipline themselves to wait and save. Most of us want what we want when we want it, but disciplined people say no to themselves.

When we sacrifice and save money for something we would like to have we really appreciate it when we get it. We enjoy it more because there is no debt attached to it.

I did not discipline myself when it came to scheduling my time, and more than once I became sick due to excess stress and pressure. I blamed it on everything imaginable, but finally had to face the truth that I needed to start saying no to many things. When I did change it required discipline because the fact was I wanted to do everything. I wanted to be involved in everything and know everything!

Not only does discipline pay dividends, but so does a lack of discipline. One is a dividend we enjoy, and the other is one we do not enjoy. I do enjoy having nice skin, but I did not enjoy the dividend of being tired, being stressed out, or having headaches, stomach problems, and hormone imbalances. I believe some of you reading this book have been reaping some dividends you don't like either, but the good news is you can change your dividends by changing your choices.

RESULTS OF AN UNDISCIPLINED LIFE

A lack of discipline never leads to anything good. While it may sound fun for a while, it ultimately leads to frustration and self-loathing. When we are disciplined, we gain self-respect; and when we are not, we don't feel good about ourselves for very long and we end up with problems.

When we are disciplined, we gain self-respect; and when we are not, we don't feel good about ourselves for very long and we end up with problems.

- If we do not take care of our bodies, we will eventually be sick. Prolonged lack of discipline and inattention to our health can even affect our lifestyles and prohibit our doing activities we enjoy.
- If we do not discipline ourselves in financial matters, we will end up with problems so serious we cannot hide them, and we may not be able to overcome them without taking very drastic measures.
- Failure to discipline ourselves in relationships—how we speak, act, and treat people—will result in the loss of those relationships.
- If we do not discipline ourselves in our work—arriving on time, taking only allowed break times, respecting company policies, and being productive—we will eventually lose our jobs.

WHAT ABOUT YOU?

I want to close this chapter with some questions for you. I encourage you to answer them honestly and use the answers to show you where you need to be more disciplined in your life. Remember, be enthusiastic about discipline, because the more disciplined you are, the more you will enjoy your life today and in the future.

Your Mouth

Do you talk too much or too little?

Do you talk too loudly, too softly, too fast, or too slow?

Do you use a harsh tone of voice when you speak? Can people tell by the way you speak when you are frustrated or irritated?

Do you gossip or tell other people's secrets?

Are you critical or judgmental in your speech?

Are you as good at listening to others as you are at talking to them?

Your Mind

Do you let your thoughts "run wild" or do you cast down every thought that is not consistent with the knowledge of God?

Do you spend time meditating on God's Word and the things He has done for you?

Do you meditate on insults and offenses?

Do you choose your thoughts carefully or merely think on whatever falls into your mind?

Your Health

Do you eat too much or too little?

Do you eat too often, or not often enough, and feel bad as a result?

Do you eat too fast, not chewing your food and thereby missing its nutritional value?

Do you eat healthily and have a well-balanced diet?

Do you eat too much sugar or other types of junk food?

Do you drink enough water?

Are you an "emotional eater," one who eats when you are depressed, lonely, or hurt? Or do you only eat when you are physically hungry?

Do you get enough exercise in your everyday life?

Do you get enough rest and relaxation?

Your Finances

Do you spend more than you make?

Do you hoard money or possessions?

Do you tithe?

Do you give offerings and help the poor and needy?

Do you keep your checkbook balanced and know the state of your finances at all times?

Do you plan ahead for large expenditures?

Do you save money?

Do you have money put away in case of an emergency?

Do you spend money for emotional reasons?

Do you use shopping as a form of entertainment and end up spending money you should not spend?

Your Time and Priorities

Do you discipline yourself to put the most time into your top priorities?

Do you pray, worship, and spend time with God on a regular basis?

Do you read the Bible and other books that will help you grow in your understanding of the ways and purposes of God?

Do you spend quality time with your family and friends?

Do you spend too much time in a relationship that needs some boundaries?

If you find you need to change in any of these areas, it is as simple as making a decision to do so. Feeling guilty won't change anything; regretting a lack of past discipline won't change anything; resenting people who are disciplined won't change anything; and dreading discipline won't change anything. The only thing that will change anything is starting right now to consistently discipline yourself. Let your new slogan in life be, "No excuses, only results!"

CHAPTER 27

Take Your Hands Off

"Worry does not empty tomorrow of its sorrow; it empties today of its strength."
—CORRIE TEN BOOM

We all know people who worry. I have observed that worriers tend to enjoy life less than any other group of people I know. Nothing drains the peace and joy out of pleasant experiences and wonderful days like having a worry-wart around! You know the scenario: An extended family gathers for a picnic in the park and they are laughing and having a wonderful time. Good food abounds; children are playing happily; adults are enjoying visiting with each other. But the grandmother—the matriarch of the family—sits at a table with a worried look on her face, totally preoccupied because she's afraid it's going to rain; she's afraid a child will get hurt while playing, or she's afraid bacteria will grow in the food if they do not eat it right away. She cannot enjoy the picnic because all she can think about is what could go wrong.

People who worry are consumed by fear, anxiety, and torment. They cannot relax and enjoy the simple pleasures of being alive, and this is one reason the Bible is full of scriptures encouraging us not to worry, but to trust God. When we are tempted to worry, we need to say to ourselves, "Take your hands off this situation! God is in control, so calm down and trust Him."

We all have troubles. We can all think of something to worry about if we want to, but that will only make us miserable. We need to deal with our concerns in godly ways, and with positive attitudes. I once read a story about a wise man who dealt with his worries and troubles in a very creative and effective way. It's called "The Trouble Tree," and I'd like to share it with you:

> When we are tempted to worry, we need to say to ourselves, "Take your hands off this situation! God is in control, so calm down and trust Him."

> The carpenter I hired to help me restore an old farmhouse had just finished a rough first day on the job. A flat tire made him lose an hour of work, his electric saw quit, and now his ancient pickup truck refused to start. While I drove him home, he sat in stony silence.
>
> On arriving, he invited me in to meet his family. As we walked toward the front door, he paused briefly at a small tree, touching the tips of the branches with both hands. When opening the door, he underwent an amazing transformation. His tanned face wreathed in smiles and he hugged his two small children and gave his wife a kiss.
>
> Afterward he walked me to the car. We passed the tree and my curiosity got the better of me. I asked him about what I had seen him do earlier.
>
> "Oh, that's my trouble tree," he replied. "I know I can't help having troubles on the job, but one thing's for sure, troubles don't belong in the house with my wife and the children. So I just hang them on the tree every night when I come home. Then in the morning I pick them up again.
>
> "Funny thing is," he smiled, "when I come out in the morning to pick 'em up, there ain't nearly as many as I remember hanging up the night before."[1]

NO ANXIETY

The apostle Paul was well acquainted with hardship and trouble. He had plenty of reasons to worry about himself, the churches he worked so hard to establish, and people he loved. At one point in his ministry he wrote, "We are hedged in (pressed) on every side [troubled and oppressed in every way], but not cramped *or* crushed; we suffer embarrassments *and* are perplexed *and* unable to find a way out, but not driven to despair. We are pursued (persecuted and hard driven), but not deserted [to stand alone]; we are struck down to the ground, but never struck out *and* destroyed" (2 Corinthians 4:8, 9). He also wrote about being hungry, thirsty, "roughly knocked about," homeless, beaten, shipwrecked, and stoned (see 1 Corinthians 4:11; 2 Corinthians 11:25).

What was Paul's attitude toward his troubles? We find it in Philippians 4:6: "Do not fret *or* have anxiety about anything, but in every circumstance *and* in everything, by prayer and petition (definite requests), with thanksgiving, continue to make your wants known to God." In these words, Paul's basic instruction is: "Do not worry or be anxious, but pray, be thankful, and tell God what you need."

Worry and anxiety cannot coexist with trusting God. We have to do one or the other. If we worry, we do not trust Him; and if we trust Him, we don't worry.

> Worry and anxiety cannot coexist with trusting God. We have to do one or the other.

Worry and anxiety are both methods by which we try to figure out what only God knows. We grow worried and anxious when we spend today trying to get tomorrow's answers. We become like the Israelites during the time when God fed them with manna every day (see Exodus 16:14–26). He gave them just enough for each day. If they tried to gather tomorrow's manna today, it became rotten and started to stink. They had to learn to trust God to provide for them when they needed provision, not before.

I believe some people have very difficult lives because they do not know how to live one day at a time, believing God is in control. Instead, they try to handle tomorrow's concerns today and end up anxious and upset. This is not God's plan. He wants us to refuse to worry and to learn to trust Him each day. Trust is not worrying, reasoning, or being afraid. Trust is rest, peace, hope, and a positive attitude. Trust says, "God is in control!"

As Paul wrote, the best way to overcome worry and anxiety is to pray. I remind you: we are not to fret about anything, but to pray about everything (see Philippians 4:6). Our first response to any problem, trial, challenge, or bad report should be to pray. Prayer opens the door for God to work in our lives. He is sovereign, and He can do anything He wants, but He wants us to invite Him to work in our circumstances through prayer.

As you pray, I encourage you to remind God of His Word because it is your covenant with Him. His Word is always effective, as we see in Isaiah 55:11: "So shall My word be that goes forth out of My mouth: it shall not return to Me void [without producing any effect, useless], but it shall accomplish that which I please *and* purpose, and it shall prosper in the thing for which I sent it." Also, as you pray, remember the great things God has done for you, and declare the end result from the beginning, according to Isaiah 46:9, 10: "[Earnestly] remember the former things, [which I did] of old; for I am God . . . and there is none like Me, declaring the end *and* the result from the beginning, and from ancient times the things that are not yet done, saying, My counsel shall stand, and I will do all My pleasure *and* purpose." Praying in these ways will increase your faith, and when faith increases, anxiety decreases.

In Philippians 4, Paul writes about a three-step process to enjoying life. The first step is to rejoice: "Rejoice in the Lord always, [delight, gladden yourselves in Him]; again I say, Rejoice!" (v. 4). The second step is to pray about everything and worry about nothing (see v. 6). The third step is to fear nothing from God and be content (see v. 7).

You may not *feel* like doing what Paul did, but if what you have been doing is not working, then you might as well try it.

HOW, GOD, HOW?

Most of the time, the reason we become anxious is we do not have the answers we want. We cannot stand uncertainty, so we worry and reason. We consider the various ways God could intervene in our circumstances and try to figure out what He should do to help us. When we think this way, we are wasting our time. When we really trust God and take our hands off the situations concerning us, we realize we don't have to have all the answers. We do not need to know what to do or what the outcome will be or how God will bring it to pass. We simply need to know God is in control and He is good. There is a wonderful verse on this subject tucked in the brief and often-overlooked book of Nahum: "The Lord is good, a Strength *and* Stronghold in the day of trouble; He knows (recognizes, has knowledge of, and understands) those who take refuge *and* trust in Him" (1:7). We don't have to know *how* God will deliver us; we simply need to trust He will.

When we really trust God and take our hands off the situations concerning us, we realize we don't have to have all the answers.

For many years, I have loved and lived by Proverbs 3:5, 6: "Lean on, trust in, *and* be confident in the Lord with all your heart *and* mind and do not rely on your own insight *or* understanding. In all your ways know, recognize, *and* acknowledge Him, and He will direct *and* make straight *and* plain your paths."

We must realize trust requires some unanswered questions. We cannot look to our own knowledge, understanding, or good ideas when we are trusting God. We have to accept that He can bring to our problems solutions we never imagined. We don't have to have all the answers; that's God's job. He will give us the answers we need when we need them. Until He does, our responsibility is to pray, rest in Him, and go on about our lives. When we can be comfortable "not knowing," we take a big step forward.

WHEN, GOD, WHEN?

People can become very impatient while trusting God. After all, trust often requires a period of waiting, and most of us do not like to wait. Remember, God's timing is an aspect of His will, and when we really want His will in our lives, we must be willing to submit to His timing.

In many years of walking with God, I have rarely seen Him intervene in a situation at a time that seemed "early," but I have never, ever known Him to be late. He is always right on time.

In many years of walking with God, I have rarely seen Him intervene in a situation at a time that seemed "early," but I have never, ever known Him to be late.

A good verse to remember during times of waiting is Galatians 6:9: "And let us not lose heart *and* grow weary *and* faint in acting nobly *and* doing right, for in due time *and* at the appointed season we shall reap, if we do not loosen *and* relax our courage *and* faint." Now I realize the words "due time" and "the appointed season" still do not give us a month, a day, and a year for something to happen, and that is often what we want. But they do build our faith and encourage us in our waiting and give us confidence that God will act at the moment He believes is best. Our part is to resist becoming impatient, to keep praying, to continue doing what is right, and to know God is in control.

Our faith is stretched when God makes us wait longer than we think is necessary. These situations are opportunities to grow in the fruit of patience. James tells us a fully patient man is lacking in nothing (see James 1:4). I believe he means nothing can upset us when we have developed the ability to patiently wait on and trust God's perfect timing in our lives.

WHY, GOD, WHY?

Sometimes God delivers us from difficult situations or circumstances that tempt us to worry, and at other times we have to go through them. If God decides we must endure them, we simply must do so, because in those situations, *the only way out is through*. Many times, God wants to develop strength, wisdom, or certain character traits in us through the process of enduring hardship.

> Sometimes God delivers us from difficult situations or circumstances that tempt us to worry, and at other times we have to go through them.

In 2003, Joyce Meyer Ministries received some bad press. The media reported things that were not true about us. They twisted facts and took things entirely out of context. People wondered if the reports would affect us negatively, but they did not. In fact, we experienced nothing but growth after that incident. It was a situation we had to go through, and I believe it prepared us for the increase we enjoyed afterward.

The situation was difficult for me because my reputation was being attacked. I learned from the trial that we must trust God with our reputations because if we try to maintain a good name on our own, we will become very upset when anyone attacks it. According to Philippians 2:7, Jesus made Himself of no reputation. He certainly did not care what people said about Him, because He knew the truth.

Sometimes, we have problems because we need to learn a lesson, pass a test, be strengthened, or gain maturity before we enter into a time of growth and expansion. Since some trials are nothing more than tests, we need to focus on passing the tests, not trying to figure out why we have to take them.

Second Corinthians 2:14 is a great verse to remember when you go through difficult situations: "But thanks be to God, Who in Christ always leads us in triumph [as trophies of Christ's victory] and through us spreads *and* makes evident the fragrance of the knowledge of God everywhere." When you go through something, remember you will get to the other side. Even if God requires you to go through difficulty, He is not leading you to defeat, but to certain triumph.

CALM DOWN

When troubled times come our way, one of our biggest challenges is to stay calm. Our *natural* tendencies are to fear, to worry, and to try to do something to fix the situation or solve the problem. But we must learn to get our emotions under control so we can think clearly, act wisely, and pray in faith.

> We must learn to get our emotions under control so we can think clearly, act wisely, and pray in faith.

In the Old Testament, Moses often had to help the Israelites calm down. One such situation took place when Pharaoh's army was gaining ground on them. They kept running, but knew they were headed straight into the Red Sea. Death seemed certain. Exodus 14:10 tells us the people were "exceedingly frightened." They were also angry with Moses, and they decided they would have been better off as slaves to the Egyptians than trying to outrun Pharaoh's forces. It was an intense situation indeed and their emotions were running wild.

Moses said to them, "Fear not; stand still (firm, confident, undismayed) and see the salvation of the Lord which He will work for you today. For the Egyptians you have seen today you shall never see again. The Lord will fight for you, and you shall hold your peace *and* remain at rest" (vv. 13, 14). In modern language, Moses was saying, "Stop it! I know the situation looks hopeless, but don't be afraid. Just be still for a minute and watch what God is going to do for you."

Before Pharaoh's army reached the Israelites, God rolled back the waters of the Red Sea so His people could cross over on dry land. When they were all on the other side, the sea closed again and Pharaoh's fighters drowned. I want to remind you that this same miracle-working God is on your side today. He still fights for His people. Your job, if you belong to Him, is simply to "hold your peace and remain at rest."

In John 14:27, Jesus clearly indicates we have the ability to manage our emotions: "Do not *let* your hearts be troubled, neither *let* them be afraid. [Stop *allowing* yourselves to be agitated and disturbed; and do not *permit* yourselves to be fearful and intimidated and cowardly and unsettled]" (emphasis mine). When our hearts are troubled, the reason is we *let* them be that way. When we are agitated, disturbed, fearful, and intimidated, we have *allowed* these emotions. Since we have the power to permit these negative feelings, we also have the ability to disallow them. Jesus never asks us to do anything impossible. If He tells us not to let ourselves be upset, He gives us the strength to do so.

Jesus never asks us to do anything impossible.

We must choose to stay calm in the midst of crises. We have to discipline our thoughts and emotions in highly charged situations in which many people would give in to tears and fears. This kind of stability and ability to maintain peace is God's will for us, and it proves we really do trust Him. He is in control of every situation, so take your hands off, and relax and enjoy your life while He works on your behalf. Instead of spending today worrying about something you cannot do anything about, why not enjoy today and be enthusiastic about your future?

We must choose to stay calm in the midst of crises.

CHAPTER 28

Embrace Tomorrow

"Every tomorrow has two handles. We can take hold of it with the handle of anxiety or the handle of faith."

—HENRY WARD BEECHER

Over my years in ministry, I have come to believe people view the future from one of two perspectives. They either look forward to it with enthusiasm and confidence, or they are concerned, unsure, or even fearful about it. Some of the ways people think about the days ahead have to do with their personalities; certain people are more optimistic than others by nature. But regardless of the way we are wired, we need to find out what God says about the future and agree with it, even if that means having to overcome a natural personality tendency.

One of the verses that clearly expresses God's view of the future is Jeremiah 29:11: "For I know the thoughts *and* plans that I have for you, says the Lord, thoughts *and* plans for welfare *and* peace and not for evil, to give you hope in your final outcome." This is a clear invitation from God for us to embrace our tomorrows. We do not need to fear anything because God's thoughts and plans for us are good, not evil. All He has for us is good, and He is determined to give us hope for the future.

When we are having trouble today, looking forward to good things in the future helps us enjoy today even in the midst of problems that must be dealt with. The Bible says, "Hope deferred makes the heart sick" (Proverbs 13:12). Stay hopeful and agree with God about your future.

SOMETHING SPECIAL

The prophet Jeremiah, to whom God spoke about His good plans and "hope in your final outcome," was called to do something special for God. He knew this, because God said to him, "Before I formed you in the womb I knew *and* approved of you [as My chosen instrument], and before you were born I separated *and* set you apart, consecrating you; [and] I appointed you as a prophet to the nations" (Jeremiah 1:5).

Just as God had a great plan for Jeremiah before he was even born, He has had a great plan for your life since before you drew your first breath. He did not wait until you were born, or until He saw what you look like, or until you began to develop talents and abilities to decide whether or not you could enjoy your life. There is a reason you are here on earth; you were not born merely to take up space. God said He called Jeremiah before he was even born, and I believe there is something, or even many things, God has in His plan for each of us.

Just as God had a great plan for Jeremiah before he was even born, He has had a great plan for your life since before you drew your first breath.

Instead of feeling anxious if you don't know exactly what those things are yet, why not be excited about the fact that no matter what they are, they are good. Finding our purpose in life is not always easy. Sometimes we have to try some things to find out where we fit. We are partners with God and He even lets us help in the decision-making process. What are you good at? What are you passionate about? What is the desire of your heart? Many times those things point the way to what we should be doing. We should also realize that we may not do the exact same thing all of our life. We have seasons in life for some things and seasons for others.

My daughter was in ministry for thirteen years, but now she is a stay-at-home mom. When her children are grown, I am sure she will do something else. Some people worry so much about what they are supposed to be doing they end up doing nothing at all except staying confused.

I firmly believe it is God's job to show us if He has a specific thing He wants us to do, and if He doesn't show us anything we should live, bear good fruit, bloom where we're planted, and enjoy every day He gives us. I really want you to understand and believe the truth that God has a great future for you. He has a more awesome plan for your life than you could ever imagine simply because He loves you—and He has had this plan in His heart since before you were born.

I really want you to understand and believe the truth that God has a great future for you.

Jeremiah knew this, and so did David, who wrote these words to God:

> For You did form my inward parts; You did knit me together in my mother's womb. . . . My frame was not hidden from You when I was being formed in secret [and] intricately and curiously wrought [as if embroidered with various colors] in the depths of the earth. . . . Your eyes saw my unformed substance, *and in Your book all the days [of my life] were written before they ever took shape,* when as yet there was none of them (Psalm 139:13, 15–16, emphasis mine).

I challenge you today to believe God's Word about your life. If you have ever doubted He has a good plan for your life, it's time to change your mind. I guarantee you: you have a great future ahead. All you have to do is believe it and embrace it. In the Bible, Amos wrote that two cannot walk together unless they agree (see Amos 3:3). God has a good plan for you, but you need to agree with Him if you want to experience it. Start thinking and saying, "God has a good plan for me and I am not only excited about today, but I am looking forward to tomorrow."

EMBRACE THE CALL

Even though God spoke plainly to Jeremiah and told him clearly what his call was, Jeremiah did not embrace it with enthusiasm. Instead, he said, "Ah, Lord God! Behold, I cannot speak, for I am only a youth" (Jeremiah 1:6). God told Jeremiah he was to be a prophet to the nations, and Jeremiah responded, "No, I can't. I'm too young."

God did not approve of Jeremiah's answer. He said, "Say not, I am only a youth; for you shall go to all to whom I send you, and whatever I command you, you shall speak. Be not afraid of them [their faces], for I am with you to deliver you, says the Lord" (vv. 7, 8).

I wonder how many times God has told somebody what an awesome purpose He has for him or her, and heard in response, "No, God! I can't do that!" In the strictest sense, that answer is true. None of us can do anything in our own strength (see John 15:5), especially fulfill God's call on our lives. But when God gives us an assignment, He also plans to give us the grace and strength we will need to accomplish it. He does not expect us to do it alone. So when we respond to Him, instead of protesting and saying no to Him, we need to say, "Okay, God. This is a big assignment, but You are a big God and I know I can do anything with Your help!"

> When God gives us an assignment, He also plans to give us the grace and strength we will need to accomplish it.

GOD ARRANGES OUR SUCCESS

Jeremiah's biggest problem when confronted with God's call on his life was that he focused on himself. Everything was about him! "*I* can't answer this call, God! *I'm* too young!" When we focus on ourselves, we will never develop confidence to fulfill God's call, but when we focus on Him—His strength, His abilities, His wisdom, His power—we realize we can do whatever He asks of us.

Later in Jeremiah's story, God speaks to him again: "But you [Jeremiah], gird up your loins! Arise and tell them all that I command you. Do not be dismayed *and* break down at the sight of their faces, lest I confound you before them *and* permit you to be overcome" (Jeremiah 1:17).

Wow! God is speaking strongly to Jeremiah, saying, basically, "Jeremiah, if you become fearful, then you are not trusting Me. If you want Me to help you, you need to trust Me. If you allow the fear of man to creep into your heart I will back off and let you be overcome. I'll have to permit your failure."

You see, God planned for Jeremiah's success. He had already made a way for Jeremiah to be strong and able to complete his assignment. Jeremiah's job was to refuse to be afraid, and to speak boldly the words God gave him to say.

God still arranges success for His people today. That includes you. You do not have to wait to see how successful you can be on your own; you do not have to beg or bargain with Him to cause you to succeed. He is waiting on you to trust and believe Him to do what He has promised you. I can assure you: God wants you to accomplish His purpose for your life. He gives you everything you need to fulfill His plan. He says you can do it!

It does not matter how you feel, what you look like, what your relatives think, what anybody says, how many obstacles are in your way, or how many times you have failed in the past. If God says you can accomplish something great, then you can! And, please remember, "something great" is not always having a big ministry, presiding over a corporation, or owning your own business. It can also be raising children, helping people everywhere you go, being an encourager, praying for others, and many other seemingly simple things.

Nothing is impossible with God, and I am living proof of this truth. Naturally speaking, there is no way for a person with my background to be where I am today. But with God, an abused little girl who became an angry housewife can be changed to the point she can preach God's Word all over the world. I don't believe I could ever fully explain all the steps I had to go through, all the battles I had to fight, all the lies of the enemy I had to overcome, all the personal fears and insecurities I had to deal with to be transformed into the woman I am right now, but I can say: It is worth the work. It's worth the fight to experience the victory God has for you.

God did tell me I could have a worldwide ministry, but even more importantly, He said I could be transformed into His image. It did not seem possible years ago, but He has brought it to pass. He does not play favorites; He can bring the same kind of miraculous transformation in your life He has brought in mine if you will just ask Him and then do what He leads you to do.

When God puts a dream in your heart or shows you what He wants you to do, you will have to commit to it and persevere. You will have to confront issues in your life that will hinder you from fulfilling it. You will not be able to simply wish them all away or have someone pray for you to make them all go away. Prayer is wonderful and important, but to develop the strength you need to embrace your destiny, you will need to stand and face the enemy and conquer him. You need to know by personal experience "He Who lives in you is greater (mightier) than he who is in the

When God puts a dream in your heart or shows you what He wants you to do, you will have to commit to it and persevere. You will have to confront issues in your life that will hinder you from fulfilling it.

world" (1 John 4:4). Your dream, your destiny, is worth your effort, but you will have to be bold and continue to work toward it with God's help. Don't get so caught up in seeing your dream come to pass you fail to realize what God does *in* you is actually more important than what He does *through* you. If you sincerely ask Him to transform you and mold you into the image of Jesus Christ, I believe the rest of what God has planned for you will occur at the right time.

WHAT'S NEW?

In the New Testament, we read about a young man who reminds me of Jeremiah. God had a great plan for Timothy's life, and like Jeremiah, he responded to it with fear instead of faith, and he thought he was too young to do what God called him to do. I believe both of these young men were not only struggling with their youth, but with the fact they were being called to do something new. By saying, "I'm too young!" they were also saying, "I don't know what to do. I don't have any experience with this. This is all new to me!"

As you move into the future God has for you, you will encounter all kinds of new opportunities and challenges. The days ahead will be full of new experiences, things you have never done before. You may not know how to do them, but you will learn. Everything you are doing today was new to you at one time—and look, now you can do it. For me there was the time when I had my first child. I did not know much of anything about raising children, but God has helped me raise four and I am very proud of all of them. There was the time when I preached my first sermon. I didn't really know how to preach, but now I do. The same will be true for you if you will be bold and step into the new things awaiting you. Soon those things will become easy and the next new experience will present itself. Continuing to face new challenges

> Continuing to face new challenges and develop new abilities is extremely important to your growth and maturity.

and develop new abilities is extremely important to your growth and maturity.

We have a strong tendency to fear or be nervous about new experiences. We think, *It's time for a change! I need something new,* and then we hesitate to embrace that new thing when it comes. We often say to God, "I'm tired of the same old thing. Could you please do something new in my life?" When He tries to do something new for us, we resist it, shrink back in fear, and ask Him to deliver us!

Part of embracing your tomorrow will be developing a positive attitude toward new opportunities. As you walk with God into your future, you will hear Him say, "You have not done this before. I'm taking you to a place you have never been before. I'm going to ask you to do something you don't know how to do. This may be a little bit over your head right now, but I will help you learn to do it."

Part of embracing your tomorrow will be developing a positive attitude toward new opportunities.

You may be on the brink of some new experiences right now. You may be a student facing graduation and the many unknowns of post-college life or a new job. You may be preparing for marriage or trying to start a family. Maybe you want to change careers and learn to do a job you have never done before. Or, perhaps you are in a desperate situation, such as having to cope with a spouse who has left you with young children and you suddenly have to support your family when you have never had to work before.

The only way for us to avoid new things is to stay trapped in the past, but there is no hope or enjoyment in that. The future is all that lies ahead of us; it's all we have to look forward to; and it is full of new horizons. I can promise you: God is with you. He will lead you. He will strengthen you. He will help you.

It may surprise you to know that at this time in my life I am aggressively praying for creativity. I want to try new things, have new ideas, face new challenges, and experience all I can before my time here on earth is finished. I calculated how many days I have lived and how many I may have left, and I felt more passionate than ever about pressing ahead with a very positive, enthusiastic, and aggressive attitude.

In this book, I have mentioned the Old Testament leader Joshua. He knew the challenges of leading people into something new. He was responsible for taking God's people into a good land God promised them, a place they had never been before. The officers of Israel said to the people, "You have not passed this way before" (Joshua 3:4). Perhaps you feel that way right now.

I want you to notice what Joshua said next: "Sanctify yourselves [that is, separate yourselves for a special holy purpose], for tomorrow the Lord will do wonders among you" (v. 5). I believe that for you. I believe God wants to do something special in your life, and I believe you are called for a holy purpose—a purpose that has been in God's heart since long before you were born. I believe your future is bright with God's promise, and that His presence will be with you in every day ahead. I believe God will do wonders in your life, as you continue to follow Him.

> I believe God wants to do something special in your life, and I believe you are called for a holy purpose—a purpose that has been in God's heart since long before you were born.

A CLOSING THOUGHT

As we near the end of this book, I want to share with you a quote by William Allen White, an American journalist who worked around the turn of the twentieth century: "I am not afraid of tomorrow, for I have seen yesterday and I love today."

Let me encourage you: love and enjoy today, make the most of every moment, and look forward with passion and confidence to the great future God has in store for you as you embrace your tomorrows.

THE SECRET

We only get one chance at life. It is not something we can redo, so we should make sure the first "go around" is great. I believe God wants us to enjoy everything we do—to experience true happiness—and I believe that is possible with His help. In this book, I have tried to share with you principles God has taught me during my journey toward learning to enjoy where I am on the way to where I am going. Keep in mind that reading alone will not change your circumstances; you must act upon what you have learned to get results. Education is the first step toward change, but action is the second step—and nothing happens without it.

I encourage you to take one thing at a time as you enjoy today and embrace tomorrow. Take one of the principles in this book and begin to pray about them and examine your life in light of them. For example, are you spending regular time with God, or do you make excuses day after day while complaining that you are not happy? Excuses keep us stuck in joyless and unproductive lifestyles. Never excuse bad behavior or bad choices, but face truth and repent, which means to turn and go in the right direction. Repentance is not merely a sad feeling, but a heartfelt decision to change.

With all of my heart I want God's people to enjoy what Jesus died to provide. It is not God's will that we merely exist and try to make it through each day. He wants us to live joyfully and expectantly. He wants us to experience true happiness. The secret is simple: Enjoy today and embrace tomorrow with enthusiasm and hope.

This is the living out of faith. It is the result of trusting God for everything and being confident that He holds the present and the future. I encourage you to begin taking life one day at a time and ask yourself what you can do to get the most out of each day. Enjoying life does not mean we must have constant entertainment, but we should enjoy every little thing and each aspect of the day because we have made a conscious decision to do so.

I have taken the challenge of enjoying the ordinary. As I wrote earlier in the book, anyone can enjoy the mountaintops of life—those special times of inspiration when everything in life seems perfect. But only the very mature can enjoy the ordinary. In his devotional book titled *My Utmost for His Highest*, Oswald Chambers writes, "Do not expect God always to give you His thrilling minutes, but learn to live in the domain of drudgery by the power of God."

Perhaps it sounds a bit odd, but I like the challenge of living ordinary life as if I were attending a wonderful party. After all, today is the day the Lord has made (see Psalm 118:24). It is His party and He invites us to attend, so why not enjoy every moment while looking forward expectantly to the day He has planned for tomorrow.

God never says, "Uh-oh!" He is not surprised by anything and is never without a solution, so start living the way Jesus intends for you to live! Hopefully your newfound happiness will rub off on all the people around you—and eventually the entire world will be a better place.

APPENDIX

Knowing Who You Are in Christ

In chapter 5, I wrote about the importance of understanding your identity in Christ. The scriptures below have been adapted as confessions for you to study, memorize, and speak aloud as you renew your mind according to the truth of what God says about you:

- I am complete in Him Who is the Head of all principality and power (Colossians 2:10).
- I am alive with Christ (Ephesians 2:5).
- I am free from the law of sin and death (Romans 8:2).
- I am far from oppression, and fear does not come near me (Isaiah 54:14).
- I am born of God, and the evil one does not touch me (1 John 5:18).
- I am holy and without blame before Him in love (Ephesians 1:4; 1 Peter 1:16).
- I have the mind of Christ (1 Corinthians 2:16; Philippians 2:5).
- I have the peace of God that passes all understanding (Philippians 4:7).
- I have the Greater One living in me; greater is He Who is in me than he who is in the world (1 John 4:4).
- I have received the gift of righteousness and reign as a king in life by Jesus Christ (Romans 5:17).
- I have received the spirit of wisdom and revelation in the knowledge of Jesus, the eyes of my understanding being enlightened (Ephesians 1:17, 18).
- I have received the power of the Holy Spirit to lay hands on the sick and see them recover, to cast out demons, to speak with new

tongues. I have power over all the power of the enemy, and nothing shall by any means harm me (Mark 16:17, 18; Luke 10:17, 19).

- I have put off the old man and have put on the new man, which is renewed in the knowledge after the image of Him Who created me (Colossians 3:9, 10).
- I have given, and it is given to me; good measure, pressed down, shaken together, and running over, men give into my bosom (Luke 6:38).
- I have no lack, for my God supplies all of my needs according to His riches in glory by Christ Jesus (Philippians 4:19).
- I can quench all the fiery darts of the wicked one with my shield of faith (Ephesians 6:16).
- I can do all things through Christ Jesus (Philippians 4:13).
- I show forth the praises of God Who has called me out of darkness into His marvelous light (1 Peter 2:9).
- I am God's child—for I am born again of the incorruptible seed of the Word of God, which lives and abides forever (1 Peter 1:23).
- I am God's workmanship, created in Christ unto good works (Ephesians 2:10).
- I am a new creature in Christ (2 Corinthians 5:17).
- I am a spirit being—alive to God (Romans 6:11; 1 Thessalonians 5:23).
- I am a believer, and the light of the Gospel shines in my mind (2 Corinthians 4:4).
- I am a doer of the Word and blessed in my actions (James 1:22, 25).
- I am a joint-heir with Christ (Romans 8:17).
- I am more than a conqueror through Him Who loves me (Romans 8:37).
- I am an overcomer by the blood of the Lamb and the word of my testimony (Revelation 12:11).
- I am a partaker of His divine nature (2 Peter 1:3, 4).
- I am an ambassador for Christ (2 Corinthians 5:20).
- I am part of a chosen generation, a royal priesthood, a holy nation, a purchased people (1 Peter 2:9).
- I am the righteousness of God in Jesus Christ (2 Corinthians 5:21).

- I am the temple of the Holy Spirit; I am not my own (1 Corinthians 6:19).
- I am the head and not the tail; I am above only and not beneath (Deuteronomy 28:13).
- I am the light of the world (Matthew 5:14).
- I am His elect, full of mercy, kindness, humility, and long-suffering (Romans 8:33; Colossians 3:12).
- I am forgiven of all my sins and washed in the blood (Ephesians 1:7).
- I am delivered from the power of darkness and translated into God's kingdom (Colossians 1:13).
- I am redeemed from the curse of sin, sickness, and poverty (Deuteronomy 28:15–68; Galatians 3:13).
- I am firmly rooted, built up, established in my faith, and overflowing with gratitude (Colossians 2:7).
- I am called of God to be the voice of His praise (Psalm 66:8; 2 Timothy 1:9).
- I am healed by the stripes of Jesus (Isaiah 53:5; 1 Peter 2:24).
- I am raised up with Christ and seated in heavenly places (Ephesians 2:6; Colossians 2:12).
- I am greatly loved by God (Romans 1:7; Ephesians 2:4; Colossians 3:12; 1 Thessalonians 1:4).
- I am strengthened with all might according to His glorious power (Colossians 1:11).
- I am submitted to God, and the devil flees from me because I resist him in the name of Jesus (James 4:7).
- I press on toward the goal to win the prize to which God in Christ Jesus is calling us upward (Philippians 3:14).
- For God has not given us a spirit of fear; but of power, love, and a sound mind (2 Timothy 1:7).
- It is not I who live, but Christ lives in me (Galatians 2:20).

NOTES

Introduction

1. http://pewresearch.org/pubs/301/are-we-happy-yet

Chapter 1

1. Jaye Lewis, "Real Health," http://www.beliefnet.com/story/220/story_22099_1.html

Chapter 2

1. Author unknown, http://www.christian-jokes.org/jokes64.html

Chapter 3

1. Michael Josephson, http://www.inspirationpeak.com/cgi-bin/stories.cgi?record=44
2. Jaye Lewis, "A Different Kind of Athlete," http://www.heartnsouls.com/stories/b/s188.shtml

Chapter 4

1. Author Unknown, "E-mail Confusion," http://www.piffe.com/jokes/email.phtml

Chapter 6

1. Author Unknown, "Wedding Plans," http://www.christianstories.com/frames.htm

Chapter 7

1. Author Unknown, http://geocities.com/Athens/Acropolis/6182/LifeLesson.html

Chapter 9

1. Author unknown, "Positive Attitude," http://www.friendsacrossamerica.com/positiveattitude.html

Chapter 11

1. Author Unknown, "And This Too Shall Pass," http://www.wscribe.com/parables/pass.html

Chapter 13

1. Author Unknown, "The Wise Woman's Stone," http://www.yuni.com/library/docs/222.html

Chapter 19

1. Lederer, Richard. "Question and Answer: These Student Bloopers Are All Genuine, Authentic and Unretouched." *National Review*, December 31, 1995.

Chapter 21

1. http://thinkexist.com/quotes/viktor_frankl/
2. http://www.msnbc.msn.com/id/6802862/site/newsweek/
3. Ibid.

Chapter 27

1. Author Unknown, "The Trouble Tree," http://members.tripod.com/~tassiedevil/Inspiration.htm

ABOUT THE AUTHOR

JOYCE MEYER is one of the world's leading practical Bible teachers. A #1 *New York Times* bestselling author, she has written more than seventy inspirational books, including *The Confident Woman, I Dare You*, the entire Battlefield of the Mind family of books, her first venture into fiction with *The Penny*, and many others. She has also released thousands of audio teachings as well as a complete video library. Joyce's *Enjoying Everyday Life*® radio and television programs are broadcast around the world, and she travels extensively conducting conferences. Joyce and her husband, Dave, are the parents of four grown children and make their home in St. Louis, Missouri.

Joyce Meyer Ministries
U.S. & Foreign Office Addresses

Joyce Meyer Ministries
P.O. Box 655
Fenton, MO 63026
USA
(636) 349-0303
www.joycemeyer.org

Joyce Meyer Ministries—Canada
Lambeth Box 1300
London, ON N6P 1T5
Canada
1-800-727-9673

Joyce Meyer Ministries—Australia
Locked Bag 77
Mansfield Delivery Centre
Queensland 4122
Australia
(07) 3349 1200

Joyce Meyer Ministries—England
P.O. Box 1549
Windsor SL4 1GT
United Kingdom
01753 831102

Joyce Meyer Ministries—South Africa
P.O. Box 5
Cape Town 8000
South Africa
(27) 21-701-1056

Other Books by Joyce Meyer

New Day, New You Devotional
I Dare You
The Penny
The Power of Simple Prayer
The Everyday Life Bible
The Confident Woman
Look Great, Feel Great
*Battlefield of the Mind**
Battlefield of the Mind Devotional
Battlefield of the Mind for Teens
Battlefield of the Mind for Kids
Approval Addiction
Ending Your Day Right
21 Ways to Finding Peace and Happiness
The Secret Power of Speaking God's Word
Seven Things That Steal Your Joy
Starting Your Day Right
Beauty for Ashes (revised edition)
*How to Hear from God**
Knowing God Intimately
The Power of Forgiveness
The Power of Determination
The Power of Being Positive
The Secrets of Spiritual Power
The Battle Belongs to the Lord
The Secrets to Exceptional Living
Eight Ways to Keep the Devil Under Your Feet
Teenagers Are People Too!
Filled with the Spirit
Celebration of Simplicity
The Joy of Believing Prayer
Never Lose Heart
Being the Person God Made You to Be

A Leader in the Making
"Good Morning, This Is God!" (gift book)
Jesus — Name Above All Names
Making Marriage Work (previously published as *Help Me—I'm Married!*)
Reduce Me to Love
Be Healed in Jesus' Name
How to Succeed at Being Yourself
Weary Warriors, Fainting Saints
*Be Anxious for Nothing**
Straight Talk Omnibus
Don't Dread
Managing Your Emotions
Healing the Brokenhearted
*Me and My Big Mouth!**
Prepare to Prosper
Do It Afraid!
Expect a Move of God in Your Life... Suddenly!
Enjoying Where You Are on the Way to Where You Are Going
A New Way of Living
When, God, When?
Why, God, Why?
The Word, the Name, the Blood
Tell Them I Love Them
Peace
*If Not for the Grace of God**

JOYCE MEYER SPANISH TITLES
Las Siete Cosas Que Te Roban el Gozo (Seven Things That Steal Your Joy)
Empezando Tu Dia Bien (Starting Your Day Right)

* Study Guide available for this title.

BOOKS BY DAVE MEYER
Life Lines